S0-BEI-044

THE SAYINGS OF JESUS IN THE TEACHING OF THE TWELVE APOSTLES

SUPPLEMENTS TO

VIGILIAE CHRISTIANAE

Formerly Philosophia Patrum

TEXTS AND STUDIES OF EARLY CHRISTIAN LIFE AND LANGUAGE

VOLUME XI

THE SAYINGS OF JESUS IN THE TEACHING OF THE TWELVE APOSTLES

BY

CLAYTON N. JEFFORD

E.J. BRILL
LEIDEN · NEW YORK · KØBENHAVN · KÖLN
1989

Library of Congress Cataloging-in-Publication Data

Jefford, Clayton N.
The sayings of Jesus in the Teaching of the Twelve Apostles / by Clayton N. Jefford.
p. cm. – (Supplements to Vigiliae Christianae, ISSN 0920-623X ; v. 11)
Thesis (Ph.D.) – Claremont Graduate School, 1988.
Includes bibliographical references.
ISBN 9004091270
1. Didache. 2. Jesus Christ – Words. 3. Bible. O.T. Matthew – Sources. I. Title. II. Series.
BS2940.T5J44 1989
270.1 – dc20 89-37998
CIP

ISSN 0920-623X
ISBN 90 04 09127 0

PRINTED IN THE NETHERLANDS BY E.J. BRILL

TO TWO INSPIRATIONS:

MY MOTHER

MY WIFE

CONTENTS

ACKNOWLEDGEMENTS

Since no book is written in a vacuum, there are numerous persons to whom I would like to express my appreciation for their guidance, encouragement, assistance and patience in the completion of this volume. My initial interest in the literature of the Apostolic Fathers and its implications for the study of the New Testament first was spawned by my mentor at Southeastern Baptist Theological Seminary in Wake Forest, NC, the late Professor John E. Steely. I am indepted to his inspiration for my continued work in these fields. Also, I would like to thank Professor James E. Goehring, who directed my first serious study of the Didache at The Claremont Graduate School in Claremont, CA. His influence upon this text remains prominent, despite his eventual departure to Mary Washington College in Fredericksburg, VA.

The present volume was conceived and produced to serve as my dissertation for the Ph.D. degree, which I received from The Claremont Graduate School in 1988. I am grateful for the time and efforts of those scholars who served as my committee advisors in that task: Professor James M. Robinson (chairperson) and Professor Karen J. Torjesen of The Claremont Graduate School, Professor James A. Sanders of the School of Theology at Claremont and Professor Karen L. King of Occidental College in Los Angeles, CA.

I owe a special gratitude to Professor Torjesen for her encouragement to seek a wider audience for the manuscript. Also, special thanks are due to Mr. J. G. Deahl of E. J. Brill for his technical assistance in the process of publication.

Finally, I wish to thank my family for their patience and encouragement throughout the years that I neglected them in order to obtain my doctorate in religious studies. My special thanks go to the two persons to whom this book is dedicated: my wife, Susan, and my mother, Beth. They continually have supported my thoughts and aspirations, both with their spiritual guidance and economic assistance. The current volume would not have been possible without their own unique and individual contributions.

Clayton N. Jefford
The Claremont Graduate School
Claremont, California, USA
January 1989

LIST OF ABBREVIATIONS

PRIMARY SOURCES

'Aboth R. Nat.	Sayings of Rabbi Nathan
AC	Apostolic Constitutions
2-3 *Apoc. Bar.*	Syriac, Greek Apocalypse of Baruch
Apoc. Pet.	Apocalypse of Peter
Athan. *ep. fest.*	Athanasius of Alexandria, *epistulorum festivalium fragmenta*
Bar	Baruch
Barn.	Epistle of Barnabas
b. Bek.	Babylonian Talmud, tractate *Bekorot*
b. Ḥul.	Babylonian Talmud, tractate *Ḥullin*
b. Sukk.	Babylonian Talmud, tractate *Sukka*
Cic. *tusc.*	Cicero, *disputationes tusculanae*
Clem. *paed.*	Clement of Alexandria, *paedagogus*
Clem. *protr.*	Clement of Alexandria, *protrepticus*
Clem. *str.*	Clement of Alexandria, *stromateis*
1-2 *Clem.*	1-2 Clement
Col	Colossians
1-2 Cor	1-2 Corinthians
Deut	Deuteronomy
Did.	Didache
Dida.	Didascalia
Dor. *doct.*	Dorotheus Abbas, *doctrinae diversae*
Dor. *ep.*	Dorotheus Abbas, *epistulae*
Eccl	Ecclesiastes
Ep. Arist.	Epistle of Aristeas
Eph	Ephesians
1-2 Esdr	1-2 Esdras
Exod	Exodus
Gal	Galatians
Gos. Thom.	Gospel of Thomas
H	Hierosolymitanus 54 (Greek version of the Didache)
Herm. Man.	Shepherd of Hermas, tractate *Mandates*
Herm. Sim.	Shepherd of Hermas, tractate *Similitudes*
Herm. Vis.	Shepherd of Hermas, tractate *Visions*
Hipp. *trad. ap.*	Hippolytus, *traditio apostolica*
Hos	Hosea
Iren. *haer.*	Irenaeus, *adversus haereses*
Isa	Isaiah
Jer	Jeremiah
Jos. *AJ*	Flavius Josephus, *antiquitates judaicae*
Josh	Joshua
Just. *dial.*	Justin Martyr, *dialogus cum tryphone judaeo*
Just. 1-2 *apol.*	Justin Martyr, *apologiae*
KO	Church Ordinances
L	*Doctrina apostolorum* (Latin version of the Didache)
Lev	Leviticus
LXX	Septuagint
M	Special Matthean source
1-2 Macc	1-2 Maccabees

Mart. Pol.	Martyrdom of Polycarp
Matt	Gospel of Matthew
Mek. Bah.	Mekilta de-Rabbi Ishmael, tractate *Bahodesh*
Mic	Micah
MT	Masoretic Text
NT	New Testament
Orig. *prin.*	Origen, *de principiis*
OT	Old Testament
1-2 Pet	1-2 Peter
Phil	Philippians
Philo *decal.*	Philo Judaeus, *de decalogo*
POxy	Oxyrhynchus papyrus
Prov	Proverbs
Ps(s)	Psalm(s)
Ps-Clem. *hom.*	Pseudo-Clementine homilies (*homiliae Clementinae*)
Q	Sayings Gospel Q
1QS	Qumran *Rule of the Community (Manual of Discipline)*
4QpPs	Psalm Scroll of Qumran Cave 4
Rom	Romans
Sib. Or.	Sibylline Oracles
Sir	Sirach
T. Asher	Testament of Asher
T. Benj.	Testament of Benjamin
T. Dan.	Testament of Dan
T. Gad	Testament of Gad
T. Isa.	Testament of Isaac
T. Iss.	Testament of Issachar
T. 12 Patr.	Testament of the Twelve Patriarchs
Tert. *virg. vel.*	Tertullian, *de virginibus velandis*
1-2 Thes	1-2 Thessalonians
1-2 Tim	1-2 Timothy
Tob	Tobit
Wis	Wisdom of Solomon
Zech	Zechariah

SECONDARY SOURCES

AASF	Annales academiae scientiarum Fennica
AB	The Anchor Bible
AF	The Apostolic Fathers: A New Translation and Commentary
AnBib	Analecta biblica
AndRev	*Andover Review*
ATR	*Anglican Theological Review*
BBET	Beiträge zur biblischen Exegese und Theologie
BETL	Bibliotheca ephemeridum theologicarum lovaniensium
Bess	*Bessarione*
BFCT	Beiträge zur Förderung christlicher Theologie
Bib	*Biblica*
BibS(F)	*Biblische Studien* (Freiburg)
BibS(N)	Biblische Studien (Neukirchen, 1951-)
BJRL	*Bulletin of the John Rylands University Library of Manchester*
BKAT	Biblischer Kommentar: Altes Testament
BSac	*Bibliotheca Sacra*
BU	Biblische Untersuchungen
CBQ	*Catholic Biblical Quarterly*
CHS	*Protocol of the Colloquy of the Center for Hermeneutical Studies in Hellenistic and Modern Culture*

CNT	Commentaire du Nouveau Testament
CQ	*Church Quarterly*
CSCO.C	Corpus scriptorum christianorum orientalium. Scriptores coptici
CSJCA	University of Notre Dame Center for the Study of Judaism and Christianity in Antiquity
EBib	Etudes bibliques
EF	Europäisches Forum
EKKNT	Evangelisch-katholischer Kommentar zum Neuen Testament
Exp	*The Expositor*
FRLANT	Forschungen zur Religion und Literatur des Alten und Neuen Testaments
FV	*Foi et Vie*
FzB	Forschung zur Bibel
HTKNT	Herders theologischer Kommentar zum Neuen Testament
HTR	*Harvard Theological Review*
ICSR	International Conference for the Sociology of Religion
JSJ	*Journal for the Study of Judaism in the Persian, Hellenistic and Roman Period*
JTS	*Journal of Theological Studies*
KIT	Kleine Texte für Vorlesungen und Übungen
KNT	Kommentar zum Neuen Testament
LCL	Loeb Classical Library
LEC	Library of Early Christianity
NovT	*Novum Testamentum*
NovTSup	Novum Testamentum, Supplements
NTAbh	Neutestamentliche Abhandlungen
NTD	Das Neue Testament Deutsch
NTS	New Testament Studies
NTS	*New Testament Studies*
OBO	Orbis biblicus et orientalis
PEQ	*Palestine Exploration Quarterly*
PETSE	Papers of the Estonian Theological Society in Exile
PFLUS	Publications de la faculté des letters de l'université de Strasbourg
RB	*Revue biblique*
RelSRev	*Religious Studies Review*
RM	Die Religionen der Menschheit
RNT	Regensburger Neues Testament
SAW	Studienhefte zur Altertumswissenschaft
SBLDS	Society of Biblical Literature Dissertation Series
SBS	Stuttgarter Bibelstudien
SBT	Studies in Biblical Theology
SC	Sources chrétienne
SD	Studies and Documents
SecCent	*The Second Century*
SGKA	Studien zur Geschichte und Kultur des Altertums
SKK.NT	Stuttgarter Kleiner Kommentar. Neuen Testament
SNTSMS	Society for New Testament Studies Monograph Series
StPatr	*Studia Patristica*
Str-B	[H. Strack and] P. Billerbeck, *Kommentar des Neuen Testament*
SVTG	Septuaginta Vetus Testamentum Graecum
TDNT	G. Kittel and G. Friedrich (eds.), *Theological Dictionary of the New Testament*
Theoph.	Theophaneia. Beiträge zur Religions- und Kirchengeschichte des Altertums
THKNT	Theologischer Handkommentar zum Neuen Testament
TQ	*Theologische Quartalschrift*

TU	Texte und Untersuchungen zur Geschichte der altchristlichen Literatur
UNT	Untersuchungen zum Neuen Testament
WBC	Word Biblical Commentary
WMANT	Wissenschaftliche Monographien zum Alten und Neuen Testament
WUNT	Wissenschaftliche Untersuchungen zum Neuen Testament
ZBNT	Züricher Bibelkommentare Neues Testament
ZNW	*Zeitschrift für neutestamentliche Wissenschaft*
ZTK	*Zeitschrift für Theologie und Kirche*

English quotations of the Bible come from *The New Oxford Annotated Bible*, edited by Herbert G. May and Bruce M. Metzger (New York: Oxford University Press, 1973). English quotations from the Didache are based upon *The Apostolic Fathers*, translated by Kirsopp Lake (LCL, no. 24/1; Cambridge, MA: Harvard University Press, 1912; London: William Heinemann, 1912) 303-33. Sigla for standard biblical manuscript references are taken from the *Novum Testamentum Graece*, edited by Kurt Aland and Barbara Aland (26th ed.; Stuttgart: Deutsche Bibelgesellschaft, 1979).

CHAPTER ONE

INTRODUCTION

The New Problem of the Didache

The discovery of the Greek text of the Didache (= H) by Archbishop Bryennios in 1873 occurred at a time when biblical scholarship was beginning to assume the reins of its own destiny. As the emergence of twentieth-century "criticisms" loomed imminently upon the horizon, scholars were poised to transcend the restrictions that dogmatics had imposed upon biblical scholarship for centuries and to open themselves to a new arena in which scripture could be evaluated, both with respect to textual integrity and with respect to historical witness.

In the face of such promise, a generation of scholars held a unique advantage within their discipline that eventually would be lost as the world of biblical studies expanded and segmented itself into specialized fields. On the one hand, biblical scholars prepared to evaluate the canon apart from the restrictions and apart from the rigors of contemporary ecclesiastical politics; on the other hand, they remained the pupils and the product of a tradition which emphasized that research into the primitive church was to be at once both biblical in orientation and ecclesial in scope. Indeed, such academicians maintained the broad perspective that existed for those to whom the study of scripture was not to be undertaken without some consideration of early church structures and of sociological development – they were at once both students of biblical studies and students of patristic investigations.

Among the primary contributions to the fervor of the age were the discoveries of papyri in Egypt that offered fresh glimpses of early Greco-Roman life and the social background of the nascent church.[1] The "modern" perception of the history and of the theology of early Christianity, which previously had been constructed through the narrow "glasses" of the Church Fathers, now was infused with fresh insights and considerations that could have arisen only through an uncensored perspective of antiquity. It was in this "age of expectation" that the Didache appeared. But unlike many of the papyri that were discovered during the mid-nineteenth to the mid-twentieth centuries, the Didache was a document that bore directly upon the situation of a specific early Christian community.

[1] For representative discussions on the status of papyrological discoveries and their application to biblical studies, see Turner, *Papyri*, 17-53, 154-71; Roberts, *Manuscript*, passim; and, White, *Letters*, 3-20.

Scholars thus welcomed the opportunity to evaluate the text of the Didache, not only with respect to its witness to the biblical tradition, but also with respect to its witness to the structure of the early church. And to both of these research arenas the Didache had much to offer. Unfortunately, however, the late nineteenth-century view of the early church milieu was far from complete, and the enigmatic nature of the Didache perhaps offered as much confusion as it offered assistance to the reconstruction of apostolic and post-apostolic congregations. This confusion is evident at once in the variously-divergent dates and histories for the text that were proffered by scholars around the turn of the century. In many respects, the newly "rediscovered" Didache was a "discovery that was ahead of its time" – a document that was eminently suited for the instruction of modern biblical scholars and church historians, yet was too much an "enigmatic" (a "unique") documentation of early Christian existence to assist in any definitive understanding of the primitive church.

Two primary issues have led to this modern characterization of the Didache as a somewhat singular witness to the early church: the question of date and the question of origin (or provenance). While these issues continually are acknowledged "in passing" by those who have attempted to decipher the Didache, and while these issues periodically have received discussion in those extended volumes that are devoted to the nature and to the background of the text, most contemporary scholars have attempted to examine various aspects of the text under the assumption that such questions already have been resolved in a definitive manner. Other inquiries that are associated with the Didache always remain available for would-be students who would launch critical investigations of the text. Thus, recent scholars consistently have chosen to examine questions that are related to sources, textual integrity, Christology, Jewish and Hellenistic motifs and terminology, thematic patterns, etc. Each of these studies, however, has been devoted in the final analysis to an examination of the Didache that is based upon the recognition that a previous generation of researchers has resolved the questions of date and of milieu, when in fact, no "objective" and conclusive determination for these questions ever has been achieved.

To compound the dilemma, the confusion among nineteenth-century scholars with respect to the questions of date and of origin for the Didache was inherited by their students, who themselves became the biblical and patristic scholars of the early- and mid-twentieth century. The onset of source criticism, form criticism and redaction criticism in turn offered these students an opportunity to examine the text of the Didache in a more exacting manner, apart from the need to persist in the resolution of the questions of date and of origin. Such issues began to receive less attention, thereby to produce a generation of students of the text who have assumed that these questions were resolved at some point in former days, or at worst, are the subject of tacit agreement within scholarship. At best, the text has been well-researched under the aegis of new methodologies, while many foundational issues have remained unresolved to any definitive degree.

The eventual result of this progressive history of modern examinations into the Didache has been an unfortunate loss of interest in this fascinating text by "the students of the students of the scholars" who first examined the writing at the turn of the century. From the beginning this has been based upon the mistaken assumptions either that all of the problems were resolved long ago or that the text is of such an enigmatic nature that it has little to offer any contemporary biblical scholar who is grounded in the quest for historical accuracy. In reality, however, the past one hundred years of research by biblical and patristic scholars have led to a more solid foundation upon which definitive statements with regard to the text of the Didache can be made. It is from these studies and their findings (though not necessarily from their conclusions) that some postulations concerning the date and the origin of the Didache now can be advanced.

The Role of Date and Sources in Contemporary Studies: A Review of Modern Research

The central axis around which scholarly assumptions concerning both the date and the origin of the Didache have been constructed is that of the sayings materials which are preserved in the text. Specifically, scholars have struggled to identify the relationship between the Synoptic Gospels, and, more recently, the growth of the Synoptic tradition, with the sayings of Jesus that are reflected primarily in chaps. 1-5 and 16 of the Didache. Those scholars who would view the Didache as a product of the first-century church must explain by necessity the nature of these sayings as a strain (tradition?) of materials that is divergent from the sayings that are preserved in the Synoptic tradition. Those scholars who would view the Didache as the product of the early second through the fourth centuries must explain the sayings as an awkward rendition of some form of the NT Gospels that we now possess.

In order to date these sayings materials, it has become necessary for many scholars to engage in a form of circular thinking. From the outset, most reviewers of the Didache have postulated a date for the sayings that is based upon the nature of the attendant ecclesial and liturgical materials that one finds elsewhere within the text. Thus, the date of the sayings, and subsequently the suggested provenance of the community from which the text derived (when such speculation indeed is attempted), is justified according to the nature of the materials that appear in chaps. 7-15 of the text, which themselves unquestionably come from the latest stages in the compositional history of the writing. Such materials can provide a *terminus ante quem* at best. They shed little light upon the earliest form of the text. Rarely are the sayings examined and then dated according to their own merits, and rarely is the nature of that community which produced the Didache judged according to the traditio-historical and sociological parameters under which these sayings materials appeared. This is unfortunate, since these sayings traditionally are acknowledged to be among the oldest portions of the text.

Before we attempt to rectify this "methodological misconception" in the study of those sayings materials that are preserved in the Didache, it is necessary to review former attempts to engage the text. Conveniently, these attempts may be classified into three dominant schools of thought, i.e., as approaches that align themselves according to the three dominant languages of the primary individual researchers.[2]

The French School of Thought

The first French scholar of record to examine the Didache was Paul Sabatier, whose work *ΔΙΔΑΧΗ ΤΩΝ ΙΒʹ ΑΠΟΣΤΟΛΩΝ: La Didachè ou L'enseignement des douze apôtres* (1885) argued that the Didache was composed at an unknown location in Syria around the middle of the first century.[3] Sabatier sought to date the text according to the following guidelines: the catechetical tradition, which differed from that of the Synoptics; the simplistic rites of baptism and eucharist; the dependence of the ecclesiastical charge upon spiritual gifts; the clearly-defined eschatological expectation; and, the Jewish character of the document. In each of these guidelines he found evidence of the primitive church in its first stages of evolution. Sabatier envisioned the Didache as an ancient ecclesiastical manual that arose in response to the needs of practical discipline prior to the composition both of the Synoptic Gospels and of the letters of Paul. According to Sabatier, it is for this reason that the sayings in the text seem to differ from those which are preserved in the Synoptic tradition.

While much of what Sabatier observed with respect to the early liturgical traditions in the Didache also was recognized both by English-speaking scholars and by their German-speaking counterparts, his dating of the text was not widely accepted. The next major examination of the Didache to be spawned from within the French tradition rejected Sabatier's dating, and adhered to the view that the sayings materials in the Didache were dependent

[2] As has been noted above, the following *Forschungsbericht* is concerned primarily with the scholarly considerations of the questions of date and of provenance for the Didache. For an excellent supplemental review of the text from the perspective of form- and redaction-critical issues, see Kloppenborg, "Sayings," 4-23.

[3] Sabatier, *Didachè*, 150-65.

directly upon the Matthean Gospel – a scholarly perspective that had achieved general recognition by the early twentieth century. In his noted monograph *Influence de l'Evangile de saint Matthieu sur la littérature chrétienne avant saint Irénée* (1950), which was devoted painstakingly to this hypothesis, Edouard Massaux insisted that the Didachist knew of the Matthean Gospel, both in its use of the sayings that were attributed to Jesus and in its reflection of early Christian moral instruction.[4] Massaux proposed that the Sermon on the Mount was a special source of interest for the Didachist, whose use of τὸ εὐαγγέλιον ("the Gospel") throughout the text was to be considered as a direct reference to the Matthean Gospel itself. He concluded in his final analysis that the Didache must be seen as an apologetic document from the period of Justin, a document that was constructed as a catechetical recapitulation of the Matthean text.

Without question, the most influential of the French scholars to undertake work upon the Didache was Jean-Paul Audet, who attacked the hypothesis that the Didache was dependent upon the Synoptics. In certain respects, he returned to many of the assumptions that had been espoused by Sabatier. In his massive commentary upon the Didache, entitled *La Didachè: Instructions des apôtres* (1958), Audet sought to divide the text into three redactional levels.[5] The earliest of these levels derived from a time before the appearance of the first written gospel. The redactor of this earliest level also was responsible for the second level of the text, which itself indicates some knowledge of a gospel that was similar to that of the Matthean Gospel. The final level of redaction was a series of interpolations that were derived from several gospel sources, though the current effect of "harmonization" that appears in the Greek version of the Didache must be attributed to a later stage in the transmission of the text (represented now by the text of H), and should not be attributed to the interpolator.[6]

Audet based many of his views concerning the Didache upon the recently discovered manuscripts from the Qumran area. It was from this corpus of distinctly sectarian literature that he traced themes and motifs which were paralleled in the Didache.[7] In a partial return to the conclusions of Sabatier (and in a complete reversal of the position of Massaux), Audet attributed the earliest materials in the Didache to the first half of the first century, since the literary and the doctrinal affinities between the text of the Didache and the materials of Qumran were so predominant. By the same token, the sayings

[4] Massaux, *Influence*, 3-6, 647-55.

[5] The levels that were delineated by Audet (*Didachè*, 104-20) are as follows: $\mathbf{D_1}$ = 1.1-3a; 2.2-5.2; 7.1; 8.1-11.2; $\mathbf{D_2}$ = 11.3-13.2; 14.1-16.8; **I** = 1.3b-2.1; 6.2-3; 7.2-4; 13.3, 5-7. Audet concluded that 1.4a and 13.4 were even later interpolations to the text.

[6] Audet, *Didachè*, 187-210.

[7] See for example, Audet, "Affinités littéraires," 219-38

materials that were preserved in the Didache clearly were distinct from the sayings tradition that is found in the Synoptics, according to Audet, though certain parallels with the Matthean Gospel seem to indicate that the two writings may have stemmed from the same general milieu, i.e., the region of Antioch.

Twelve years after Audet's monumental contribution, Stanislas Giet published *L'énigme de la Didachè* (1970), which relied heavily upon the extensive research of the French tradition and upon the conclusions of Audet. Giet's efforts were directed toward specific methodological approaches to the Didache, as well as toward the determination of internal structures within the text. From these analyses he concurred with Sabatier and with Audet in their recognition of the primitive elements within the materials, particularly in comparison with the writings of the NT. In his arguments for an early date of composition, he too placed the text in Syria.[8]

The latest development concerning the Didache that has arisen from within the arena of French thought[9] is the recent commentary by Willy Rordorf and André Tuilier, *La doctrine des douze apôtres* (1978).[10] This study is largely an attempt to refine the text of the Didache that was established previously by Audet. Rordorf and Tuilier date the text upon a *terminus ante quem*, which they recognize to be the final chapters of the text, i.e., chaps. 14-16. They conclude with Audet that the composition of the text must have been undertaken within the first century, primarily because of the primitive nature of the regulations and of the early ecclesiastical materials that are found in these final chapters. While they find it difficult to believe that the work derived from an Antiochene origin, they do agree with the general view of the French school of thought that the text should be attributed to western Syria.[11]

A review of the research that has derived from French examinations of the Didache reveals the continual return to a central understanding of the text: the materials of the Didache and their composition both are early and probably can be attributed to the first century; the provenance is most likely that of Syria, and possibly is even Antioch itself. While the tone for the standard French argument was established before the turn of the century by the work of Sabatier, the work of Massaux alone stands apart from this uniform understanding of the date and of the origin of the text. Ultimately, however,

---

[8] Giet, *L'énigme*, 257-65. For a more recent, though brief, statement of Giet's approach, see Giet, "L'énigme," 84-94.

[9] The volume is classified here by language and by the predominant influence of the French School, though the authors themselves are Swiss.

[10] Rordorf and Tuilier, *La doctrine*, 83-101.

[11] See also, Tuilier, "Une nouvelle édition," 31-36, and Rordorf, "Une nouvelle édition," 26-30.

the contributions of Audet have served without question as the primary influence upon subsequent French conclusions[12] in this area of research.

The German School of Thought

Among the more important studies of the text of the Didache that were undertaken after the publication of Bryennios' *editio princeps* in 1883 were those examinations which investigated the text from the position of source-critical analysis. The undisputed leader in this early approach to the Didache was Adolf Harnack, who quickly responded to Bryennios with the volume *Die Lehre der zwölf Apostel nebst Untersuchungen zur ältesten Geschichte der Kirchenverfassung und des Kirchenrechts* (1884). In his quest to establish a literary foundation of sources for the Didache, Harnack identified four texts, which he believed to be the basis for those materials that were preserved in H: the Old Testament; a gospel harmony (= The Gospel of the Egyptians); the Epistle of Barnabas; and, the Shepherd of Hermas.[13] With these four sources in view, Harnack felt assured in his conclusions that the text should be dated to 120-165, a time which fell shortly after the composition of all four texts, yet was early enough to influence subsequent strains of developing Christian literary traditions. He attributed the text to Egypt.[14]

Several important studies accompanied the appearance of Harnack's extensive monograph in 1884. An influential article by Adam Krawutzcky ("Ueber die sog. Zwölfapostellehre, ihre hauptsächlichsten Quellen und ihre erste Ausnahme") also explained the Didache as a text that was formulated upon Barnabas, Hermas and the *Duae Viae* (*Judicium Petri*). The Didachist's gospel source, however, was assumed to be the Gospel of the Hebrews. With the evidence of such written sources, Krawutzcky, like Harnack, assigned the Didache to a date shortly after the middle of the second century.[15] Adolf Hilgenfeld (*Novum Testamentum extra canonem receptum*) also agreed that the text should be dated during the period of 120-160, though he only placed its origin within Asia Minor generally. Hilgenfeld speculated that the Didache served as a transitional link between Barnabas and *AC* 7, and further, that the text was used by the Montanists.[16] F.X. Funk ("Die Doctrina Apostolorum"), who rejected the foundations of Hilgenfeld's "Montanist theory," opted against the opinions of his many German colleagues, and, consequently, he came into agreement more with subsequent French and British/Ameri-

[12] The work of Audet also is evident as an influential building-block within the German and British/American schools of research.

[13] Harnack, *Lehre*, 76-80.

[14] Harnack, *Lehre*, 168-70.

[15] Krawutzcky, "Zwölfapostellehre," 585.

[16] Hilgenfeld, *Novum Testamentum*, 88-94.

can thought. He assigned the text to the first century, prior to the composition of Barnabas. He too placed the origination of the Didache in the area of Egypt.[17] Finally, Theodor Zahn, one of the finest scholars of patristic studies at the turn of the century, likewise assigned the text to an Egyptian provenance in his *Forschungen zur Geschichte des neutestamentlichen Kanons und der altkirchlichen Literatur*.[18] He dated the work, however, to a period between the years 80-130. This date, which has been reflected again in more recent years by Hans Lilje (*Die Lehre der zwölf Apostel* [1956]),[19] basically has established the standard for current investigations of the text within the scholarly community.

While Harnack continued in subsequent publications to maintain his belief that the Didache was dependent in part upon some form of gospel harmony (*Realencyklopädie für protestantische Theologie und Kirche* [1896]),[20] G. Wohlenberg argued, instead, that the Didachist was aware of numerous NT texts, which included the Pauline epistles (*Die Lehre der zwölf Apostel in ihrem Verhältnis zum neutestamentlichen Schrifttum* [1888]). Based upon his contention that the Didache was composed at the beginning of the canonization of the NT, Wohlenberg placed the origin of the text to 100-110. Again, he agreed upon an Egyptian provenance.[21]

The basic elements of date and of provenance (i.e., early second-century Egypt) that were suggested in Harnack's seminal work upon the Didache were firmly in place within German scholarship by the turn of the century. Based upon Harnack's presuppositions, German scholars began to examine the Didache from the perspective of non-Greek literary sources and in light of the liturgical traditions that appeared within the text. Such studies included the research of L.E. Iselin, who examined the form of the Two Ways motif that is preserved in the Life of Schnudi (*Eine bisher unbekannte Version des ersten Teiles der "Apostellehre"* [1895]), Joseph Schlecht's review of the Greek and Latin traditions in the early church (*Die Apostellehre in der Liturgie der katholischen Kirche* [1901]), Leo Wohleb's study of the Latin text (*Die lateinische Übersetzung der Didache* [1913]) and eventually, Carl Schmidt's examination of the Coptic fragment of the Didache text ("Das koptische Didache-Fragment des British Museum" [1925]).[22] Finally, Gregor Peradse ("Die 'Lehre der zwölf Apostel' in der georgischen Überlieferung" [1932])

---

[17] Funk, "Doctrina Apostolorum," 381-85.

[18] Zahn, *Forschungen*, 278-89.

[19] Lilje, *Lehre*, 14-15.

[20] Harnack, *Realencyklopädie*, 1.727; and also, *Geschichte*, 1.88 (where he gives more credit to the role of the Matthean Gospel in the composition of the text of the Didache).

[21] Wohlenberg, *Lehre*, 91-94.

[22] On this last subject, also see Benigne, "Didachê Coptica," 311-29; and Horner, "Fragment," 225-31, upon whose analysis Schmidt was dependent. Also important, though antecedent to the work of Schmidt, is Lefort, *Pères Apostoliques*, ix-xv, 25-34.

published a collation from a previously unknown Georgian version of the Didache against the Greek version of H – but this study has become almost meaningless, since the Georgian reading no longer can be verified. While these studies ultimately were important to the expansion of research efforts into the history and into the transmission of the Didache's basic text, they have not contributed significantly to the primary concern of our current study, i.e., the discussion concerning the date and the provenance of the Didache's original composition.

In 1904 Paul Drews initiated a new discussion of the final chapter of the Didache that attempted to show that the source of this concluding section of the text was from the same Jewish apocalyptic source which appears in Mark 13 ("Untersuchungen zur Didache").[23] Thus, while the work of Drews contributed to the developing tradition of source-critical approaches, he betrayed the early influence of Funk, who sought to associate the text with specific early Christian traditions. Through his efforts, Drews noted that some influence from Matt 10 and 24 was evident in *Did.* 16, which thereby suggested that the Didachist used this material within a post-Synoptic milieu. This is to say that the Didachist had certain written versions of the Synoptic Gospels which have survived to the present. He also investigated the significance of possible connections between other biblical traditions and the Didache, especially with respect to the virtue/vice catalogs that are shared by the Didache and the Pauline epistles.[24]

J. Leipoldt (*Geschichte des neutestamentliche Kanons* [1907]) soon returned to the traditional German school of thought with his notation that 1.3b-2.1 was derived from a Matthean-Lucan harmony, a text that had circulated as an independent book of sayings materials. Leipoldt focused upon POxy 1.654 and 1.655 as examples of such early books.[25] The unique nature of 1.3b-2.1 had been observed previously by Harnack, and with various degrees of acceptance, the scholarly world has come to agree with the Harnack-Leipoldt position on this passage. Rudolf Knopf (*Die Lehre der zwölf Apostel; Die zwei Clemensbriefe* [1920]) subsequently agreed that Matthean and Lucan influence could be found throughout the Didache, though he postulated that 1.3b-2.1 might come either from a free rendering of the Synoptics or from an unknown collection of sayings. Knopf argued again that the Didache probably should be dated to 100-150 and that the provenance was Egypt.[26]

By the time of Knopf's research, the German school had resigned itself

---

[23] Drews, "Untersuchungen," 68-79.
[24] Drews, "Untersuchungen," 53-63.
[25] Leipoldt, *Geschichte*, 138.
[26] Knopf, *Lehre*, 2-4.

primarily to the understanding that the Didache derived from an Egyptian provenance, and that the text had incorporated several early written sources. Because of the presence of these sources, most scholars chose to date the Didache in the first half of the second century. Harnack previously had altered his original conclusions concerning the text, at which time he determined that the Didachist had used both the OT and the Matthean Gospel. Further, he argued that 1.3-2.1 revealed traces of either a gospel harmony or, more likely, the Gospel of Peter (*Geschichte der altchristlichen Literatur bis Eusebius* [1893]).[27]

The greatest challenge to the German synthesis that was offered from within the German school of thought itself was provided in the *Habilitationsschrift* of Helmut Köster (*Synoptische Überlieferung bei den apostolischen Vätern* [1957]). Köster argued that the Didache, in addition to the general corpus of the Apostolic Fathers, primarily was dependent upon oral tradition. Through an analysis of form-critical considerations, Köster struggled to break the barrier that written sources had imposed upon contemporary scholarship. From his examinations he concluded that while three (possibly five) passages in the text of the Didache reveal the specific influence of the Matthean Gospel, almost eighty percent of the materials were derived from an independent tradition, from the OT and/or Judaism, or from within the early Christian community itself.[28] While Köster was dependent to a large extent upon previous examinations of the individual *logia*, he emphasized the value of comparisons among numerous textual parallels for any given saying. He concluded, as with those before him, that 1.3b-2.1 was dependent upon some form of harmony, though he emphasized that the remainder of the text must be considered to be the product of the same tradition as that in which the Synoptics arose, and not the product of the Synoptics themselves. Köster's conclusions thus would date the Didache to the time of its oral usage and to the period in which oral traditions were combined with the written texts that existed within the community, i.e., presumably during the end of the first century or at the beginning of the second century. As a methodological advance over previous German scholarship, Köster's work ultimately led to the German capstone date of c. 90-130.

Since the work of Köster, two other important studies have appeared that should not be overlooked. In 1984 Klaus Wengst undertook an extensive analysis of several early Christian writings in which he analyzed the development of textual sources and early traditions within the texts (*Schriften des Urchristentums*). Wengst observed that the early traditions and the primitive

[27] Harnack, *Geschichte*, 1.86-92.

[28] For the specific results of his analysis upon the texts of the Apostolic Fathers, see Köster, *Überlieferung*, 260 (chart).

theology of the Didache in many respects paralleled those of the Matthean Gospel. He concluded that the Didache must have stemmed from second-century Syria.[29]

Three years after the publication of Wengst, Wolf-Dietrich Köhler studied the Didache with a more specific emphasis upon the Matthean tradition (*Die Rezeption des Matthäusevangeliums in der Zeit vor Irenäus* [1987]). Köhler concluded that the Didache, based upon an analysis of external considerations, cannot be dated through its association either with Hermas or with Barnabas, but only through its relationship with the NT corpus. With respect to internal grounds, Köhler followed Harnack in the recognition that the text comes from a time between the early roots of the Christian movement and the dominance of the catholic church – sometime around the end of the first century and the beginning of the second century. From an analysis of the traditions that are preserved in the Didache, he decided that the text most likely arose in the area of Syria/Palestine, rather than in the region of Egypt.[30] While the conclusions of Wengst and Köhler continue to date the origin of the Didache to the turn of the first century (in a consistent perspective with the original view of Harnack), both authors represent a shift away from the typically German hypothesis of Egyptian provenance and toward an understanding of the Didache in its relationship to the Matthean Gospel in Syria.[31]

The British/American School of Thought

The research of English-speaking scholars has not come to any unified consensus concerning either the date or the provenance for the Didache. To be sure, there has been little agreement with the early dates that have been offered by the French, on the one hand, and there has been a mixed response to the Egyptian provenance that has been offered by the Germans, on the other. It is within both the British and the American range of perspectives that the widest panorama of conclusions regarding the date and the milieu for the Didache has been registered.

Among the earliest responses in English to the discovery of the Didache was that of F. W. Farrar ("The Bearing of the 'Teaching' on the Canon" [1884]). Farrar argued that much of the Didache was derived from memory, but that the Didachist knew portions of the NT, including the Matthean Gospel and probably the Lucan Gospel. He dated the text to the end of the first century,

[29] Wengst, *Schriften*, 61-63.

[30] Köhler, *Rezeption*, 29-30.

[31] The most recent contribution to the discussion among the Germans is the work of Kurt Niederwimmer, *Die Didache* (Kommentar in den Apostolischen Vätern, Band I), which was due for publication by Vandenhoeck & Ruprecht in September 1988. Unfortunately, I did not have an opportunity to examine this particular work prior to the publication of my volume.

and assigned it to Egypt, in agreement with the views of Harnack and Krawutzcky.[32]

Farrar was followed by several studies from British scholars in 1885. Philip Schaff (*The Oldest Church Manual Called the Teaching of the Twelve Apostles*) argued that the text could be placed to c. 90-100, since the Didache seems to reveal no knowledge of the NT canon but was used by the authors of Barnabas and Hermas. He believed that either Syria or Palestine (most likely Jerusalem) could be likely candidates for the provenance of the text.[33] Canon Spence (*The Teaching of the Twelve Apostles*), in agreement with the considerations that were offered by Schaff, dated the Didache to c. 80-90. He claimed that the unique nature of the document and the theological positions of its teachings argued for a community of Jewish Christians as that source from which the text derived. He chose the church at Pella, in Palestine, as this community.[34] At the end of 1885, R. D. Hitchcock and Francis Brown prepared an in-depth revision to their earlier announcement of the Didache, which they had published in haste the previous year (*The Teaching of the Twelve Apostles*). They noted the use of the OT and of the Synoptic sources by the Didachist, though they argued that only the Matthean Gospel probably was ever quoted – the remaining materials were cited from memory. Because the text was used as a source both by Barnabas and by Hermas, they dated the text to c. 100. With Farrar, they placed the composition of the Didache in Egypt.[35]

In the following years, both British and American scholars contributed vigorously to the debate concerning the Didache. Among the more focused studies of the period were two sets of lectures by Charles Taylor (*The Teaching of the Twelve Apostles with Illustrations from the Talmud* [1886] and *An Essay on the Theology of the Didache* [1889]). Taylor sought to explain the Jewish nature of the document through a comparison with early Jewish sources. While he offered no specific date or provenance, he determined that the text must derive from primitive Christian traditions. His conclusions in this specific field of study were most influential, particularly among the French.

Also in 1886, B. B. Warfield undertook a short, though insightful, analysis of the text in his article "Text, Sources, and Contents of 'The Two Ways' or First Section of the Didache." Warfield detected the influence of the Matthean Gospel, and added his view that 1.3-6 was taken from the Diatessaron.[36] In conjunction with a view of the Two Ways that was offered by

[32] Farrar, "Bearing," 84-85.
[33] Schaff, *Manual*, 119-25.
[34] Spence, *Teaching*, 87-100.
[35] Hitchcock and Brown, *Teaching*, xc-ci.
[36] Compare the work of Connolly, "Use," 147-57.

Krawutzcky four years previously, he decided that the Two Ways source had served as a separate textual basis for both Barnabas and the Didache, though the different Latin and Greek forms of the Didache had developed within two distinctive traditions, viz., Egyptian and Syrian. Warfield saw the influence of numerous OT and NT texts in the Didache, which he dated to c. 100.[37] In reaction to Warfield and to Harnack and under the firm influence of Taylor's conclusions, J. Rendel Harris (*The Teaching of the Twelve Apostles* [1887]) soon published a collection of related studies upon the text. While he would not offer a provenance for the Didache, he noted that it must stem from an ancient tradition, since it had been used so extensively by authors in the second century.[38]

A study of scriptural sources behind the writings of the Apostolic Fathers, which was directed by Kirsopp Lake of the Oxford Society (*The New Testament in the Apostolic Fathers* [1905]),[39] did little to advance theories concerning the date, the sources and the provenance of the Didache. Lake noted that throughout the text the Didachist seems to use the Synoptic tradition apart from any direct references to the Synoptic Gospels proper. A strong affinity with the sayings of the Matthean Gospel was noted, however. Subsequently, it was argued that the phrase τὸ εὐαγγέλιον ("the Gospel"), which appears throughout the Didache, refers to the Matthean text. In his analysis of 1.3b-2.1, Lake saw four possible sources, which in themselves have formed a foundation for the basic theories that consistently have arisen in analyses of the text by later scholars: a blending of gospel passages; a separate *logia* source; oral tradition; and, an early harmony.

In accordance with the central thrust of English-speaking scholarship in the early years of the twentieth century, J. B. Lightfoot offered his views concerning the nature of the text in his classic volume *The Apostolic Fathers* (1912). His position was in fact a restatement of his previously-stated position upon the Didache, which had appeared in an 1885 article that was entitled "Results of Recent Historical and Topographical Research Upon the Old and New Testament Scriptures." Lightfoot dated the work to the beginning of the second century, since he perceived 1) that there was no "permanent localized ministry"; 2) that episcopacy was not universal; 3) that the *agape* was still part of the eucharist; and, 4) that the exhortations in the text reveal a certain "archaic simplicity." He acknowledged with his peers that the text probably derived from Syria or Palestine.[40]

In an effort to consolidate the conclusions that were offered by Lightfoot

---

[37] Warfield, "Text," see especially 100-10.

[38] Harris, *Teaching*, see 90-94.

[39] Oxford Society, *New Testament*, 24-36.

[40] Lightfoot, "Results," 8-9, and *Apostolic Fathers*, 215-16.

with other English-speaking scholars, Jan Greyvenstein undertook a discussion of the Didache in his Chicago dissertation of 1919 ("The Original 'Teaching of the Twelve Apostles': Its Text and Origins"). From his observations of the "Hebraic ancestry" of the work and of the remarkable association of the text with numerous NT passages, Greyvenstein concluded that the Didache must have derived from the school of James. He placed the text in Antioch, which he saw to be the center of Gentile Christianity and which he believed to be that location to which the Jerusalem Christians had fled after the rebellion of C.E. 70. In this light he dated the Didache to the end of the first century.[41]

After the work of Greyvenstein, two important studies arose. In 1920 J. Armitage Robinson determined to establish with some assurance the relationship of the Didache with other contemporary texts (*Barnabas, Hermas and the Didache*). As a corrective to an article that he published in 1912 (republished as "Appendix A" in his 1920 study), Robinson argued that the Didachist borrowed both from Barnabas and from Hermas, and thus, that the Didache could not have been composed prior to 140 – possibly, it was even a third-century document.[42] Because such a late date left the Didache open to the possible influence of numerous written sources and of divergent Christian traditions, Robinson did not seek to argue on behalf of a specific provenance for the writing. His insistence upon a late date set a precedent for subsequent studies. In 1929, James Muilenburg produced his Yale dissertation (*The Literary Relations of the Epistle of Barnabas and The Teaching of the Twelve Apostles*) upon the same theses as those of Robinson. He, too, saw that the central problem with modern attempts to date the Didache was that of the relationship of the text to Barnabas. Muilenburg argued that the text was a literary unity which was dependent upon Barnabas and which reflected knowledge of the written Matthean and Lucan Gospels – not some unknown "*ur*-text" or hypothetical gospel source.[43]

Positive responses to the views of Robinson and of Muilenburg were immediate. In 1932, F. C. Burkitt ("Barnabas and the Didache") announced his support for the findings of both scholars. That same year, R. H. Connolly ("The *Didache* in Relation to the Epistle of Barnabas") elaborated and expanded these views with a more detailed examination of the Way of Death that appears in *Barn*. 20 and *Did*. 5. Robinson in turn responded to the observations of Burkitt and Connolly with an expansion of his earlier work ("The Epistle of Barnabas and the Didache" [1934]), though he did little toward the revision of his original conclusions.

[41] Greyvenstein, "'Teaching,'" 123-30.
[42] Robinson, *Barnabas*, 69-83.
[43] Muilenburg, *Relations*, 165-68.

In reaction against the Robinson-Muilenburg thesis, J. M. Creed continued the cause of Lightfoot in 1938 ("The Didache"). He argued that the Didache probably stemmed from the first three decades of the second century, since the document was primitive both in character and in phraseology. Further, he issued a challenge to any who would prove that the Didache could be attributed to a period that was later than this date.[44] In the following year, W. Telfer ("The *Didache* and the Apostolic Synod of Antioch" [1939]) responded in his reconstruction of a scenario in which he characterized the Didachist as "a leader in the church at Antioch, and an elder contemporary of Theophilus" (thus, no earlier than c. 180).

Perhaps the most extreme response to the Robinson-Muilenburg thesis was published in the study of F. E. Vokes (*The Riddle of the Didache: Fact or Fiction, Heresy or Catholicism?* [1938]). Vokes found evidence that the Didachist had used Acts, the Matthean Gospel, Barnabas, Hermas and Justin's *Apology*. He characterized this compiler of ancient texts as a Montanist ("of a very mild type"), and therefore a person who lived and who wrote around the end of the second century or at the beginning of the third century, since the text predates the Didascalia and since, according to Labriolle (as was noted by Vokes), "the first spark of Montanism was kindled in A.D. 172." For various and multifacited reasons, he placed the text in Syria.[45] The late dating for the text that was offered by Vokes had been surpassed only by Charles Bigg (*The Doctrine of the Twelve Apostles*), who already in 1898 had proposed that the Didache was "a romance of the fourth century."[46] Vokes undoubtedly was influenced significantly by the conclusions of Bigg.

The more recent responses to the Robinson-Muilenburg thesis among English-speaking scholars have appeared in two basic streams of thought. The first approach had been initiated by the work of B. H. Streeter some years earlier (*The Four Gospels* [1924]), which was continued briefly by Streeter a short time after the work of Robinson and Muilenburg in 1936 ("The Much-Belaboured Didache"). Streeter argued that the Didache was used within the Matthean community and that it arose as a compilation of the Sayings Gospel Q (though for Streeter it was not necessarily a written text), which was known within the community and was transmitted by the elders of the community through oral tradition. He indicated that the text must have been derived from Syria or Palestine and that the witness to the tradition must be very old (prior to 100).[47] In 1958, Richard Glover ("The Didache's Quotations and the Synoptic Gospels") sought to refine the position of Streeter and to explain the

---

[44] Creed, "Didache," 302-307.

[45] Vokes, *Riddle*, see the extended discussion of 129-76. Also, see his subsequent article upon the contemporary debate over the text; "Didache," 57-62.

[46] See Arthur John Maclean, "Introduction" to the 1992 reprint of Bigg, *Doctrine*, xxvi-xxvii.

[47] Streeter, *Gospels*, 507-11.

appearance of apparent Lucanisms within the text. Through an analysis of the individual sayings of the Didache, Glover determined that the Didachist was not dependent either upon the Matthean[48] or upon the Lucan Gospels, but instead, that the Didachist had borrowed from the sources that were used in those Gospels. Specifically, he found that the Didache reflects only the Marcan Gospel in those instances where the Lucan and the Matthean redactors use the Marcan text in combination with the Sayings Gospel Q. Further, the Didachist follows the Lucan wording whenever materials that were common to both the Matthean and the Lucan Gospels appeared alone. Thus, Glover argued for the Sayings Gospel Q as the source for the sayings in the Didache, a source which also is found in Justin.[49]

Finally, the more recent Masters thesis of John S. Kloppenborg ("The Sayings of Jesus in the Didache: A Redaction-Critical Approach" [1976]) revealed a certain dependence upon the work of Glover, though he also was influenced strongly by the examinations and the conclusions of Audet and Köster. After an exhaustive analysis of the NT traditions that purportedly lie behind the sayings of the Didache, Kloppenborg decided that the text "was compiled in Syria in fairly close contact with the community in which Matthew's gospel arose." He chose a date of c. 100-120 for the earliest redaction of the text and the mid-second century for the final redaction of the materials.[50]

The second trend of thought, and one which has been assumed more readily among scholars, was an attempt to understand the Didache within an expanding tradition of development. In this respect, the multifarious diversities of the text could be explained both in terms of early tendencies and in terms of later influences. Edgar J. Goodspeed represented the onset of this movement among British and American researchers in his brief analysis of the Didache in its relationship to contemporary texts ("The Didache, Barnabas and the Doctrina" [1945]). Based upon his earlier arguments of 1942, Goodspeed reiterated the opinion that a short Greek Didache appeared early in the second century, followed by a Greek Barnabas (c. 130), which itself was used to expand the Didache into its current configuration (c. 150 [=H]), a configuration which in turn was used to redevelop Barnabas into that form which we now possess! Since 1.3-2.1 was composed from the Matthean Gospel, the Lucan Gospel, 1 Peter, Hermas and an unknown text, the Didache is a secondary construction, "not a primary work."[51]

The primary support for Goodspeed's traditio-historical approach, though

---

[48] Streeter finally conceded to Connolly that the Didachist was dependent to some extent upon the Matthean Gospel in addition to the Sayings Gospel Q ("Didache," 372-73).

[49] Glover, "Quotations," 25-29. Also see Smith, "Justin," 287-90.

[50] Kloppenborg, "Sayings," 211.

[51] Goodspeed, "Didache," 228-29.

certainly not for Goodspeed's interpretation itself, came in the form of the more recent commentary upon the text by Robert A. Kraft (*Barnabas and the Didache* [1965]). Kraft, who coined and applied to the Didache the phrase "evolved literature," noted that[52]

> the Didache contains a great deal of material which derives from very early (i.e., first-century and early second-century) forms of (Jewish-) Christianity; but it would be difficult to argue convincingly that the *present form* of the Didache is earlier than mid-second century.

Based upon this analysis of the text and its history, Kraft determined 1) that one must choose Egypt over Syria as the point of origin, since the majority of the textual tradition that is in existence stems from Egypt, and 2) that one cannot determine the identity of the author-editor.[53]

Apart from these studies of the Didache in English, a number of examinations have been dedicated to specific aspects of the document, the most noteworthy of which are George Eldon Ladd's Harvard dissertation on eschatological elements in the text ("The Eschatology of the Didache" [1949]), Bentley Layton's redaction-critical study of the materials in 1.3b-2.1 ("The Sources, Date and Transmission of Didache 1.3b-2.1" [1968])[54] and Arthur Vööbus' analysis of liturgical traditions (*Liturgical Traditions in the Didache* [1968]). While such analyses have offered much new evidence concerning the specificities of the text, including some indication of the sources that may have been used by the Didachist, they have not proven to effect greatly the questions of date and of provenance for the earliest form of the Didache.

Thesis and Objectives

Twentieth-century analyses of apocryphal and pseudepigraphical materials, which have been inspired largely by recent considerations of the tractates from the Nag Hammadi library and the scrolls from the Qumran area, have indicated the need to investigate non-canonical materials in a new light. This is to say that such writings, while often previously excluded from the authoritative canons of a more recent normative Judeo-Christian tradition, should not be judged *de facto* as late developments within that tradition and, therefore, should not be considered to be only of secondary value in examinations of scripture.[55]

---

[52] Kraft, *Barnabas*, 76.

[53] Kraft, *Barnabas*, 77.

[54] Cf. the reaction against Layton by Mees, "Bedeutung," 55-76.

[55] As has been noted by Crossan in his introduction to a discussion of four Gospels that lie outside of the biblical canon (the Gospel of Thomas, Egerton Papyrus 2, the Secret Gospel of Mark and the Gospel of Peter): "The canon is neither a total nor a random collection of early Christian texts. It is both deliberate and selective and it excludes just as surely as it includes. I

Instead, such writings may derive from the earliest sources of the Christian tradition. Current efforts to incorporate these materials into contemporary investigations of the first-century world of Christianity are numerous. In these efforts, however, the text of the Didache has been ignored to a large extent: firstly, because of its previous acceptance into an informal canon of early Christian literature, i.e., the Apostolic Fathers; secondly, because of the presumptions of recent scholars that all the questions of background which pertain to the Didache have been answered.

As we have observed in the *Forschungsbericht* that appears above, the questions of date and of provenance most certainly have not been answered beyond the need for further examination. Instead, the text has been categorized according to several common assumptions about which most scholars would agree uncritically – assumptions that are based upon the investigations and the recommendations of others: 1) since there appear to be both early features and late features, the text should be dated to a "mid-point" in the history of the early church tradition, perhaps c. 80-120 (with Ignatius?!); 2) because the text has been preserved in Greek and in Coptic texts, and because additional Greek and Latin fragments have been discovered in Egypt, the text should be attributed either to someplace in Syria or to some provenance in Egypt; and, 3) by reason of the enigmatic form in which the sayings of the Didache are preserved and because of the unique nature of the liturgical elements and of the ecclesial questions that are addressed by the Didache, the document must represent a single community within Christian history whose ideas and approaches quickly disappeared before the encroachment of developing orthodoxy.

The purpose of the present study is to further investigations into the sources and into the elements that were used in the construction of the earliest layer of the Didache. The specific focus for this examination will be the sayings materials that are preserved in *Did.* 1.1-6.1a and 16, where evidence of an early "sayings tradition" appears in conjunction with a modified version of the decalogue. It is proposed that this tradition of sayings comes from among the earliest collections of materials that were preserved by the same community from which the Matthean Gospel was produced.[56] The Matthean redactor has chosen in most cases to present parallel sayings either from the Sayings Gospel

---

would even say that you cannot understand what is included in the canon unless you understand what was excluded from it. When the four other gospels are played over against the four canonical gospels, both the products and the processes of those latter texts appear in a radically different light" (*Gospels*, 10). As true as this may be for the literature that Crossan has chosen to review, it is equally as true for the materials of the Didache, which the early Church Fathers even chose to *include* in a post-apostolic canon of primitive Christian texts.

[56] So too, this agrees in part with the thesis of Glover ("Quotations," 18), though he chose the Sayings Gospel Q as the source here, a perspective that I will reject in the discussion below.

Q or from the Marcan tradition, and has not utilized the form of these sayings that was original to the earliest collection of "Jesus materials" which were collected and preserved by the Matthean community. It will be argued here that the remaining liturgical and ecclesial materials in chaps. 7-15 also preserve practices and traditions that were commonly acknowledged within the community, but that are not represented in the Matthean Gospel. The reason why these practices and traditions were included in the Didache is determined by the practical use to which the writing was put in the concluding years of the first century, i.e., the text became a "handbook" for the training of community presbyters.

The objectives of the study will include the following: 1) to analyze the sayings materials with a view toward the determination of those elements that bind the sayings together into a single tradition; 2) to indicate the manner in which the remaining materials stem from a community milieu that provided an appropriate occasion for the collection and for the preservation of this sayings tradition; and, 3) to suggest a scenario in which the apparently disjunctive features of the Didache may be explained within the development of the early church.

Considerations of Methodology

The methodological approaches that have been applied to the Didache in the past are basically the same as those that have accompanied the development of modern investigations of the biblical canon, as have been demonstrated above. Thus, much of the primary considerations of the Didache with respect to source, form and redaction criticism already has been investigated.[57] While it is true that such approaches have been helpful in attempts to discover the secrets of the text, they have not been conclusive. Most notably, there has been a resistance among scholars to speculate concerning the nature of the community that produced the Didache based upon the results of these approaches. Among those persons who have made such speculations, brief though those speculations have been, they have not sought to characterize the community through the informative insight that is provided by these traditio-historical approaches themselves.

The current study examines the problems of the Didache through an analysis of that element which has provided the greatest deterent to scholars of the text, i.e., the so-called "enigmatic character" of the sayings. While the

[57] While Kloppenborg has not advanced significantly upon the foundations and conclusions that are represented by Audet, Glover and Köster, his Masters thesis is an excellent presentation of the use of source, form and redaction methods in investigations of the Didache's sayings; cf. "Sayings," passim.

results of previous examinations in source, form and redaction criticism are incorporated, the sayings will be examined further in an attempt to determine two basic elements: 1) the common denominator that exists among these specific sayings and 2) the nature of a tradition that would have contained and/or transmitted this common denominator.

As with previous examinations of the Didache, the present study assumes several presuppositions from the outset:

1) With Kraft[58] and the consensus of more recent scholars, the Didache is the product of an "evolving tradition." Hence, it is the product of several layers of redaction. There may be as many as four layers in this tradition, but our concern rests primarily with the first layer – that stratum in which the bulk of the sayings materials was incorporated.

2) With Robinson, Muilenburg, Burkitt and Connolly, it is admitted that there are numerous elements of the Didache which *could* be the product of a late tradition (third-fourth centuries). A survey of these elements, however, indicates that they as easily may be the product of an early tradition (first century), though they probably stem from different decades within that time-frame, i.e., some elements probably are much earlier than are others.

3) The text of the Didache presents two different perspectives with respect to the written Synoptic Gospels, viz., certain portions betray a knowledge of these gospels in some literary form, while other portions reflect only a knowledge of sayings and of liturgical traditions that were independent, though parallel to, the Synoptics or that were derived from the source traditions which also were incorporated by the Synoptics.

4) Though there are various witnesses to the tradition of the Didache proper or to the Two Ways source that is contained within the Didache, the Greek text of H (which in most cases is taken directly from the reading of Lake[59] throughout the present study) will be used as the core witness for the sayings materials. Admittedly, this is a late text (eleventh century) that may reflect some development within the tradition; however, the variations to H that are attested by the L source, POxy 1782, the Apostolic Constitutions, the Church Ordinances, etc., in most cases do not offer textual variants which differ significantly from H so as to justify a primary dependence upon one of these other sources. At those places where major variants are attested, these will be noted and discussed.

5) The text of the Didache will be considered in the present study with an understanding that there are six (versus the usual five) primary topical divisions, which themselves reveal minor redactional alterations. These divisions are:

---

[58] Kraft, *Barnabas*, 1-3.

[59] Lake, *Apostolic Fathers*, 1.309-33.

a) The Two Ways	1-3a, 2.2-6.1a
b) The Apostolic Decree	6.1b-3
c) The Liturgical Section	7.1-10.6
d) The Community Rules	11.1-15.4
e) The Apocalypse	16.1-8
f) The Sayings Interpolation	1.3b-2.1

Within the development of the tradition, these divisions may represent the intrusion of several basic redactional strata, though random redactional elements certainly appear throughout each section. This indicates that no portion of the text automatically can be considered to be free from later textual adjustments or from theological manipulation.[60]

Apart from these presuppositions, the study will explore a new set of questions for scholarly considerations of the Didache. From the outset it is assumed that if the sayings which appear in the Didache can be placed in the wider tradition of first-century sayings materials, both with respect to the Sayings Gospel Q and in relationship to the broader biblical canon, then the sayings will serve as a valid source for a description of the community that maintained the sayings tradition itself. Further, if a community "ethos" can be reconstructed, then sociological considerations, Christological examinations and questions concerning community hierarchy and ecclesial structure may be addressed with new benefits.

[60] The following chapters assume that the text of the Didache developed in three basic stages. The redactor of the first stage is referred to both as the "Didachist" and as the "first redactor" (while this person is not assumed to have collected the sayings of 1.1-6.1a, s/he is responsible for their association with the current Two Ways format that appears in those chapters); the redactor of the second stage is known as the "second redactor" (= chaps. 7-15, which probably were added to the original materials of 1.1-6.1a in two phases [7-10 and 11-15], though under the same hand); the redactor of 1.3b-2.1, most of chap. 16 and probably 6.1b-3 (i.e., the latest materials of the text) is called the "final redactor."

CHAPTER TWO

REVIEW OF TEXTS

Didache 1.1: The Two Ways

Introduction

Perhaps the best-known saying in the corpus of the Didache is that one which appears at the beginning of the work:

> Ὁδοὶ δύο εἰσί, μία τῆς ζωῆς καὶ μία τοῦ θανάτου,
> ("There are two ways, one of life and one of death,")[1]

And as the compiler of the text notes immediately thereafter:

> διαφορὰ δὲ πολλὴ μεταξὺ τῶν δύο ὁδῶν.
> ("and there is a great difference between the two ways.")

The bold assertion of this saying compels an immediate response from the modern exegete, much as it probably did from the early Christian reader/hearer. In a single and vibrant statement, the Didache opens with an exhortation that establishes the ethical guideline for the remainder of the text. Indeed, this Two Ways "saying" not only introduces a Two Ways "motif," whose influence reverberates throughout chaps. 1-5, but probably introduces a Two Ways literary "source" upon which these chapters were fabricated by the Didachist. At least, this is the common assumption of contemporary scholars. While this interpretation of the text in fact may be a correct analysis, some care must be taken to avoid any undue confusion with respect to the three elements of "saying," "motif" and "source" that traditionally are associated with the Two Ways concept in *Did.* 1-5.[2]

Both the Two Ways source and the Two Ways motif are restricted primarily to the materials of chaps. 1-5 (and 16, according to some authorities). This

---

[1] For a complete critical discussion of the NT sources that lie behind the "Two Ways" saying which is paralleled here, see "Appendix A." The format of the appendix derives from specific textual research currently underway in Claremont, CA.

[2] In the following discussion the "Two Ways" label is attached to three different concepts: 1) an individual saying that was incorporated from a separate sayings tradition by the Didachist and that appears at *Did.* 1.1; 2) a literary document that was shared by the Epistle of Barnabas and that was used by the Didachist as the structural framework upon which *Did.* 1.1-6.1a was constructed; and, 3) an early Christian motif that dominates the discussion of *Did.* 1-5 in its entirety.

restriction often has lead scholars to two conclusions: 1) chaps. 1-5 (and 16?) probably reflect the earliest form of the Didache (i.e., the Two Ways source) to which chaps. 6-15 were added subsequently, and 2) the statement that appears in *Did.* 1.1 is a saying which originally was an integral part of that source. While the former conclusion surely is correct, the latter conclusion probably is incorrect.

With respect to the first conclusion, chaps. 6-15 do not reveal any dependence either upon the Two Ways motif or upon the Two Ways source. The majority of materials in these chapters focus upon considerations of ritual and of community structure that, upon initial examination, seem far-removed from the Two Ways focus of chaps. 1-5. Scholars commonly have assumed with some justification, therefore, that the composition of the Didache occurred in at least two phases, the latter of which was constructed by a second redactor who had no particular interest in the Two Ways motif.

By this same logic, one safely may assume that the Two Ways motif that appears in chaps. 1-5 of the Didache is not the product of a later redactional hand, since later redactors appear to have been interested primarily in liturgical and ecclesial concerns, on the one hand, and since the structure of chaps. 1-5 is dependent upon a specific Two Ways source text that does not underlie chaps. 6-15, on the other hand. According to the typical scholarly argument, if one can assume, therefore, that chaps. 1-5 were constructed originally upon a specific Two Ways literary source and around a basic Two Ways motif, then one also must assume that the Didachist found the specific Two Ways saying of *Did.* 1.1 in that Two Ways source which was incorporated into the text of the Didache.

With respect to this second conclusion, one should consider the presence of the Two Ways motif and a similar Two Ways literary structure that also appear in *Barn.* 18-20. The consensus of scholarly opinion now argues that the Didache and Barnabas are dependent upon a common literary source for these materials, at least insofar as they have been preserved for us in both writings. But while the Two Ways section of Barnabas opens with an elaborately descriptive statement of the Two Ways motif, that statement is characterized by an apocalyptic concern for light/darkness images and for angelology (*Barn.* 18:1) that is not paralleled in *Did.* 1.1. The Two Ways saying of the Didache instead appears as a simple exhortation to follow the path of life, a concept that is consistent with the ethical emphases of early wisdom literature in ancient Israel.

Because there is a Two Ways saying at the beginning of *Did.* 1-5 and at the opening of *Barn.* 18-20, there is little question that the Two Ways source that was used by these texts began with some form of Two Ways exhortation. The nature of that exhortation is unknown, however, and numerous reasons have been offered for the differences in form and content that appear between Barnabas and the Didache.[3] The key to this difference probably is best explained through the influence of a sayings tradition that existed separately from the Two Ways source itself. Thus, *Did.* 1.1 may not only reflect the presence of a general Two Ways motif, such as that which was associated with the Didachist's Two Ways source, but it also may reflect a specific Two Ways saying from early Jewish wisdom tradition that the Didachist perceived to be significant. Furthermore, as will be argued below, it also is quite likely that this saying was drawn from an early collection of sayings, many of which have been chosen by the Didachist to appear throughout chaps. 1-5.[4]

Comparison of Sources

There is little question that the Two Ways motif appears consistently throughout the OT and the Apocrypha. Indeed, it is in these collections of literature that many of those who have reviewed *Did.* 1.1 have sought the *Grundschrift* for the form of the saying that appears here.[5] As a source for

---

[3] While previous scholars have labored to explain the reason for the divergencies between the Two Ways statements of Barnabas and the Didache (cf. for example, Kraft, *Barnabas*, 134-36; Kloppenborg, "Sayings," 51-56 [who is highly dependent upon the view of the French school that, somehow, the Didache and Barnabas are influenced by the texts of Qumran; so Audet, *Didachè*, 252-56, and "Affinités littéraires," 226-32), the appearance of sayings materials throughout *Did.* 1-5 would seem to support the idea that here too in 1.1 an individual Two Ways saying was incorporated by the Didachist. As will be argued below, this is not to argue that the Two Ways motif was not already suggested to the Didachist at the opening of the Two Ways source. Instead, the Didachist may have known of a specific saying that was considered suitable for placement at this position in the text.

[4] Traditionally, scholars have assumed that the presence of the Two Ways saying in *Did.* 1.1 signifies that chaps. 1-5 were used by the early church as a text for catechetical instruction to be given prior to the performance of a baptismal ritual. While it also is assumed throughout the following discussion that *Did.* 1.1-6.1a was constructed for a specific early Christian community which eventually used the materials for the instruction of catechumens, it is only fair to recognize that this does not imply by necessity that the text originally was constructed for this purpose.

There always is the possibility that the sayings materials of 1.1-6.1a were assembled originally simply as a recollected record of aphorisms that was attributed to the historical Jesus and that this record did not include a saying concerning the Two Ways. Instead, such a saying could have been added later (by an early Christian prophet?; cf. Boring, *Sayings*, passim, and Aune, *Prophecy*, 242-44) in order to shape 1.1-6.1a into a format that could have been utilized more readily in catechetical instruction.

While this possibility can never be discounted, the following discussion will argue that the presence of the Two Ways statement at *Did.* 1.1, while not original to the Two Ways source that was received by the Didachist, can be explained as an addition by the Didachist him/herself (not a later redactor), who attached a separate saying to the Two Ways source at 1.1 in the same manner in which other sayings were added throughout the remainder of 1.2.-6.1a.

[5] Cf. Prov 12:28; Sir 15:17; Bar 4:1; *T. Asher* 1.5-9; 2 *Enoch* 30:15. Other writings are oriented around this theme for the purpose of structure: Ps 1; Prov 1-9; Wis 14. For an excellent discussion of the history of the Two Ways theme in early Jewish and Christian literature, see Suggs, "Tradition," 60-74; see also the comments of Greyvenstein, "'Teaching,'" 97-101, and, Giet, *L'énigme*, 71.

Did. 1.1, among the more probable texts that have been suggested are the following:

> Deut 30:15 – Ἰδοὺ δέδωκα πρὸ προσώπου σου σήμερον τὴν Ζωὴν καὶ τὸν θάνατον, τὸ ἀγαθὸν καὶ τὸ κακόν.
>
> ("See, I have set before you this day life and good, death and evil.")[6]
>
> Jer 21:8 – And to the people you shall say: Thus says the LORD:
> Ἰδοὺ ἐγὼ δέδωκα πρὸ προσώπου ὑμῶν τὴν ὁδὸν τῆς Ζωῆς καὶ τὴν ὁδὸν τοῦ θανάτου·
>
> ("See, I set before you the way of life and the way of death.")[7]

It is probable that Jer 21:8 itself is a reflection of Deut 30:15, as is suggested by the introductory phrase of "thus says the LORD." Since, as we shall see below, the majority of sayings in *Did.* 1-5 are to some degree dependent either upon OT materials or upon related Jewish traditions, it is difficult to imagine that the Didachist has not drawn upon one or upon both of these sayings in order to formulate *Did.* 1.1. This observation is reinforced further by the evidence that is preserved in the witness of the NT texts.

The NT pericope that consistently has been indicated as the source of *Did.* 1.1 is Matt 7:13-14 (par. Luke 13:23-24).[8] Of course, one could as easily attribute the source of this material in the Didache to the Sayings Gospel Q itself, and not to the Synoptic witness for Q.[9] As is argued in "Appendix A" below, however, the Two Ways motif is not a common element to the Sayings Gospel Q at all. Instead, it is restricted to the Matthean version of the Q saying. The omission of the Two Ways emphasis in the Lucan Gospel, the highly stylized parallelism in which the Two Ways theme appears in Matt 7:13-14 and the ease with which the motif can be excised from the Q saying ("Enter through the narrow door"), all three of these elements suggest that the Mat-

---

[6] Hitchcock and Brown, *Teaching*, xlviii; Schaff, *Manual*, 18; Muilenburg, *Relations*, 102; Audet, *Didachè*, 226; Kohler, *Origins*, 248; L'Eplattenier, "Présentation," 50; Köhler, *Rezeption*, 42.

[7] So Schaff, *Manual*, 18; Taylor, *Teaching*, 7; Harnack, *Lehre*, 1; Lightfoot, *Apostolic Fathers*, 217; Greyvenstein, "'Teaching,'" 101 (used to reshape Matt 7:13-14); Robinson, *Barnabas*, 46-47 (used by the Didachist to alter Barnabas); Muilenburg, *Relations*, 102; Audet, *Didachè*, 226; Kohler, *Origins*, 248; Köhler, *Rezeption*, 42.

[8] Schaff, *Manual*, 18; Greyvenstein, "'Teaching,'" 101 ("In fact a careful comparison of the two leaves a strong impression that the former [*Did.* 1.1] is merely a simplified and symmetrically compressed statement of the latter [Matt 7:13-14], having been shaped in part by the author's recollection of Jeremiah [21:8] . . . "); Muilenburg, *Relations*, 73 (the Didachist used both *Barn.* 18.1 and Matt 7:13-14); Vokes, *Riddle*, 19 (the Didachist abridged Barnabas and altered Matt 7:13-14).

[9] It is most interesting, however, that the person who has "found Q" under every foundational saying in the Didache (i.e., Richard Glover) has not considered Q as a source for *Did.* 1.1 (cf. "Quotations," and "Patristic Quotations"). Most likely, this is not an oversight on the part of Glover, but instead, this omission seems to result from the fact that Glover does not argue that *Did.* 1.1 is based upon any biblical text or upon any known source for a biblical text.

thean redactor must have drawn upon a special source (M?) for this specific motif.[10] Of course, it would be preferable if one could indicate additional instances of the Two Ways motif within the text of the Matthean Gospel, which thus would lend weight to the argument that the Matthean redactor consciously has chosen to incorporate this motif as a crucial aspect of his theology. But while it is unfortunate that no such theme is repeated in the Gospel, on the one hand, the unique appearance of this Two Ways motif at Matt 7:13-14 in fact may indicate the utilization of a specific Two Ways saying here – a saying which may have circulated within the community of the Didachist.

A Question of Baptismal Practices

The immediate and practical relevance of the Two Ways motif within the Didache derives from the claim that modern authors continually have associated with chaps. 1-5(6), i.e., that these chapters were intended to serve as a text for the ritual of baptism. In Matt 7:13-14, therefore, one discovers that the original nature of the Two Ways motif has been readjusted in a radical manner through its association with the Q saying of Luke 13:24 ("Enter through the narrow door"). Both redactors have inserted the Q saying of the "narrow door" (στενός θύρα) into an eschatological setting whose dualism of a future judgment provides the rhetorical framework in which the hearer/reader is to understand the message of Jesus.

The Two Ways saying of the Didache, however, bears no such marks, except as they are inferred from the Synoptic Gospels by the synthesizing mindset of the modern reader. Instead, we should not assume that the Two Ways source which was incorporated by the Didachist was necessarily dualistic. More correctly, we discover that the Two Ways motif of the Didache is formulated upon the simple, classical image of Israel's wisdom tradition: a righteous existence leads to "life" (ζωή); a life of iniquity results in "death" (θάνατος).[11] Thus, while the Didachist has placed this wisdom saying into a dualistic setting, its true context is not one of eschatological judgment, such as has been forced upon the saying by the Matthean redactor.

There are numerous arguments in support of the use of the Two Ways motif as an introduction to a ritual of baptism here. Firstly, in his Festal Epistle 39, Athanasius lists the Didache as one of several tractates that were appointed for catechumens.[12] Secondly, apart from the list of exhortations and instruc-

---

[10] For more focused discussions upon the nature of the Matt 7:13-14/Luke 13:23-24 passage, see especially Denaux, "Spruch," 305-35; Marguerat, *Le jugement*, 175-82; Hoffmann, "Πάντες," 188-214; and, Luz, *Matthäus*," 395-400 (see especially his note on the "community relationship" between this text and that of *Did.* 3.7 on p. 397).

[11] So Audet, *Didachè*, 255. See Wis 14.

[12] Athan. *ep. fest.* 39. Also listed by Athanasius as representatives of this "catechetical genre"

tions that are offered in chaps. 1-6, chap. 7 follows immediately with an elaborate discussion upon the proper wording and upon the correct practice for the ritual of baptism. The blunt introduction of this topic in chap. 7 would seem to imply that the previous materials (chaps. 1-6) are to be understood as texts that were related to baptismal ritual.[13]

Finally, a pattern of initiation instruction appears in chaps. 1-5(6) that parallels such instruction in other early Jewish-Christian literature.[14] In 1QS 3.13-4.26 there appears to be a pre-Christian pattern of initiation that finds certain correspondences in *Did.* 1-6:

1. Dualistic introduction
2. Virtue and vice lists
3. Concluding eschatological exhortation

The first element of this schema within the Didache itself diverges from many other catechetical documents in that the elements of *dualistic cosmology* and *angelology* are missing. In this respect the Didache is closer to Deut 30:15ff.[15] The absence of these elements (i.e., a dualistic cosmology and an angelology) either may be the result of the process of textual transmission or may be the intended effort of the Didachist to lend an ethical tone to *Did.* 1.1. The second element appears in *Did.* 2-3, 5 (separated by a short *Haustafel* section in chap. 4), where a collection of community rules is assembled. The NT catalogs of virtues and vices also show a "high incidence of baptismal language,"[16] which suggests that their use in the Didache may have been related to the practice of immersion ritual. Finally, the third element is not apparent in chaps. 1-5(6), but in fact, it may be assumed to be represented in *Did.* 16, if one can agree with those scholars who argue that chap. 16 originally belonged with the earliest materials that were associated with *Did.* 1-5(6).[17]

---

are the writings of Judith, Tobit, Sirach, the Wisdom of Solomon, Hermas and Esther. See the discussion of baptism in relationship to the Didache by Schaff, *Manual*, 29-57; and more recently, Noakes, "Times," 80-94, and Meeks, *Christians*, 150-57.

[13] In this observation Suggs agrees, "Tradition," 72. While it is true that *Did.* 7.2-4 *may* be a later insertion into the text, as has been suggested by Audet (*Didachè*, 58-62), this does not serve as an argument against the ultimate use of the text for baptismal instruction within the community, but only against the original use of the text for such ritual instruction.

[14] See Baltzer, *Covenant Formulary*, 127-32.

[15] Baltzer, *Covenant Formulary*, 128. Compare *Barn.* 18.1-2.

[16] Suggs, "Tradition," 69 (based upon the work and the observations of Kamlah, *Form*, see especially 210-14).

[17] For an extensive comparison of these three elements as they are understood in the work of Baltzer, Kamlah and Suggs, see the discussion in Kloppenborg, *Sayings*, 27-31. Following Kamlah's schema of a "Two Angels/Two Ways" myth that has been incorporated by Jewish-Christian literature from Iranian mythology, Kloppenborg outlines the resultant pattern, as follows (set in comparison with the 1QS 3.13-4.26, *T. Asher* 1-7 and Gal 5:17-24):

	Didache	1QS	*T. Asher*	Galatians
Two Ways intro.	1.1	3.13-4.1	1.3-9	5:17-18
Double list of sins	2.1-4.14; 5.1-2	4.2-6, 9-11	2.1-6.6	5:19-21a, 22-23
Admonition	6.1	4.7-8, 12-26	7.1-7	5:21b, 24

The Two Ways tradition, as it appears in *Did.* 1-6, combines both the elements of dualism that are common to the immersion ritual of 1QS 3.13-4.26 and the parenetic character of sapiential literature that was spawned within the Jewish wisdom tradition (as for example, the Testament of the Twelve Patriarchs and the Book of Enoch). Unfortunately, it is difficult to see in these writings the direct antecedents to the Didache;[18] however, it is obvious that the Didachist has drawn upon both traditions freely. Further, the Didachist has cast both of these traditions into an ethical framework, the purpose of which has been overlooked completely by those tradents who transmitted the later recensions of the text.[19] Most appropriately, if the immediate issue for the Didachist was one of baptism (or some other form of ritual immersion), the redactor of the later Apostolic Constitutions, which incorporated the framework of the Didache, may well have chosen to refashion the text to meet the requirements of his/her own time and situation. (One assumes that the circumstances of the person who compiled the Apostolic Constitutions were not oriented toward baptism *per se*, but probably were focused upon the pressing concerns of ecclesial hierarchy.)

Conclusions

It is quite difficult to place the Two Ways tradition of the Didache into a specific historical trajectory, simply because the Two Ways motif was so widespread among early Mediterranean cultures.[20] Contrary to those scholars who would argue for the Sayings Gospel Q (i.e., Matt 7:13-14/Luke 13:23-24) as the source of *Did.* 1.1, it is quite apparent that Q did not in fact contain the Two Ways motif. Instead, the Matthean redactor probably has drawn the motif from the M source, which we presumably may attribute to the resources of the Matthean community.

Neither is it an easy task to determine the exact form of any Two Ways saying through an analysis of Matt 7:13-14, since the Matthean redactor probably altered the original form of the saying in a manner that was consistent with the format of the "narrow door" *logion* in the Sayings Gospel Q. Since the saying *does* seem to stand apart within the framework of Matt 7:13-14, however, one might suggest an early form such as that which is rendered here:

> πλατεῖα ἡ πύλη καὶ εὐρύχωρος ἡ ὁδὸς ἡ ἀπάγουσα εἰς τὴν ἀπώλειαν·
> στενὴ ἡ πύλη καὶ τεθλιμμένη ἡ ὁδὸς ἡ ἀπάγουσα εἰς τὴν ζωὴν.

---

[18] Rordorf and Tuilier, *Doctrine*, 24.

[19] Rordorf and Tuilier, *Doctrine*, 26-27. This is most evident in the recension of *AC* 7, where the redactor of the Apostolic Constitutions appears to have no use for the ethical considerations of the Didachist, and thus has chosen to omit them.

[20] See the discussion that is offered by McDonald, *Kerygma*, 177-78 n. 23.

("Wide is the gate and easy is the way which leads to destruction; narrow is the gate and hard is the way which leads to life.")

While this reconstruction certainly does not bring us to a form of the Two Ways saying that is equivalent to the specific saying that appears in *Did.* 1.1, there is no question that the basic Two Ways motif which appears in Matt 7:13-14 is also the same as that which is found in *Did.* 1.1.[21] The rendering of the Two Ways saying that appears in the Matthean Gospel and that which appears in the Didache both probably stem from an early strand of materials that came from OT/Jewish sources. Presumably this strand also incorporated the forms of the saying that appeared in Deuteronomy and/or Jeremiah, which themselves were commonly used in early Jewish literature.[22] As we will continue to argue below with respect to other sayings in the Didache that are paralleled in the OT and in the Synoptic Gospels, the Didache is more likely to be dependent upon OT sources that have been preserved through Jewish traditions than either upon the Matthean Gospel or upon the Sayings Gospel Q.

Didache 1.2: The Way of Life

Comparison of Sources

H 1.2a-b	**Matt 22:37-39**	**Mark 12:30-31**	**Luke 10:27**
. . .			
πρῶτον		ὅτι πρώτη ἐστίν·	
		. . .	
ἀγαπήσεις	ἀγαπήσεις	ἀγαπήσεις	αγαπήσεις
	κύριον	κύριον	κύριον
τὸν θεὸν	τὸν θεόν	τὸν θεόν	τὸν θεόν
τὸν ποιήσαντά			
σε	σου	σου	σου
	. . .	. . .	. . .
	αὕτη ἐστὶν		
	ἡ μεγάλη καὶ		
	πρώτη ἐντολή.		
δεύτερον	δευτέρα δὲ	δευτέρα	
	ὁμοία αὐτῇ	αὕτη	καὶ

[21] As will be seen below, the Didachist has drawn from a specific Two Ways source *document* which the Matthean redactor also reflects (particularly in Matt 7), but which the redactor does not incorporate directly. Thus, it may be that the Matthean redactor did not insert any single Two Ways saying into Matt 7:13-14 at all, but instead, that s/he simply may reflect the *spirit* of the Didache's Two Ways source in these verses of the Matthean Gospel. This is not likely though.

[22] Thus one finds that Pirke Rabbi Eleazar itself is a midrash upon Deut 30:15ff.

		ἀγαπήσεις	ἀγαπήσεις
τὸν πλησίον	τὸν πλησίον	τὸν πλησίον	τὸν πλησίον
σου	σου	σου	σου
ὡς σεαυτόν·	ὡς σεαυτόν.	ὡς σεαυτόν.	ὡς σεαυτόν.
H 1.2c	**Matt 7:12**		**Luke 6:31**
πάντα δὲ	πάντα οὖν		καὶ
ὅσα ἐὰν	ὅσα ἐὰν		καθὼς
θελήσῃς	θέλητε		θέλετε
μὴ			
γίνεσθαί	ἵνα ποιῶσιν		ἵνα ποιῶσιν
σοι,	ὑμῖν		ὑμῖν
	οἱ ἄνθρωποι,		οἱ ἄνθρωποι
καὶ σὺ	οὕτως καὶ ὑμεῖς		
	ποιεῖτε		ποιεῖτε
ἄλλῳ	αὐτοῖς·		αὐτοῖς
μὴ			
ποίει.			ὁμοίως.

There is little question that the "double love commandment" of Matt 22:37-39/Luke 10:27 is derived from Mark 12:30-31 (and perhaps from the Sayings Gospel Q),[23] which itself is dependent upon the texts of Deut 6:5 (καὶ ἀγαπήσεις κύριον τὸν θεόν σου ["and love the Lord your God"]) and Lev 19:18 (καὶ ἀγαπήσεις τὸν πλησίον σου ὡς σεαυτόν ["and love your neighbor as yourself"]). Against the witness of *Did.* 1.2, all three Gospels agree upon the inclusion of κύριος (["Lord"], as does Deuteronomy), though the Lucan redactor agrees with the format of the Didachist in those instances where both texts omit the second ἀγαπήσεις, a term which also is suggested from Leviticus. This element of omission does not indicate necessarily that the Lucan Gospel and the Didache share a unique source at this point (especially since this is their only true agreement against the Marcan/Matthean formula). Instead, this common element indicates that both the Didachist and the Lucan redactor chose a more abbreviated and a more concise format for the presentation of these materials. The Marcan Gospel agrees with the Didache that these sayings are to be introduced by the use of πρῶτος ["first"]. The Matthean redactor, however, concludes the "love of God" statement with the announcement that "this is the greatest and first [πρῶτος] commandment," which indicates some knowledge of this element of "ordering" within the tradition.[24]

---

[23] Most of the arguments for the presence of the Sayings Gospel Q here are based upon elements that appear in the background or context to the sayings proper, and are not based upon elements within the sayings themselves; see Fuller, "Double Commandment," 42.

[24] This discussion, with respect to the text of the Didache, is not particularly meaningful, however, if in fact the "first . . . second" (πρῶτος . . . δεύτερος) distinctions of the Didachist's witness derive from a later redactional hand; see Draper, "Tradition," 271-72. Compare the position of Köhler (*Rezeption*, 43), who sees "first . . . second" as an emphasis upon priority, not upon order.

The parallels to *Did.* 1.2c that occur in the Synoptic Gospels appear, as with *Did.* 1.1, to be based upon the Sayings Gospel Q.[25] As is most often characteristic of Q materials, this saying of the "Golden Rule" is not dependent upon an OT citation, but instead, it reflects an element of the common wisdom tradition that occurs throughout the early wisdom literature of the ancient Near East and the Mediterranean basin.[26] Though the wording of the Matthean form parallels that of the Didache in certain respects, the Lucan/ Matthean texts agree upon an interesting presentation of the saying in a positive formula, while the Didachist presents the more typical *negative* form of the saying.

The Question of a Tradition

The Love of God (Didache 1.2a)

Scholarly opinion is divided concerning the question of which source the Didachist used for this saying.

While the text is remarkably close to that of the Synoptic Gospels, the addition of the phrase τὸν ποιήσαντά σε ("who made you") suggests that the Didachist has used or incorporated a different source here.[27] Since this phrase typically has been seen as a sign of direct Jewish influence,[28] it often has been suggested that at this point the Didachist has drawn either upon the writings of Justin Martyr or upon Justin's source.[29] This may be the case, but if so, this is one of only a few instances where the Didachist might be dependent upon Justin. On the other hand, the source of *Did.* 1.1, which we have seen above is a specific saying whose position was suggested to the Didachist by the arrangement of the Two Ways source (as can be judged against *Barn.* 18-20), may have supplied the "who made you" phrase as readily. While the Two Ways source, at least according to the witness of Barnabas, does not include the "love of God" saying that is found here, the phrase ἀγαπήσεις τὸν ποιή-

[25] For representative discussions with regard to the original position of the Golden Rule in the Sayings Gospel Q, see Lührmann, "Liebet," 416, and Syreeni, *Making*, 1.138-39.

[26] Audet, *Didachè*, 260. Taylor (*Teaching*, 10) lists among the extensive parallels to the "Golden Rule" two examples that appear in the Confucian Analects 15.23 and the Doctrine of the Mean 13.3-4. See Dihle, *Goldene Regel*, 80-127.

[27] Among those scholars who believe that the Didachist is dependent upon the Synoptics for all the sayings in *Did.* 1.2 are Spence, *Teaching*, 9 (the Synoptics were quoted from memory); Harnack, *Lehre*, 76 (the Didachist inserted τὸν ποιήσαντά σε into *Did.* 1.2a); Vokes, *Riddle*, 92; and, Massaux, *Influence*, 606-607.

[28] So, for example, Oxford Society, *New Testament*, 26.

[29] Just. 1 *apol.* 1.16: προσκυνήσεις . . . κύριον τὸν θεὸν τὸν ποιήσαντά σε (["revere . . . the Lord God who made you"]; Harnack, *Lehre*, 70; Butler, "Quotations," 13). Even here, however, Justin has maintained the word κύριος in agreement with the LXX and the Synoptics against the witness of the Didache!

σαντά σε does appear in the source (cf. *Barn.* 19.2a). To be sure, the Two Ways source was a likely and probably a more readily available source for the Didachist than was Justin. This influence from the Two Ways source is suggested by the consistent usage of the source throughout *Did.* 1-5. Otherwise, *Did.* 1.2a appears to parallel closely the witness of the Synoptic Gospels, which is based upon the Marcan and/or Q traditions. Admittedly, however, the κύριος of the LXX and of the Synoptics is not repeated in *Did.* 1.2a, which may be viewed as an unexpected circumstance if one is to argue that the Didachist depended either upon the LXX or upon the Synoptics for these materials. The significance of this minor disagreement will be addressed below.

The Love of Neighbor (Didache 1.2b)

Comments concerning the Didache's "love of God" saying hold true with respect to the "love of neighbor" saying as well. With reference to form, there is no dispute between the Synoptic witness and that of the Didache, since all of the relevant texts repeat the exact same wording.

Because the two elements of "love of God" and "love of neighbor" appear in tandem in the Synoptics, we are no longer surprised to see them together in other contexts. While it must be noted that the union of these sayings was not unknown in first-century Judaism,[30] their juxtaposition most certainly had become a convention within certain circles of early Christianity. On the other hand, one discovers numerous texts in which the "love of neighbor" saying appears by itself as a primary representative of the Torah, thus:

Rom 13:9	**Gal 5:14**	**Jas 2:8**	***Gos. Thom.* 25**
ἀγαπήσεις	ἀγαπήσεις	ἀγαπήσεις	ἀγαπήσεις
τὸν πλησίον	τὸν πλησίον	τὸν πλησίον	τὸν ἀδέλφον
σου ὡς	σου ὡς	σου ὡς	σου ὡς
σεαυτόν.	σεαυτόν.	σεαυτόν	τὴν ψυχήν σου.

In the above NT passages the wording is precisely that of Lev 19:18. The Gospel of Thomas offers several minor divergencies in wording (and probably in theological perspective), but not necessarily in basic intent. An argument may be made that these illustrations of the "love of neighbor" saying, in addition to a parallel example that appears in Pirqe Aboth 1.12, attest to an early tradition that arose both within early Judaism and within nascent Christianity apart from the Marcan tradition of Mark 12:30-31 and its Synoptic parallels. The further appearance of the commandment at Matt 19:19 (absent from the

[30] As is noted by Kraft (*Barnabas*, 137), the close association between the "love commandments" appears in the Testaments: *T. Iss.* 5.2, 7.6; *T. Dan* 5.3; *T. Benj.* 3.3; Pirqe Aboth 6.1. See the discussion of Köhler, *Rezeption*, 43.

parallel passages of Mark 10:19 and Luke 18:20) also may attest to such an early tradition. Since the Didachist reflects the association of the "double love commandment," however, it would seem reasonable to assume that s/he depends upon a "double love commandment" tradition such as that which is reflected in Mark 12, rather than that s/he has chosen to unite the "love commandments" (in addition to the Golden Rule saying) through his/her own initiative.[31]

The Golden Rule (Didache 1.2c)

The Golden Rule saying is found commonly throughout both Jewish and Hellenistic sources. The rare occurrence of the saying in its *positive* form in the Matthean and Lucan Gospels,[32] however, argues that the redactors of those texts are dependent upon a common source, which is most likely the Sayings Gospel Q. The Didache, on the other hand, reveals the *negative* form of the saying, which is a form that is predominant throughout the tradition of the Golden Rule.[33] Though there is the possibility that the Didachist is dependent upon the Q tradition as it is reflected in the Synoptics and that s/he consciously has chosen to change the format into one that is negative,[34] this hardly seems likely. Instead, it would appear that the Didachist is dependent upon a form that was distinct from the form which was derived from the Sayings Gospel Q.

A Suggestion from the Matthean Gospel

A discussion has arisen among NT scholars concerning the probability that the Matthean and Lucan redactors shared another source for the "double love commandment" in addition to that which is provided by the Marcan tradition. On the one hand, there is no certainty that the Lucan redactor used the Marcan tradition at all; on the other, the Matthean version contains several features which do not derive from the Marcan tradition. While the Lucan sayings may be attributed to a Q source that varied from the Marcan tradition,[35]

---

[31] In this assertion I consciously am expressing some resistance to the view of Giet (*L'énigme*, 67), who believes that both the "love of neighbor" commandment and the Golden Rule have been added to a saying which does not need them (i.e., the "love of God"). While it may be the case that the "love of God" saying does not "require" these additions, the Marcan tradition seems to argue for at least the addition of the "love of neighbor" saying in certain strains of the tradition. See Ps-Clem. *hom.* 7.4-7 for an interesting example of where the Two Ways motif has been juxtaposed with the Golden Rule.

[32] See also 1 *Clem.* 13.2c; Just *dial.* 93.1.

[33] Compare Tob 4:15, *Ep. Arist.* 15.5; Acts 15:20 [sa, Ir, D]; Iren. *haer.* 3.12.14; Clem. *str.* 2.23; Alexander Severus 51. See Dihle, *Goldene Regel*, 107.

[34] Vokes (*Riddle*, 92) suggests that this was undertaken in order to "conceal the borrowing."

[35] An excellent and concise summary of this discussion appears in Kloppenborg ("Sayings,"

there are several indications that the Matthean redactor also may have used a third source that was not incorporated either by the Marcan or by the Lucan texts.[36]

A simple proposal for the identification of sources in the Matthean tradition may explain this additional source. As is attested in the Testaments material, the "double love commandment" circulated widely within early Jewish and Christian communities without the associated Christian context of "what is the greatest commandment," which is represented now in the Synoptic witnesses. Such a "free-floating" version easily may have existed in some "early stage of the Matthean material," prior to the influence of the Marcan Gospel. Even without the Marcan "greatest commandment" context, such a "double love commandment" would have functioned as a complete unit in itself.

> . . . Two reasons can be given [in justification that this commandment could have functioned as a unit without the Marcan context]. First, the double commandment of love would have been a characteristic and rather important teaching (whether from Jesus, or attributed to him). We have other examples in which Jewish teachers of the period summarized the Torah, and one can expect that the same would have been done by Jesus or the teachers of the primitive community (as Rom 13:9 gives evidence for the latter). Furthermore, this summary could be used on various occasions and in several connections. We have independent traditions in which it is used, viz., Mk and Q. We are here proposing that there was a third as well (special M).[37]

With the incorporation of the Marcan framework into the Matthean materials, the Matthean redactor reconstructed his/her version upon the Marcan context of the commandment, in addition to the Marcan position within the general framework of the text. Divergencies with the Marcan tradition occurred here, both with respect to the inclusion of the special M materials, and subsequently, with respect to the influence of the Q tradition. Such a development within the tradition of the Matthean materials may well-explain the disparate elements of the Matthean version of the "double love commandment." Further, if one can believe that the Didachist has drawn upon sayings that were known by the Matthean redactor from the special M source, the use

---

60-69), who cites the arguments of Manson, *Sayings*, 259-61 (the Lucan redactor here used the special Lucan source); Lohmeyer, *Matthäus*, 327-30; Jeremias, *Parables*, 202-204; Bornkamm, *Doppelgebot*, 85-93 (the Matthean and Lucan redactors used a pre-Shema form of the Marcan tradition); Furnish, "Commandment," 24-45; Schramm, *Markus-Stoff*, 47-49 (the Matthean redactor used Mark; the Lucan redactor used Q); Fuller, "Doppelgebot," 317-29 (with Schramm); Ellis, "Directions," 299-315 (with Schramm); Strecker, *Weg*, 135-37 (with Schramm); Grundmann, *Matthäus*, 475-77; Stendahl, *School*, 76; and, Gundry, *Use*, 22-24 (Matthean redactor used Mark). Kloppenborg's arguments for this pericope are aligned with those of Bornkamm.

[36] These observations and the reconstruction of a separate source in the Matthean tradition come from the perceptive observations of Hultgren, "Double Commandment," 373-78.

[37] Hultgren, "Double Commandment," 376.

of such a commandment in the Didache without the Marcan context lends further evidence for this reconstruction.

With respect to *Did.* 1.2a, there is little question that the Didachist here is dependent upon a Two Ways source for his/her ordering of elements, as with *Did.* 1.1. In the Two Ways segment of Barnabas one finds hints of the "double love commandment" as well, though the two elements of the saying do not occur together and the wording of each varies considerably from the witness of *Did.* 1.2a:

> *Barn.* 19.2a – ἀγαπήσεις τὸν ποιήσαντά σε
> ("love the one who made you")
>
> *Barn.* 19.5c – ἀγαπήσεις τὸν πλησίον σου ὑπὲρ τὴν ψυχήν σου.
> ("love your neighbor more than your own life.")

On the one hand, the Didachist did not find these sayings *together* in the Two Ways source (as is attested by the reading of *Barn.* 19.2a, 5c, where the sayings appear separately), though s/he obviously is dependent to some extent upon that source for the occurrence of 1.2a-b itself within the text of the Didache and for the positioning of 1.2a-b near to the beginning of the Two Ways materials.[38] Yet, the Didachist did not construct *Did.* 1.2a-b with the assistance of the Two Ways source alone, since the wording of the "double love commandment" in Barnabas does not indicate a knowledge of materials that could have led to the more complete rendering of the "double love commandment" that appears in the Didache. The Didachist also does not appear to know of the controversy that surrounds these materials within the Marcan (and Q?) tradition, since s/he does not betray any contextual framework in *Did.* 1.2a-b that is reminiscent either of the Matthean, the Marcan or the Lucan versions of the pericope. The logical assumption, therefore, is that the Didachist was inspired by the Two Ways source to provide a specific rendering of the "double love commandment" (apart from the mere hint of the commandment which existed in the Two Ways source itself[39]) at the beginning of the Didache and in close proximity to the opening Two Ways statement of *Did.* 1.1. The Didachist, however, also knew of an independent "double love

[38] The saying that appears at *Barn.* 19.2a is noticeably different from the *Did.* 1.2a version of the saying. If the Two Ways source indeed was used for catechetical purposes early in the Christian tradition, this might explain why the Didachist would have chosen to incorporate the Barnabas version of the saying into *Did.* 1.2a (Greyvenstein, "'Teaching,'" 102).

[39] One can only guess concerning the nature of the original Two Ways source by means of a comparison of those materials that are preserved in *Did.* 1-5 and *Barn.* 18-20. Throughout this study, the text of Barnabas is assumed to represent a more accurate preservation of the Two Ways source than does the text of the Didache, since the materials in *Barn.* 18-20 do not indicate any major redactional concerns.

commandment" that existed within a tradition that was distinct from the Marcan tradition.[40]

With respect to the Golden Rule, we have seen above that the version which appears in *Did.* 1.2b is not necessarily dependent upon the Q form of the saying as it is preserved in the Matthean or in the Lucan Gospels. More likely, the source that was used by the Didachist also stems from a non-Q tradition, one that was more common in early Jewish/Christian circles.[41]

With respect to *Did.* 1.2, we thus are left with a situation whereby: 1) the Didachist is dependent upon the Two Ways source for the *ordering* of the individual sayings and for the suggestion of the inclusion of the "double love commandment" near to the motif of the Two Ways; 2) the Didachist knew and used a tradition of the double love commandment that did not stem from the Marcan tradition or from the Sayings Gospel Q; 3) the Didachist knew and used a tradition of the Golden Rule that also did not stem from the Sayings Gospel Q; and, 4) the presence of the Golden Rule in *Did.* 1.2 was not suggested by either the Two Ways source or by the "double love commandment" of the Marcan tradition.

Several features of the Matthean Gospel suggest that the Matthean redactor recognized to some extent the same set of elements as that from which the Didachist derived *Did.* 1.2: 1) the Matthean redactor, alone among the Synoptic writers, places the Golden Rule in close proximity to a statement of the Two Ways (Matt 7:12-14);[42] 2) the Matthean redactor probably knew and incorporated a tradition of the "double love commandment" that did not stem from the Marcan or Q traditions (as is argued above); 3) though the Matthean redactor used the Q version of the Golden Rule, much of the terminology of the Matthean rendering is similar to that of *Did.* 1.2b; and, 4) the Matthean redactor appears to recognize the significance of the "double love commandment" in connection with the Golden Rule, as is indicated by the uniquely Matthean conclusion that appears in each instance:

---

[40] Köster classifies this source as a *free tradition* (*Überlieferung*, 260). It is difficult to agree with the presumptuous opinion of Greyvenstein ("'Teaching,'" 101), however, that: "Here it is once more evident that Jesus and the author of the 'Teaching' have been the first to bring these two commandments together."

[41] Various scholars naturally opt for different sources: Sabatier, *Didachè*, 24 n. 2 (oral tradition); McGiffert, "Relations," 434 (oral tradition); Wohlenberg, *Lehre*, 21 (Acts 15:20 [D]); Schlecht, *Doctrina*, 46 (Tob 4:16); Oxford Society, *New Testament*, 26 ("If the saying be part of the true text of the Acts, it would here most naturally be attributed to the use of the Acts. If it be regarded as a gloss in Acts, the *Didache* may have originated such a gloss."); Robinson, *Barnabas*, 48-49 (an early tradition that was associated with the prohibition against certain foods – as with Acts 15:20 [D] – and that subsequently was used here for the instruction of Gentile converts as a word of the Apostles); Köster, *Überlieferung*, 168-69 (an earlier form than the positive format, perhaps from ancient Palestinian Judaism).

[42] Massaux (*Influence*, 607-608) makes this point, though he argues, based upon his analysis of the Matthean Gospel, that the Didachist is responsible for the ordering of *Did.* 1.1-2, instead of both redactors using a common source. The divergent order of the elements is inconsequential.

Matt 7:12b – οὗτος γάρ ἐστιν ὁ νόμος καὶ οἱ προφῆται.
("For this is the law and the prophets.")

Matt 22:40 – ἐν ταύταις ταῖς δυσὶν ἐντολαῖς ὅλος ὁ νόμος κρέμαται καὶ οἱ προφῆται.
("On these two commandments depend all the law and the prophets.")

This notation concerning the "double love commandment" and the Golden Rule as the summation of "the law and the prophets" appears only here in the Gospels, and thus may imply that the Matthean redactor was familiar with a tradition in which the "double love commandment" and the Golden Rule were recognized as two elements of a single *inclusio* concerning the parameters of the OT Law.[43] For our purposes, it is *not* significant that the phrase was used as an indicator of the summation of the Law, since this was a common practice in early Jewish circles. It *is* significant that the Matthean redactor uses this phrase to underscore two sayings that came from different OT sources, which the Didachist also considered to be the essence of the "Way of Life," since this lends some support for the position that the Didachist and the Matthean redactor are dependent upon a common tradition of scriptural interpretation.

Conclusions

In accordance with the order of the Two Ways source (as is suggested by the witness of Barnabas), upon which much of *Did.* 1-5 was constructed, the Didachist chose to place the "love of God" saying in close proximity to the Two Ways statement of *Did.* 1.1. While the witness of *Barn.* 19.2a, 5c indicates that the "love of God" saying was not associated with the "love of neighbor" saying in the text of the Two Ways source, the Didachist in fact has placed them together. This "double love commandment" also appears in the Synoptic Gospels, where it is derived primarily from the Marcan tradition and secondarily from the Sayings Gospel Q and/or from separate special Matthean/Lucan sources. Since the Two Ways source did not provide sufficient terminology for that reconstruction of the "double love commandment"

[43] The phrase "law and prophets" rarely occurs elsewhere among the writings of the Synoptic redactors. At three points in Acts (13:15; 24:14; 28:23) mention is made of "the law and the prophets" as an indication of the OT. Also, Matt 11:13 and Luke 16:16 appear to share a Q saying that notes the existence of "the law and the prophets" as an authoritative principle prior to John the Baptizer. Finally, in Matt 5:16 the Matthean redactor attributes to Jesus the exhortation "Think not that I have come to abolish the law and the prophets; I have come not to abolish them but to fulfil them." Since this last citation is a significant motif in the Matthean Sermon on the Mount that appears to stem from the M source, there may be some further justification to consider that the Matthean redactor has relied upon "the law and the prophets" theme as a major building block throughout the composition of the Sermon.

which appears in *Did.* 1.2a (as again is suggested by the witness of Barnabas), and since the Didachist seems unaware of the Marcan context for the commandment (and contains some divergent terminology), the Didachist must have known of a separate saying from which *Did.* 1.2a was borrowed. The Didachist also must have attached to the "double love commandment" a version of the Golden Rule saying that came from a separate tradition than that which was associated with Q, since the form of the Didachist's saying diverges from the *positive* format of the Q source.

It is likely that the Matthean redactor also was familiar with the "double love commandment" and with the Golden Rule traditions that were used by the Didachist, since both sayings are underscored by the redactor in distinction from the witness of the remaining Synoptic Gospels. The Matthean redactor has chosen to rely primarily upon the Marcan and upon the Q traditions for his/her rendering of the "double love commandment" and for his/her formation of the Golden Rule, instead of upon the tradition that was incorporated by the Didachist.[44] The reason for this choice by the Matthean redactor will be discussed below. In any case, the association of the "double love commandment" with the Golden Rule apparently held a significance both for the Didachist and for the Matthean redactor that was not shared by the Marcan or the Lucan redactors. The Matthean redactor chose to indicate this association through the addition of "the law and the prophets" phrase, even though s/he consciously had chosen to separate these sayings in the final construction of the Gospel itself.[45]

Didache 1.3b-2.1: Positive Admonitions

Introduction

From the outset, students of the Didache have been hesitant to attribute 1.3b-2.1 to the earliest form of the text, since these materials are in many respects unique to the writing.[46] There is little question that, unlike the majority of verses in the first five chapters of the Didache, 1.3b-2.1 derives from more re-

---

[44] With respect to the "double love commandment," this allegiance to the Marcan tradition would explain why the Matthean redactor chose to incorporate the term κύριος, even though it did not appear in the tradition that was used by the Didachist.

[45] So, Fuller ("Double Commandment," 45) misses the point of this phrase as it is used by the Matthean redactor when he comments that "Matthew is particularly fond of the expression . . . ."

[46] So Warfield, "Reviews," 596: "on internal grounds it can hardly have been part of the original text." Others since Warfield who have denied the originality of this section include Greyvenstein, "'Teaching,'" 25, 69-71 (based upon both internal and external evidence); Muilenburg, *Relations*, 5 (he notes, however, that external evidence suggests that it indeed was original [47]); Creed, "Didache," 376.

cent sources within Intertestamental Judaism and early Christianity, and not from long Judeo-Christian traditions of textual transmission.[47] One notes a distinct break here with the remainder of the Didache in regard to several points: 1) there is no distinct appeal to a specific interpretive motif as with the rest of the early chapters;[48] 2) the background texts around which the section is constructed reflect a knowledge of some form of the Sayings Gospel Q as it has been preserved in the Matthean and in the Lucan Gospels (a somewhat unique feature of the Didache apart from the Lord's Prayer in chap. 8 and scattered materials in chap. 16); and, 3) while the texts are set in a logical sequence within the broader context of *Did.* 1-2, their concerns are strictly Christian, bearing only minor reflections of any Jewish concerns. This absence of Jewish foci appears to be atypical of the remainder of chaps. 1-5.

Yet, as has been argued recently, some care must be taken before one can attribute every element of this interpolation in a "wholesale" manner to the final redaction of the Didache.[49] The segment obviously reflects a conscious (though awkward) attempt to integrate it with respect both to nascent Christian motifs and to Jewish wisdom themes. Indeed, these efforts have produced a workable, complete literary unity within the section. Each saying within the segment must be examined and considered on its own merit before a determination can be made concerning the role of the unit within the larger context of the Didache.

Comparison of Sources for 1.3b-4[50]

Matt 5:43-48, 38-42	**H 1.3b-4**	**Luke 6:27-28, 29-30, 32-36**
(v 43) 'Ηκούσατε ὅτι ἐρρέθη· ἀγαπήσεις τὸν πλησίον σου καὶ		

[47] See Layton, "Sources," 343-83.

[48] Thus, one finds a dependence upon the Mosaic Law (specifically the decalogue) and its use as an ethical guideline elsewhere throughout chaps. 1-5. This reliance upon the decalogue as a framework around which the Two Ways motif is oriented in *Did.* 1.1-6.1a is illustrated in the discussion below.

[49] A thoughtful challenge to such early attempts to dismiss the section as part of the final stage of Christian redaction that was undertaken by the final redactor recently was offered by Pickett, "Eschatology," 10: ". . . the composition of the sayings section in 1.3b-4 is very similar to that found in *Did.* 16. Both sections cite traditional material but not its source. Both change and adapt this material freely. The author does not need to cite an authority, he does not need to quote the sayings exactly, yet they are authoritative for him. Evidently he believed either that the material was familiar enough to his audience that it spoke for itself, or that his personal authority as a teacher gave him the right to cite and adapt such material at will, or even that he, as a representative of God (cf. Ignatius) needed no further authorization."

[50] Throughout the following discussion we will refer to the text as H (versus the Latin text of L), since the L witness omits 1.3b-2.1. *(note 50 continued on p. 40)*

μισήσεις τὸν ἐχθρόν σου.		
(v 44)		**(v 27)**
ἐγὼ δὲ λέγω ὑμῖν·		Ἀλλὰ υμῖν λέγω τοῖς ἀκούουσιν·
ἀγαπᾶτε *τοὺς* *ἐχθροὺς ὑμῶν**		ἀγαπᾶτε *τοὺς* *ἐχθροὺς ὑμῶν,**
		καλῶς ποιεῖτε τοῖς μισοῦσιν υμᾶς,
	(v 3)	**(v 28)**
	εὐλογεῖτε τοὺς **καταρωμένους** **ὑμῖν**	**εὐλογεῖτε τοὺς** **καταρωμένους** **ὑμᾶς,**
καὶ προσεύχεσθε ***ὑπὲρ τῶν*** ***διωκόντων ὑμᾶς,****	**καὶ προσεύχεσθε** **υπὲρ *τῶν*** ***ἐχθρῶν ὑμῶν,***	**προσεύχεσθε** περὶ **τῶν** ἐπηρεαζόντων **ὑμᾶς.**
	νηστεύετε δὲ *ὑπὲρ τῶν* *διωκόντων ὑμᾶς·***	
(v 45) etc.		
(v 46)		**(v 32)**
ἐὰν γὰρ **ἀγαπήσητε τοὺς** **ἀγαπῶντας ὑμᾶς,** τίνα μισθὸν ἔχετε;	***ποία* γὰρ *χάρις,*† ἐὰν** **ἀγαπᾶτε τοὺς** **ἀγαπῶντας ὑμᾶς;**	καὶ εἰ **ἀγαπᾶτε τοὺς** **ἀγαπῶντας ὑμᾶς,** *ποία* ὑμῖν *χάρις* † ἐστίν;
οὐχὶ καὶ οἱ τελῶναι **τὸ αὐτὸ** **ποιοῦσιν;**		**καὶ** γὰρ οἱ ἁμαρτωλοὶ τοὺς ἀγαπῶντας αὐτοὺς ἀγαπῶσιν.

H has been placed in the center position here to indicate more readily its associations both with the Matthean and with the Lucan forms of the Q text. It is not necessary to argue that the passage comes from Q, since the parallels between the Matthean and the Lucan texts are so strong, and since the sayings are unique within the early Christian tradition. Exact verbal and position agreements between one or both Gospel sources and H, with the exception of minor tense or declension variants, are indicated in bold type. Agreements between the Gospels and H with a variance in position are indicated by italics. Parallels that appear in different sequences throughout the text are highlighted through the use of asterisks and cross patterns.

(v 47)		(v 33)
καὶ ἐὰν ἀσπάσησθε τοὺς ἀδελφοὺς ὑμῶν μόνον,		καὶ γὰρ ἐὰν ἀγαθοποιῆτε τοὺς ἀγαθοποιοῦντας ὑμᾶς,
τί περισσὸν ποιεῖτε;		*ποία* ὑμῖν *χάρις* † ἐστίν;
οὐχὶ καὶ οἱ ἐθνικοὶ τὸ αὐτὸ ποιοῦσιν;	**οὐχὶ καὶ τὰ ἔθνη τὸ αὐτὸ ποιοῦσιν;**	**καὶ οἱ ἁμαρτωλοὶ τὸ αὐτὸ ποιοῦσιν.**
		(v 34) etc.
		(v 35)
	ὑμεῖς δὲ **ἀγαπᾶτε τοὺς** μισοῦντας **ὑμᾶς**,	πλὴν **ἀγαπᾶτε τοὺς** ἐχθροὺς **ὑμῶν**
	καὶ οὐχ ἕξετε ἐχθρόν.[51]	καὶ ἀγαθοποιεῖτε καὶ δανίζετε μηδὲν ἀπελπίζοντες· καὶ ἔσται ὁ μισθὸς ὑμῶν πολύς, καὶ ἔσεσθε υἱοὶ ὑψίστου, ὅτι αὐτὸς χρηστός ἐστιν ἐπὶ τοὺς ἀχαρίστους καὶ πονηρούς.
(v 48)		(v 36)
ἔσεσθε οὖν ὑμεῖς *τέλειοι* †† ὡς ὁ πατὴρ ὑμῶν ὁ οὐράνιος τέλειός ἐστιν.		Γίνεσθε οἰκτίρμονες καθὼς καὶ ὁ πατὴρ ὑμῶν οἰκτίρμων ἐστίν.
Ἠκούσατε ὅτι ἐρρέθη· ὀφθαλμὸν ἀντὶ ὀφθαλμοῦ καὶ ὀδόντα ἀντὶ ὀδόντος.		

[51] Contrary to the view of Köster that this most likely is a redactional addition for the purpose of clarification (*Überlieferung*, 221), I have placed this phrase of the Didache in parallel with the extended wording of the Lucan text, since both texts serve the same form-critical roles, viz., they serve as a justification for the appearance of the previous exhortation.

(v 39)		
ἐγὼ δὲ λέγω ὑμῖν μὴ		
ἀντιστῆναι τῷ		
πονηρῷ·		
	(v 4)	
	ἀπέχου τῶν σαρκικῶν	
	καὶ σωματικῶν	
	ἐπιθυμιῶν·	
		(v 29)
ἀλλ' **ὅστις σε**	ἐάν **τίς σοι** δῷ	Τῷ τύπτοντί σε
ῥαπίζει εἰς	**ῥάπισμα εἰς**	ἐπὶ
τὴν δεξιὰν	**τὴν δεξιὰν**	**τὴν**
σιαγόνα σου,	**σιαγόνα,**	**σιαγόνα**
στρέψον αὐτῷ	**στρέψον αὐτῷ**	πάρεχε
καὶ τὴν ἄλλην·	**καὶ τὴν ἄλλην,**	**καὶ τὴν ἄλλην,**
	καὶ ἔσῃ τέλειος·††	
	ἐὰν *ἀγγαρεύσῃ* σέ τις	
	μίλιον ἕν, ὕπαγε	
	μετ' αὐτοῦ δύο·***	
(v 40)		
καὶ τῷ θέλοντί σοι	ἐὰν **ἄρῃ** τις	καὶ ἀπὸ τοῦ
κριθῆναι καὶ		αἴροντός σου
τὸν *χιτῶνά* †††	**τὸ ἱμάτιόν******	**τὸ ἱμάτιον**
σου λαβεῖν,	**σου,** δὸς	
ἄφες **αὐτῷ**	**αὐτῷ**	
καὶ τὸ	**καὶ τὸν**	**καὶ τὸν**
ἱμάτιον·****	**χιτῶνα**· †††	**χιτῶνα**
		μὴ κωλύσῃς.
(v 41)		
καὶ ὅστις σε		
ἀγγαρεύσει μίλιον		
ἕν, ὕπαγε μετ'		
*αὐτοῦ δύο.****		
(v 42)		**(v 30)**
τῷ αἰτουντί	ἐὰν λάβῃ τις ἀπὸ	παντὶ αἰτοῦτί
σε δός,	σου τὸ σόν,	σε δίδου,
καὶ τὸν θέλοντα		καὶ
ἀπὸ σοῦ δανίσασθαι		ἀπὸ τοῦ αἴροντος
		τὰ σὰ
μὴ ἀποστραφῇς.	**μὴ ἀπαίτει·**	**μὴ ἀπαίτει.**
	οὐδὲ γὰρ δύνασαι.	

From the above outline one may visualize quite readily the many points of correspondence between the text of H and its Matthean/Lucan parallels. In this correspondence, H 1.3-4 at first glance appears to reflect some form of the Q source as its *Vorlage*. Three factors in the comparison of the texts traditionally have caused problems for scholars in reconstructing this Q *Vorlage*, however: 1) the disagreements among the texts of the Didachist, the Matthean Gospel and the Lucan Gospel that are evidenced in the additions and alterations which appear in H; 2) the verbal agreement of H with the Matthean/ Lucan texts, even where the ordering varies; and, 3) the individual agreements of H with either the Matthean or the Lucan Gospel to the exclusion of the other Gospel. Specifically within these verses, H appears to reflect some knowledge of Q in five *stichoi*, some knowledge of the Lucan text in four *stichoi* and some knowledge of the Matthean text in three *stichoi*. From this evidence one must conclude that there is a broad awareness of the Synoptic Gospels and of their sources throughout the verses. There is, however, a special association with the Matthean tradition, which will be outlined below.

Vv 3-4 at several points betray some knowledge of NT texts that fall outside of the Gospels or of their sources. Thus, it has been suggested that the rationale "and you will have no enemy" is a conscious reflection of 1 Pet 3:13,[52] while the phrase "abstain from carnal and bodily lust" is aptly paralleled in 1 Pet 2:11.[53] The presence of such late parallels may argue for the influence of later traditions upon the Didache at this point.

Evidence of a Matthean Tradition

Several features of the content and the ordering of H consistently serve to make the witness of the Didache unique. When these elements are compared with Synoptic parallels, they are commonly ascribed to an unknown, mysterious redactor of the Didache text. When these elements are considered together, they suggest that *Did.* 1.3b-2.1 should be considered as an integral part of the Matthean tradition. The specific elements under consideration here are as follow:

1) The association of εὐλογέω ("to praise"), προσεύχομαι ("to pray") and νηστεύω ("to fast")
2) The reference to ἔθνος ("heathen, pagan, Gentile")
3) The focus upon the antithesis motif in Matt 5-6
4) The call to perfection: καὶ ἔσῃ τέλειος ("and you will be perfect")

---

[52] Hitchcock and Brown, *Teaching*, 33.

[53] ἀπέχεσθαι τῶν σαρκικῶν ἐπιθυμιῶν ("abstain from the passions of the flesh"). As noted by Vokes (*Riddle*, 23), POxy 1782 (i.e., the single papyrus witness to the Greek Didache) omits καὶ σωματικῶν, thereby to produce a phrase in exact parallel to 1 Peter. The *AC* 7 rendering of κοσμικῶν in the place of σωματικῶν for the purpose of avoiding repetition with σαρκικῶν probably has been influenced by the phrase κοσμικὰς ἐπιθυμίας ("worldly passions") in Titus 2:12.

5) The acknowledgment of powerlessness: οὐδε γὰρ δύνασαι ("for you are not able")

1) From the outset, the triad of praise, prayer and fasting that opens the H version of these materials immediately recalls the similar triad of almsgiving, prayer and fasting (= the Three Rules) that appears in Matt 6:2-6, 16-18. There is no question that the assemblage of the Three Rules derives from Jewish tradition[54] and that this tradition appeared widely both within Jewish wisdom texts and within early Christian writings. Thus, in Tob 12:8 one finds the clearest statement of this association between the elements of "alms/prayer/fasting" that occurs among various references in the biblical canon (LXX) and in later rabbinic discussions of this singular collection of elements:[55]

> ἀγαθὸν *προσευχὴ* μετὰ *νηστείας* καὶ *ἐλεημοσύνης* καὶ δικαιοσύνης· ἀγαθὸν τὸ ὀλίγον μετὰ δικαιοσύνης ἢ πολὺ μετὰ ἀδικίας· καλὸν ποιῆσαι ἐλεημοσύνην ἢ θησαυρίσαι χρυσίον.
>
> ("*Prayer* is good when accompanied by *fasting*, *almsgiving* and righteousness. A little with righteousness is better than much with wrongdoing. It is better to give alms than to treasure up gold.")

Elsewhere, one finds in *Gos. Thom.* 6a, 14a the same Three Rules motif, though the elements are presented in reverse order:

> ⲁⲩϫⲛⲟⲩϥ ⲛ̄ϭⲓ ⲛⲉϥⲙⲁⲑⲏⲧⲏⲥ ⲡⲉϫⲁⲩ ⲛⲁϥ ϫⲉ ⲕⲟⲩⲱϣ ⲉⲧⲣⲛ̄ⲣ̄ⲛⲏⲥⲧⲉⲩⲉ ⲁⲩⲱ ⲉϣ ⲧⲉ ⲑⲉ ⲉⲛⲁϣⲗⲏⲗ ⲉⲛⲁϯ ⲉⲗⲉⲏⲙⲟⲥⲩⲛⲏ ⲁⲩⲱ ⲉⲛⲁⲣ̄ⲡⲁⲣⲁⲧⲏⲣⲉⲓ ⲉⲟⲩⲛ̄ϭⲓⲟⲩⲱⲙ . . .
>
> ("His disciples asked him, saying: Do you wish that we *fast*, and how shall we *pray*, and how shall we give *alms*, and what diet shall we eat . . .")
>
> ⲡⲉϫⲉ ⲓ̄ⲥ̄ ⲛⲁⲩ ϫⲉ ⲉⲧⲉⲧⲛ̄ϣⲁⲛⲣ̄ⲛⲏⲥⲧⲉⲩⲉ ⲧⲉⲧⲛⲁϫⲡⲟ ⲛⲏⲧⲛ̄ ⲛ̄ⲛⲟⲩⲛⲟⲃⲉ ⲁⲩⲱ ⲉⲧⲉⲧⲛ̄ϣⲁ̄ ϣⲗⲏⲗ ⲥⲉⲛⲁⲣ̄ⲕⲁⲧⲁⲕⲣⲓⲛⲉ ⲙ̄ⲙⲱⲧⲛ̄ ⲁⲩⲱ ⲉⲧⲉⲧⲛ̄ϣⲁⲛϯ ⲉⲗⲉⲏⲙⲟⲥⲩⲛⲏ ⲉⲧⲉⲧⲛⲁⲉⲓⲣⲉ ⲛ̄ⲟⲩⲕⲁⲕⲟⲛ ⲛ̄ⲛⲉⲧⲙ̄ⲡⲛ̄ⲁ̄ . . .
>
> (Jesus said to them: If you *fast* you will bring sin to yourselves and if you *pray* you will be condemned, and if you give *alms*, you will do evil in your spirits . . .)

Matt 6:1-18 preserves the Three Rules in a special setting that betrays specific redactional interests. Most notably, the Three Rules have been cast into a catechetical framework,[56] and they have been expanded through the ad-

---

[54] Gerhardsson, "Opferdienst," 73; Betz, *Essays*, 62; Dietzfelbinger, "Frömmigkeitsregeln," 189. Syreeni (*Making*, 1.164-65) ascribes this triad of elements to the peculiar form of the Matthean version of the Q sermon (i.e., Q^{mt}).

[55] Cf. Jer 14:11-12; 2 Esdr 11:4; 1 Macc 3:46-47; Sir 7:10; 34:26. For a discussion of the rabbinic elements, see Gerhardsson, "Opferdienst," 73-75.

[56] Bultmann, *History*, 133 n. 1; Grundmann, *Evangelium*, 190; Strecker, *Bergpredigt*, 100.

dition of the Q source (vv 9-13 par. Luke 11:2-5), Marcan materials (vv 14-15 par. Mark 11:25-26) and, probably, additional sayings from elsewhere in the M source.[57] Though it is difficult to know whether v 1 should be considered as an original element of the Three Rules motif, as is suggested by the appearance and use of δικαιοσυνή ("righteousness") both here and in Tob 12:8, there is little question that the Matthean redactor[58] considers this verse to be a foundation for the Rules as they are presented in the Matthean text, since it is through the Rules that righteousness may be obtained.[59]

The Matthean version of the Three Rules presents both an explicit and an implicit scenario. Explicitly, the historical Jesus is in direct conflict with the "halachic authority" of Judaism, the proponents of which are more concerned with the observance of Torah than they are with the acceptance of the will of the Spirit. Implicitly, the post-C.E. 70 church seeks to define a cultic standard for public worship – based upon its Jewish background and traditions but in distinction from the practices of the contemporary synagogue[60] – by which community ritual can be both ordered and vibrant at the same instant. The central emphasis of each scenario is that of eschatological expectation, which has been established for the Matthean redactor in v 1 through the conscious incorporation of the term "righteousness," i.e., that goal which is achieved through the correct observance of the Three Rules.[61] Presumably, this is a primary concern of the Matthean redactor alone, and is not a concern of the tradition proper, since the element of eschatological expectation is not associated with the Three Rules elsewhere in the tradition.

It is difficult to know the original form and nature of the Three Rules schema that existed within the tradition that was received by the Matthean redactor;[62] however, it appears that the redactor was content to use the Three Rules in the regular literary pattern and parallelism that now characterizes these materials. Most importantly, the Three Rules are constructed as antitheses, much like the Antitheses that appear in Matt 5:20-48. While it may be incorrect to argue from this antithetical pattern that the Antitheses and the

---

[57] Brooks, "History," 65: "The disjunctions in grammar, supported by analysis of style and content, establish that vv. 7-8 are removed from their original context, and that Matthew is probably responsible for their inclusion within a piece of material in vv. 1-6, 16-18. The lack of redactional elements and the disjunction mentioned above [i.e., the shift from singular to plural and other stylistical peculiarities] also indicates that vv. 7-8 are probably an M saying."

[58] Presumably the final redactor; Gerhardsson, "Opferdienst," 70.

[59] See Betz, *Essays*, 60.

[60] Dietzfelbinger, "Frömmigkeitsregeln," 191.

[61] Brooks, "History," 68. Even if the term "righteousness" was originally associated with the Three Rules motif, there is no question that the term possesses a special role in the construction of the Sermon on the Mount for the Matthean redactor.

[62] Dietzfelbinger believes that the Rules may come from an oral tradition ("Frömmigkeitsregeln," 191), though there is no need to speculate that such a tradition would have come to the redactor apart from those materials that were already to be found within his community.

Three Rules were connected originally, it is not unreasonable to think that they came from the same background materials.[63]

It is this very antithetical format that serves as the point of contact between Matt 6:1-18 and *Did.* 1:3b-4, since it is the final Antitheses of Matt 5 (vv 38-48), i.e., the Antitheses that fall immediately prior to Matt 6:1-18, which are paralleled in the text of the Didache. To be accurate, the Didache does not mention almsgiving here as an element in the triad, but instead, the interpolator of 1.3b-2.1 *has* chosen to incorporate "bless" (= "glorify" [δοξάζω] in Matt. 6:2?) in this position. But the theme of "almsgiving" has not been ignored in the Didache. Indeed, it appears at two points in the text: at *Did.* 15.4 the reader is exhorted to perform "prayers, alms and acts" (εὐχας, ἐλεημοσύνας, πράξεις); and more importantly, "almsgiving" becomes the primary concern of *Did.* 1.5-6, where it serves as the focus of the concluding admonition for the 1.3b-2.1 interpolation! Despite the late nature of this interpolation, it well may be that *Did.* 1.3b-4 preserves remnants of an early Jewish tradition which came from the same source as that from which the Matthean redactor borrowed and restructured into the pattern that now appears at Matt 5:20-6:18.

2) The Matthean Gospel makes extended use of the term ἔθνος, most often in a negative sense.[64] This, of course, stands in tension with the anti-Jewish polemic that appears on occasion throughout the Gospel. One assumes that the two strands of thought derive from divergent layers in the Matthean tradition, with the anti-Jewish polemic as a later element in that tradition. It is most interesting to note, therefore, that while the Didache itself presents an anti-Jewish element in subsequent layers of the text (specifically 8.1), an element which presumably is the product of a later tendency in the tradition, 1.3b preserves an *anti-Gentile* bias.[65] This in fact may be a simple reflection of the phrase "do not also the Gentiles do the same" (οὐχι καὶ οἱ ἐθνικοὶ τὸ αὐτὸ ποιοῦσιν;), which appears in the Synoptic parallel to the interpolation, i.e., Matt 5:47 (versus Luke's *sinners* in Luke 6:33), and which the Matthean redactor has altered in 5:46 to include the more intense and heinous figure of the "tax collector" (τελώνης). But if the interpolation of 1.3b-2.1 is among the latest layers of the Didache, which it most probably is, one would not expect the interpolator to have reverted back to a Jewish sympathy. One further finds at this juncture that an anti-Gentile bias not only exists in 1.3, but indeed, that the anti-Gentile element has been placed in the middle of an ABCB′A′ pattern, which thus suggests that it holds some special meaning for the interpolator:[66]

---

[63] Wrege, *Überlieferungsgeschichte*, 94.
[64] Cf. Matt 6:7, 32; 10:5, 18.
[65] Glover, "Quotations," 14.
[66] Layton, "Sources," 354.

ποία γὰρ χάρις,
("For what credit is it to you")

ἐὰν ἀγαπᾶτε τοὺς ἀγαπῶντας ὑμᾶς;
("if you love those who love you?")

οὐχὶ καὶ τὰ ἔθνη τὸ αὐτὸ ποιοῦσιν;
("Do not even the Gentiles do the same?")

ὑμεῖς δὲ ἀγαπᾶτε τοὺς μισοῦντας ὑμᾶς,
("But you should love those who hate you,")

καὶ οὐχ ἕξετε ἐχθρόν.
("and you will have no enemy.")

It is quite likely that the interpolator does not seek to strengthen the "Jewishness" of chaps. 1-5 at all, but instead, as with the discussion of the Three Rules above, has preserved here an element of early Christian tradition that was recognized to be very old or was believed to maintain a special authority. While it is true that this tradition was preserved both in Matt 5:46 and in Luke 6:32, and therefore presumably comes from the Sayings Gospel Q, the Didache has preserved the ἔθνος (ἐθνικός) of the Matthean witness (cf. Matt 5:37).

3) With *Did.* 1.4 one again returns to the Q saying on retaliation (Matt 5:38-42; Luke 6:29-30). In its minimal form (with Luke), the saying speaks of two elements – "turning the other cheek" and "giving both the shirt and coat" – and indeed, the interpolator agrees with the Lucan redactor in the ordering of the latter saying: first "coat" (ἱμάτιον), then "shirt" (χίτον). Matthew reads: first shirt, then coat. The interpolator, however, includes a third element from the tradition ("going the extra mile") that is found only in the Matthean Gospel. While one can argue here that the interpolator has chosen simply to expand the saying by means of a comparison between the Lucan and the Matthean sources that were available, it may as easily be true that the interpolator has preserved a form of the Q saying that was known by the Matthean redactor but which was not a form of the saying that was known by the Lucan redactor.[67]

4) In *Did.* 1.4 another Q saying is preserved (Matt 5:48; Luke 6:36), though here the Didache preserves a much shorter version, which is couched in the wording of the Matthean Gospel. As with item 3 above, it is most likely that

[67] Of course, the consideration of the original Q text is most important here, though opinions among scholars differ widely. For example, both Schulz (*Q*, 123) and Lührmann ("Liebet," 418) argue that the Matthean redactor has composed this element of the tradition, while Schürmann (*Lukasevangelium*, 348 n. 41) insists that the Lucan redactor omitted it. It seems reasonable to agree with Kilpatrick here (*Origins*, 20) that the Matthean redactor has added this element to the Q materials from a separate M source.

the interpolator has preserved a form of the saying that was known to the Matthean redactor alone.[68]

5) Finally, these verses in the Didache conclude with the mysterious admonition that the reader/hearer is "unable to refuse a request." While scholars have sought in various ways to explain this exhortation, it is quite possible, of course, that this is simply the result of a transmissional error on the part of an early scribe.[69] As such, the original text probably read "ωδε" for "ουδε," and thus this phrase would have been seen as a structural and a rhetorical parallel to "and you will be perfect," i.e., "thus you will be able (to be perfect)."

Analysis of 1.5

The handiwork of the interpolator is quite evident in the structure of 1.5. Here one finds a combination of three elements: 1) the preservation of an early Christian tradition (formulated upon the Sayings Gospel Q); 2) a concern for contemporary ethics; and, 3) the formulation of a redactional framework. This verse is attached to 1.4 through the catchword "give" (δίδωμι), a term which both parallels the previous discussion and incorporates the core materials of v 5. On the other hand, the verse concludes with an observation upon the perils that are risked by those who "receive" (λαμβάνω). The structure of the verse may be viewed in three segments:

A. Give to everyone who asks of you, and do not refuse;
   for the Father desires that we give to all from our gifts.

B. Blessed is he who gives according to the *commandment* (ἐντολή),
   for he is innocent.
   Woe to him who receives;
   for if anyone receives from need, he is innocent.
   But he who receives without need shall be tried as to why he took and for what,

C. And being in prison he shall be examined concerning his actions and he shall not come out until he pay the last penny.

In part A one discovers the basic ethical tenet upon which the remainder of the verse is constructed. The first portion of part A is itself a continuation of the Q materials that are paralleled in *Did.* 1.3b-4 – specifically here, the saying that appears in Matt 5:42 and Luke 6:30:

---

[68] Köster likewise argues that καὶ ἔσῃ τέλιος ("and you will be perfect") was in the interpolator's source as a reflection of Matt 5:48, though he believes that the same phrase in *Did.* 6.2 probably comes from a redactor (*Überlieferung*, 222).

[69] For example, Hitchcock and Brown (*Teaching*, 33) point to the rule of Paul that denied Christians to "go to law before the unrighteous." For a brief review of arguments, see Layton, "Sources," 345-49.

Matt 5:42	**H 1.5**	**Luke 6:30**
	παντὶ	παντὶ
τῷ αἰτοῦντί σε	τῷ αἰτοῦντί σε	αἰτοῦντί σε
δός, καὶ	δίδου καὶ	δίδου, καὶ
τὸν θέλοντα ἀπὸ		ἀπὸ τοῦ αἴροντος
ἀπὸ σου δανίσασθαι		τὰ σὰ
μὴ ἀποστραφῇς.	μὴ ἀπαίται·	μὴ ἀπαίτει.

There is little question that the interpolator again is dependent upon the form of Q that is found in the Lucan saying. Whether one can say with certainty that the interpolator is dependent upon the Lucan Gospel itself, as seems to be indicated by the preservation of the three "Lucanisms" of παντί, δίδου, ἀπαιτέω,[70] it is difficult to say. One likewise is confronted with the fact that the Synoptic redactors agree in their preservation of additional materials in the saying (though they disagree concerning the wording of those materials), while the interpolator of the Didache seems to be unaware of any such materials. But it is most probable that the interpolator has omitted these materials in order to use this saying as the introductory foundation for the remainder of 1.5.

The remainder of part A is a rationale for this introductory exhortation, which reflects the materials that follow in parts B-C. It is most likely that this statement is the work of the interpolator, though it easily may have been drawn from the ethical consciousness of the interpolator's community.

In part B one finds the rule upon which part A is shaped. This rule, which is called the "commandment," traditionally has been seen as a reflection of one of several other early Christian texts.[71] Since this verse is among the latest strata of the Didache,[72] it is quite possible that part B here refers to the saying that is preserved in Acts 20:35, which purportedly is included by the Lucan redactor from an independent collection of sayings from the historical Jesus:[73]

μακάριόν ἐστιν μᾶλλον διδόναι ἢ λαμβάνειν.

("It is more blessed to give than to receive.")

---

[70] See a summary of this argument by Kloppenborg, "Sayings," 199-200.

[71] Sabatier sees oral tradition as the source (*Didachè*, 26 n. 3).

[72] Kraft (*Barnabas*, 60-61) notes that *Did.* 1.5-6 is missing both from the Apostolic Constitutions and from the Georgian version of the Didache. He thus assigns these two verses to "the most recent if not the final redactional level," which would explain the unique nature of this closing portion of 1.3b-2.1. Draper argues that this level still was added before the end of the first century, since there are no specific doctrinal points that are made and since the Greek is awkward ("Tradition," 271-76).

[73] So Hitchcock and Brown, *Teaching*, 33; Köster, *Überlieferung*, 230; Glover, "Quotations," 15-16; Draper, "Tradition," 276.

If this is to be considered as the source of the interpolator's words, this presents an interesting situation with respect to the Didache's relationship with the special sources of Acts (see the discussion of *Did.* 6 below). Thus, one finds here a possible reflection of a saying that is preserved by the Lucan redactor. In *Did.* 1.2c and 6.3 the Didachist parallels two elements that appear in another special source of the Lucan redactor, i.e., the Apostolic Decree of Acts 15. These two elements are, of course, the negative form of the Golden Rule (*Did.* 1.2c; Acts 15:29 [D 614 *al* h p sy^h sa; Ir]) and the prohibition against eating food that is offered to idols (*Did.* 6.3; Acts 15:29). While one is hesitant to claim that the Didachist has borrowed from Acts for these materials, especially in light of the early nature of the remainder of *Did.* 1-5, it would be quite possible for the Didachist to have acquired such materials if the first stage of the Didache was constructed in Antioch, which was the location to which the Apostolic Decree was directed, according to the witness of Acts.[74]

In *Herm. Man.* 2.4-6 one finds another parallel to this section of part B that has been argued as a possible source for the appearance of these materials in the interpolation:[75]

> Give to everyone, for to all God wishes to give from his own stores.
> Those then who receive shall be accountable to God for why they took and for what; for those who received in distress will not be punished, but those who accept in hypocrisy shall pay the penalty.
> He therefore who gives is innocent . . .
> (v. 7) Therefore keep this "commandment" (ἐντολή)

There is little question that the interpolator knows this text, or at least is familiar with the source from which it has been derived. If this is indeed the case, there is probable evidence that the interpolation, or at least this portion of the interpolation, is as late as the beginning of the second century. Apart from the parallel wording between the Didache and Hermas here, the use of the term "commandment" serves as a key element. Traditionally this term has been the hook upon which commentators have indicated Hermas to be a

---

[74] In light of this hypothesis, the question of "food offered to idols" thus would not need to be explained as the influence upon the Didachist by materials that are found in the Pauline letters.

[75] So McGiffert, "Relations," 437-38 n. 3; Layton, "Sources," 363-67. Of interest, Betz (*Essays*, 48 n. 44) makes a further cogent comment upon the use of ἐντολή in the Sermon on the Mount, which is that portion of the Matthean materials from which so much of the interpolation of 1.3b-2.1 is derived: ". . . in the [Sermon on the Mount], νόμος refers to Torah collectively, while ἐντολή, which appears only once (in 5:19), refers to Jesus' own interpretation of an individual command." This distinction would argue well for the secondary nature of *Did.* 1.3b-2.1, which otherwise does not adhere well to the general Jewish and Torah-oriented framework of *Did.* 1-5. This also lends further support to the position of Draper that the interpolation is a redefinition of the "first commandment," wherein the rule of Jesus is given priority for the Christian churches over against the rule of Torah.

source for the Didache. One is compelled to agree, however, that the text of Hermas itself is based upon some source for this saying and that it is possible, if not likely, that the interpolator of the Didache is dependent upon this common source, rather than upon Hermas itself. It is likely indeed that the source for both texts is Acts 20:35.[76]

The remainder of part B is an obvious reflection of contemporary moral speculation – the acceptance of unnecessary charity is depicted as a heinous sin. It is with part C, however, that one finds an interesting use of early Christian literature to support this speculation. Here one discovers a blatant quotation of the materials that appear in the Sayings Gospel Q (Matt 5:26; Luke 12:59):[77]

> (Matthew: ἀμὴν) λέγω σοι, οὐ μὴ ἐξέλθῃς ἐκεῖθεν, ἕως (Matthew: ἂν ἀποδῷς τὸν ἔσχατον κοδράντην. [Luke καὶ τὸ ἔσχατον λεπτὸν ἀποδῷς.])
>
> ("[Truly] I say to you, you will never get out until you have paid the last penny/copper.")

The interpolator makes no attempt to incorporate into the Didache the remainder of this Q segment, which constructs a setting for the exhortation with its "admonition to come to an agreement with an accuser quickly."[78] Instead, there is a rough and a crude attachment of the exhortation onto part B with the words ἐν συνοχῇ δὲ ("and being in prison"), whereby the occasion of the original Q setting is ignored. One finds a similarly rough textual insertion of this Q passage in the Lucan text, though the Matthean redactor obviously has managed to incorporate these verses into a suitable milieu.

Analysis of 1.6

The concluding saying of 1.3b-2.1 is unique within the interpolation in that it reflects a knowledge of early Jewish wisdom tradition, yet is not primarily dependent upon the Synoptic Gospels or upon their sources. After numerous early examinations of this mysterious saying, there is little question now that the exhortation is constructed upon a second rescension of Sir 12.1.[79] This

---

[76] Köster (*Überlieferung*, 231) speculates that 1 *Clem.* 2.1 (ἥδιον διδόντες ἢ λαμβάνοντες ["giving more gladly than receiving"]) likewise is a reflection of the saying in Acts.

[77] Because the Didache reflects the κοδράντην ("penny") of the Matthean version, most commentators indicate that the Matthean form must be the source for this reading in the text; so, Oxford Society, *New Testament*, 33-36.

[78] Kloppenborg, "Sayings," 203.

[79] See the discussions of Taylor, "Traces," 115-17 (a review of the Latin sources); Hitchcock and Brown, *Teaching*, 34 ("A homely but graphic injunction of carefulness in giving" = Sir 12.1); Sabatier, *Didachè*, 27 n. 1 (the phrase περὶ τούτου εἴρηται ["concerning this it was said"] indicates that this is not cited from scripture but alludes to a popular proverb = Sir 12.1); Muilenburg, *Relations*, 73-74 (following Taylor above); Vokes, *Riddle*, 21-22 (this is probably a restrictive correction to 1.5 = Sir 12.1); Köster, *Überlieferung*, 238 (from an unknown Jewish say-

text also is reflected in Hermas, which indicates that the saying was popular in certain circles of the primitive church. A brief comparison of texts indicates that there is no direct dependence between Hermas and the Didache, but more probably, that each text has incorporated the saying from divergent traditions of Sirach:

H 1.6	**Sir 12.1**	***Herm. Man.* 2.4b**
Ἱδρωσάτω ἡ		πᾶσιν ὑστερουμένοις
ἐλεημοσύνη σου εἰς		δίδου ἁπλῶς, μὴ
τὰς χεῖράς σου,	Ἐὰν εὖ ποιῇς	διστάζων,
μέχρις ἂν		τίνι δῷς ἢ
γνῷς,	γνῶθι	
τίνι δῷς.	τίνι ποιεῖς	τίνι μὴ δῷς.

From the above comparison one readily notes that the similarity between H and Hermas is in content alone, not in wording or structure. H is much closer to Sirach, however, and this dependence is unmistakable. Because 1.6 is presented as a direct quotation and since it has been conjoined so abruptly with 1.5, there is some reason to think that 1.6 derives from an even later hand than that of the interpolator. The overlap with Hermas argues against this assumption,[80] however, as does the presence of the basic Three Rules structure, which forms an *inclusio* to 1.3b-6 here through the reference to "alms" in 1.6.

Conclusions

From the above examination we may conclude the following with respect to 1.3b-2.1: 1) with the exception of minor redactional alterations and the isolated wisdom saying in 1.6, the section consistently is dependent upon Synoptic texts that are derived from the Sayings Gospel Q; 2) the hand of the interpolator is most evident both in 1.5-6, where a brief digression or commentary upon Matt 5:42/Luke 6:30 appears, and in the use of the Three Rules as a structural *inclusio* for the section; and, 3) the interpolator writes from within the same tradition as that of the Matthean Gospel, not only because s/he shows an awareness of that Gospel's text (s/he seems to know the Lucan Gospel as well), but because s/he uses a simple form of the Three Rules structure in a manner which diverges from that of the Matthean redactor.

There is no question that the Greek text of the Didache (H), versus the Latin text (L), has been "more thoroughly Christianized – brought up to date – by insertion of the passage."[81] Firstly, the message of the interpolation is uni-

ing); Di Lella, "Qumrân," 245-67; Skehan, "*Didache* 1,6," 533-36 (= Sir 12.1); Grant, *Apostolic Fathers*, 75 (= Sir 12.1); Layton, "Sources," 367-69 (= Sir 12.1).

[80] See the discussion of Layton, "Sources," 368-69.

[81] Layton, "Sources," 380.

quely "Christian," versus the nature of the remaining Two Ways materials. Secondly, the origin of sources for the interpolation (apart from 1.6) stems only from the canonical texts, versus the many OT and early Jewish wisdom sources in the remaining Two Ways material. It is quite evident that the Didachist is familiar with a broad background of religious texts for the basis of the Didache's religious tradition. So too, the interpolator borrows from the "holy texts" of his/her times, which are a much more restricted selection of materials.[82] While the nature of this section betrays an intent and a method that differs from those of the Didachist,[83] the familiarity with the peculiarities of the Matthean tradition suggests that this section need not be dated especially late, and certainly need not be considered as a derivation from a second-century Gospel harmony.[84] The concerns of the interpolator also are not those of the secondary redactor, who is responsible for the majority of chaps. 7-15.[85]

Didache 2.2-7: The Law

Introduction

As with 1.3b-6, *Did.* 2.1 has been assigned to a later hand by the general consensus of scholarship. The purpose of this verse is to bridge the transitional gap between the introduction of secondary materials at 1.3b-6 and the resumption of materials, now preserved at 2.2-7, which came from an earlier form of the text. The indication within the verse that the following materials are in fact the explication of a "second commandment" probably refers back to the πρῶτον . . . δεύτερον ("first . . . second") elements that are found in 1.2. Thus 2.1 implies that 2.2-7, at the minimum, and chaps. 2-4, at the maximum, are meant to serve as a commentary upon the theme "love of neighbor." This assumes, of course, that the final redactor intended for 1.3b-6 to serve as a commentary upon the "love of God" command in 1.2.[86]

---

82 Drews, "Einleitung," 186.

83 The question of whether this section should be attributed to the Didachist or to a secondary hand continues otherwise as an important issue of debate; cf. Köster, *Überlieferung*, 218, and Audet, *Didachè*, 109.

84 The discussion of a gospel harmony as the source for 1.3b-2.1 continues with arguments on all sides; cf. Warfield, "Reviews," 596; Robinson, *Barnabas*, 20; Vokes, *Riddle*, 62-64; Kline, *Sayings*, 19-20; Layton, "Sources," 377; Kloppenborg, "Sayings," 205.

85 So too, Kloppenborg, "Sayings," 205-206.

86 This is the traditional view; cf. Giet, *L'énigme*, 64. Audet argues that the phrase "second commandment" in fact means a second consideration of the Way of Life, rather than what the restrictive term "commandment" normally might suggest to the modern reader, i.e., "love your neighbor as yourself" (*Didachè*, 281). On the other hand, Draper ("Tradition," 271) believes that the latest redactional phase of the Didache (1.3b-2.1, 8 and 15:3-4, according to him), which has been incorporated into the text of the Didache "to subordinate the [earlier] teaching contained

While the collocation of the Two Ways, the Golden Rule and the decalogue does not appear commonly within Jewish-Christian literature,[87] these three elements in fact are placed together within the Matthean Gospel, two in the Sermon and one in each of the pericopae of Matt 19:16-19 and 22:34-40.[88] Since we have argued above that the interpolation at 1.3b-6 has been inserted into the Didache with the purpose of aligning the theology of the text with the perspective of the Matthean Gospel, it does not follow that 1.1-3a, 2.2-7 was ordered according to the Gospel as well. Instead, the Didachist and the Matthean redactor each may be dependent upon a common tradition. If this indeed is the case, the Matthean redactor also may have found these three motifs joined together within the community tradition.[89]

With 2.2 the Didachist begins an explication of the Way of Life that is based upon a review of the second table of the decalogue.[90] One finds similar listings of the decalogue at 3.2-6 and 5.1 – the former couched within the special considerations of the Jewish wisdom tradition and the latter constructed to serve as an explication of the Way of Death.[91] The text of the decalogue that is found at 2.2-7 is in fact only an abbreviated version of its OT parallels, but it is expanded by additional elements, which no doubt stem from the contemporary milieu of the Didachist. Our initial concern, therefore, is to establish whether this framework indeed does stem from an OT text, or instead, from a later source, that has been significantly modified by the early church community.

---

in the Didache to the authority of the Gospel," is best observed at this very point in the text. Thus he notes that "the teaching of Jesus becomes the 'first teaching' of the Way of Life (1:3), displacing the Torah to a 'second teaching' (2:1)."

[87] Oesterley (*Background*, 150-51) offers the interesting observation that the decalogue typically was recited after the shema in the early synagogue: "therefore the assumption is justified that the first Jewish Christians did the same; indeed, this is practically proved by the fact that the Synagogue abrogated the liturgical use of the Decalogue 'on account of the cavilling of the heretics,' i.e. Christians. If this was so, however, the custom must have ceased at an early period; for it does not appear, as far as can be ascertained, that any trace of the liturgical use of the Decalogue is to be discovered in any early Christian Liturgy." [p. 150 n. 3: "The references to the Decalogue in *Did.* ii and *Barn.* xix do not offer any evidence for its liturgical use."])

[88] Warfield, "Text," 140; Greyvenstein, "'Teaching,'" 107-108; Audet, *Didachè*, 282.

[89] If Paul also had contact with the early Matthean community, a likely possibility should that community be identified with Antioch, the apostle's collocation of the decalogue, "love of neighbor" and Golden Rule motifs at Rom 13:8-10 also might stem from this same hermeneutical tradition which existed within the community. On the other hand, Spence (*Teaching*, 14) believes that the Didache in fact is dependent upon the text of Romans here. This is unlikely, however, since there appears to be no other allusion to the epistle in the Didache.

[90] Muilenburg (*Relations*, 145) calls this section of the text, i.e., 2.2-3, "redundant" when considered in relation to the materials of chap. 3. Audet correctly notes, however, that there is specifically a literary unity here which reflects a "legal" style in distinction from the "sapiential" format of 3.1-4.14. Further, Audet observes that there is in general a lack of awareness in chap. 2 with respect to motifs that were influenced by the sapiential tradition.

[91] It must be agreed with Warfield, however, that while each of these lists ultimately must be perceived in relation to one another, "we must guard against erecting an artificial harmony between the three lists" ("Texts," 145).

Comparison of Sources for 2.2-3[92]

H 2.2	Exod 20:13-16	Exodus text [A]	Deut 5:17-20
φονεύσεις,		φονεύσεις.	
μοιχεύσεις,	μοιχεύσεις.	μοιχεύσεις.	μοιχεύσεις.
			φονεύσεις.
. . .			
κλέψεις,	κλέψεις.	κλέψεις.	κλέψεις.
	φονεύσεις.		
. . .			
ψευδομαρ-τυρήσεις,	ψευδομαρ-τυρήσεις	ψευδομαρ-τυρήσεις	ψευδομαρ-τυρήσεις
. . .			

As can be observed readily above, the various OT parallels of the decalogue show a form that usually is slightly divergent from that of the Didache. That version which is identical to the ordering of the Didache, as a result of the reversed order that is given to the elements of "murder" (φονεύσεις) and "adultery" (μοιχεύσεις) – a consistent ordering throughout the Didache (cf. 2.2, 3.2 and 5.1) – is the particular arrangement of Exod 20:13-16 which is found in Codex Alexandrinus. The significance of this ordering in Codex Alexandrinus is that the manuscript most accurately preserves the MT form of the decalogue in both Exodus and Deuteronomy. While the elements in the Greek witnesses do not identify readily on a one-to-one basis with respect to the order of elements that are found in the Didache, apart from Codex Alexandrinus, a close parallel indeed does appear in that tradition which is based upon the MT. It is upon this comparison that most scholars have indicated the OT to be the source from which the Didachist has drawn the framework of *Did.* 2.2.[93]

H 2.2	Matt 19:18	Mark 10:19	Luke 18:20
			μὴ μοιχεύσῃς,
οὐ φονεύσεις,	οὐ φονεύσεις,	μὴ φονεύσῃς,	μὴ φονεύσῃς,
οὐ μοιχεύσεις,		οὐ μοιχεύσῃς,	μὴ μοιχεύσῃς,
. . .			
οὐ κλέψεις,	οὐ κλέψεις,	μὴ κλέψῃς,	μὴ κλέψῃς,
. . .			
οὐ ψευδομαρ-τυρήσεις,	οὐ ψευδομαρ-τυρήσεις,	μὴ ψευδομαρ-τυρήσῃς,	μὴ ψευδομαρ-τυρήσῃς,
. . .		. . .	

[92] In order to conserve space in the opening analysis of OT parallels, negative particles are not provided before individual elements. In each case that particle is οὐ.

[93] Hitchcock and Brown, *Teaching*, lxxix; Sabatier, *Didachè*, 29 n. 2 (Exod 20:13-17); Harnack, *Lehre*, 65 (Deut 5:17-19); Funk, *Patres Apostolici*, 1.xv-xvi; Köster, *Überlieferung*, 162-63;

As with our previous consideration of OT parallels, one also finds in the witness of the Synoptic Gospels a close association with the elements of *Did.* 2.2. The Matthean form of the text is without question the closest Synoptic parallel, while the Lucan version has followed the Marcan tradition in its use of the negative particle μή.[94] Further, the Lucan redactor has made an obvious effort to follow that version of the decalogue which is presented in the Deuteronomic tradition. Several scholars thus have opted for Matt 19:18 as the probable source text that was used by the Didachist.[95]

Analysis of 2.2-5

The structure of the decalogue has been expanded by the Didachist at *Did.* 2-3 to include specific prohibitions against contemporary threats to the ethical perspective of the community.[96] Included in this expansion are short lists of specific vices that were developed upon the more general themes of the decalogue. Thus one finds the following structure in vv 2-3:

Audet, *Didachè*, 282; Glover, "Quotations," 17 (LXX Exod 20:13-14); Giet, *L'énigme*, 64; Draper, "Tradition," 272. Köhler (*Rezeption*, 47-48) also points to Exod 20:14-17 MT as the source here.

[94] The Western text of Mark 10:19 includes an additional element in its framework which appears after μὴ μοιχεύσῃς, i.e., μὴ πορνεύσῃς ("do not commit fornication"). This shows some parallel with *Did.* 2.2, where one reads after οὐ μοιχεύσεις the prohibitions οὐ παιδοφθορήσεις, οὐ πορνεύσεις ("do not commit sodomy, do not commit fornication"). The element of "fornication" appears elsewhere in the texts of *Herm. Man.* 8.3 and *Barn.* 19.4. There are, of course, those scholars who have argued that the Didachist is primarily dependent upon the text of Barnabas for its reconstruction of the decalogue; cf. Knopf, *Lehre*, 10-12; Robinson, *Barnabas*, 60; Muilenburg, *Relations*, 145 (though Muilenburg's statement is most confusing: "The procedure of the compiler is apparent. On the basis of the precepts in the Epistle he sets to work to adapt his materials to the setting of the O.T. commands (Deut 5:17ff) cited by Matthew. Nor is there anything extraordinary in his method, for he simply groups together kindred precepts, thus separating members of the same source (e.g. Matthew or Barnabas) from each other."); Vokes, *Riddle*, 92 (*Did.* 2.2 possibly uses Exod 20:17 here as it is quoted in Barnabas); Massaux, *Influence*, 638-39 (while the Didache is couched here in a Matthean format and inspired by Matt 19:16-19, it is informed by Barnabas); Kraft, *Barnabas*, 186. Against these scholars, Köster argues that the order of elements in the Didache is earlier than that which is found in Barnabas (*Überlieferung*, 162).

[95] Schaff, *Manual*, 18 (one finds here an echo of the Sermon on the Mount with "peculiar features derived from oral tradition"); Iselin, *Version*, 15-17; Warfield, "Texts," 144 ("An enlarged, explained, and enforced decalogue, on the model of our Lord's words as reported by Matthew, seems to be the author's purpose."); Funk, *Patres Apostolici*, 1.7; Greyvenstein, "'Teaching,'" 108-109; Muilenburg, *Relations*, 145.

[96] Scholars have been "at pains" to make this notation – cf. Sabatier, *Didachè*, 28 n. 2 ("In the first century, Christianity struggled continually against superstition equally profuse amongst the Jews and pagans." [translation mine]); Knopf, *Lehre*, 10-11 (the list of sexual sins comes from the ethic of Hellenistic Judaism); Klevinghaus, *Stellung*, 136; Audet, *Didachè*, 286 (following Seeberg, *Wege*, 8-9, Audet believes that these additional materials arose within a Jewish milieu as a hedge against threatening "Greek" offenses).

GENERAL	GENERAL	GENERAL
SPECIFIC	SPECIFIC	SPECIFIC
1) murder	5) theft	10) covetousness
2) adultery	6) magic	11) perjury
3) sodomy	7) philtres	12) false witness
4) fornication	8) abortion	13) speaking evil
	9) infanticide	14) bear malice

There does not appear to be an obvious rationale for this structure, though it is apparent that the redactor has taken the opportunity to "build" upon those elements of the decalogue which were most pertinent to the community situation.

With the conclusion of *Did.* 2.2 (οὐκ ἐπιθυμήσεις τὰ τοῦ πλησίον ["you shall not covet your neighbor's goods"]) one discovers a theme that is resumed later in 2.6a, that of "covetousness" (οὐκ ἔσῃ πλεονέκτης ["do not be covetous"]). The appearance of this theme of "covetousness" at 2.2 and again in 2.6a forms an *inclusio* around three verses (vv 3-5) that focus upon the sin of "false witness" (οὐ ψευδομαρτυρήσεις ["you shall not bear false witness"]), which itself is taken from the decalogue. These three verses utilize the motif of "false witness" through the presentation of a series of prohibitions against the incorrect use of speech, or perhaps more accurately said, against the "sins of the tongue." The unique attention that is given to "the spoken sin" in vv 3-5 suggests that the Didachist purposefully may have opted to construct this series of prohibitions in order to combat against the dangers of harmful speech which had become a contemporary threat within the community in which the Didache was constructed.[97] If the NT is to serve as a guide here,[98] one is led to believe that the "ordering" of the early Christian community, both with respect to its internal structure and with respect to its association with "the world," required considerable attention!

While there is little question that vv 3-5 are hinged upon the motif of "false witness," an element that is common to most forms of the decalogue in early Christian literature, the appearance of the prohibition οὐ ἐπιορκήσεις ("you shall not commit perjury") in a position that is immediately prior to the prohibition against "false witness" in v 3 is most interesting. The term is found in the biblical canon only at Matt 5:33. This suggests either that this element has been borrowed from the Matthean text for use in the Didache (which thus would lead one to argue that vv 3-5 must be attributed to the second redactor

[97] Interestingly, *Dida.* 2.6.1 subsequently has defined this issue around a figure who could have controlled such issues, that of the bishop: "And let him [the bishop] not be double-minded nor double-tongued"!

[98] See Matt 5:22-26; 18:15-20; Acts 15:36-41; etc.

of the Didache)[99] or that the term is derived from the same source as that which was used by the Matthean redactor in the composition of the Antitheses at Matt 5:21-48 (which thus would lead one to argue that vv 3-5 may be attributed to the Didachist, who used that source as well). There is no additional evidence within these verses to support the former position.[100] One thus may argue with some assurance that the Didachist not only based the structure of 2.2-3 upon some form of the decalogue which appears in the OT and/or Matt 19:18, as is indicated above, but also, that the source which provided this form of the decalogue was used by the Matthean redactor in the construction of the Sermon on the Mount.[101]

Analysis of 2.6-7

Did. 2.6a serves a dual function within the structure of chap. 2. On the one hand, it serves as a thematic *inclusio* to vv 3-5 in conjunction with the term ἐπιθυμήσεις, which is found in v 2 (see the above discussion). On the other hand, it functions as a "hook" upon which several thematically-related prohibitions are attached, i.e., "extortion" (ἅρπαξ), "hypocrisy" (ὑπόκρισις), "malignance" (κακοήθης) and "pride" (ὑπερήφανος). This pattern, of course, is evident in vv 2-5 as well.[102]

Did. 2.6b is not attached to 2.6a with respect to structure, but serves as an introduction to the chapter's concluding admonition in v 7. In 2.6b-7 one finds the concern for neighbor that was exhibited previously in the saying to "love thy neighbor" at 1.2b; however, it is the *practical* implications of the saying that are of primary concern here. These implications first appear in the form of negative exhortations ("you shall make no evil plan against your neighbor; you shall hate no man" [οὐ λήψῃ βουλὴν πονηρὰν κατὰ τοῦ πλησίον σου. οὐ μισήσεις πάντα ἄνθρωπον]), and appear secondly in the

---

[99] Robinson, *Barnabas*, 59.

[100] Indeed, while 2.3 prohibits "perjury," there is no prohibition against swearing in general, such as is found with Matt 5:33-37! This would suggest, then, that the Didachist had no knowledge of the tradition against the concept of swearing, the prohibition of which is advocated both in Matthew and Jas 5:12; cf. Harnack, *Lehre*, 51; Knopf, *Lehre*, 11.

[101] This observation would appear to support the position of Bultmann (*History*, 135-36) that the Matthean redactor used a source which included those elements in the decalogue that are reflected by Antitheses 1, 2 and 4 in Matt 5:21-48, upon which Antitheses 3, 5 and 6 were subsequently added. This view stands in contradiction to the position of Strecker ("Antithesen," passim), who argues that it is Antitheses 1, 2 and 3 which are to be attributed to this earlier source.

With respect to the decalogue and its forms, one must remember that the period in which the Didache was composed, whether the first, second or third centuries, was a period of textual fluidity. While it is difficult to know the nature of specific sources that may have been used by the Didachist, those forms that are preserved for us in the major biblical witnesses are considered here as likely representatives of the format that was incorporated and used by the early church.

[102] Knopf, *Lehre*, 12.

form of positive exhortations ("reprove/convince" . . . "pray" . . . "love" [ἐλέγχω . . . προσεύχομαι . . . ἀγαπάω]). Vv 6b-7 thus reveal a certain pattern whereby the gravity and the intensity of the text ascends and descends – the lighter tone of 2.6b becomes the warning of 2.7a, and the command to "reprove/convince" becomes the admonition to "love" in 2.7b-d:[103]

2.6b – οὐ *λήψῃ βουλὴν πονηρὰν* κατὰ τοῦ πλησίον σου.
("do not *make an evil plan* against your neighbor")

2.7a – οὐ *μισήσεις* πάντα ἄνθρωπον,
("do not *hate* any person")

2.7b – ἀλλὰ
("but")

οὓς μὲν *ἐλέγξεις,*
("*reprove/convince* some")

2.7c – περὶ δὲ ὧν *προσεύξῃ*
("and *pray* for some")

2.7d – οὓς δὲ *ἀγαπήσεις* ὑπὲρ τὴν ψυχήν σου.
("and *love* some more than your own life.")

V 6b has been taken directly from the Two Ways source, as is indicated by an exact word-for-word parallel which appears in *Barn.* 19.3c. Using v 6b as an introduction, v 7 has been constructed upon a second source, i.e., Lev 19:17-18. This becomes immediately obvious upon a comparison of the verbal patterns that are found in Lev 19:17-18 and *Did.* 2.7a-b,d:

Lev 19:17 – οὐ *μισήσεις* τὸν ἀδελφόν σου τῇ διανοίᾳ σου, ἐλεγμῷ *ἐλέγξεις* τὸν πλησίον σου . . .
("You shall not *hate* your brother in your heart, but you shall *reason* with your neighbor . . .")

Lev 19:18 – . . . καὶ *ἀγαπήσεις* τὸν πλησίον σου ὡς σεαυτόν·
(". . . but you shall *love* your neighbor as yourself.")

Since *Did.* 2-3 already is highly dependent upon the OT in general and upon the decalogue in particular, it certainly is conceivable that 2.7 has been structured around this section of Leviticus in order to incorporate the use of the "love of neighbor" motif which is found here in the scriptures. The additional use of "pray" by the Didachist at 2.7c may simply have derived from the Didachist's concern to restructure the passage into its current pattern, as was noted above.[104]

---

[103] Audet, *Didachè*, 294; cf. Harnack, *Lehre*, 52.

[104] One notes that the initial half of Lev 19:18 has not been included by the Didachist. It is at this very point that *Did.* 2.7c has been inserted. *(note 104 continued on p. 60)*

Significant Parallels Outside of the Synoptic Gospels

Prominent parallels to *Did.* 2 appear throughout the NT and early Christian literature which no doubt should be reviewed quickly here. With respect to those elements that are found in vv 2-3 which do not appear in the decalogues of the OT, numerous examples abound, though their significance is difficult to ascertain.[105] Of particular interest is the fact that Clement of Alexandria includes παιδοφθορήσεις in one of his renderings of the decalogue, but omits it from two other renderings.[106] This inconsistent usage of elements by the same author reminds one that divergent forms of the decalogue circulated independently within Judeo-Christian circles, often reflecting the addition of scattered exhortations into the framework of the text. Further, one is reminded that many authors had access to more than one form of the decalogue, which today is generally recognized only in its "ten-point" pattern!

Numerous parallels also exist for various elements in vv 4-5 which suggest the particular influence of Proverbs (6:2; 11:13; 14:27; 21:6) and Sirach (1:28; 2:22; 5:9; 5:14; 28:13-15; 51:2).[107] Here one can find the influence of a strong wisdom tradition, much like that which dominates the rendering of the decalogue in *Did.* 3.

Finally, at vv 6-7 scholars traditionally have noted some relationship between the Didache and the NT text of Jude 22-23.[108] Indeed, in both passages one discovers a common exhortation to "reprove/convince" (Didache = οὓς μὲν ἐλέγξεις ["some you shall reprove/convince"]; Jude = οὓς μὲν ἐλεᾶτε ["reprove/convince some"]), which perhaps suggests some direct relationship between the two texts. In addition, each text lists three elements by which the reader is compelled to respond in a positive manner toward those who are weak or who have fallen. The Didachist includes within the parameters of its

---

There is little question that Matt 18:15ff. is likewise based upon Lev 19:17. Interestingly, however, while the Didachist has revealed a much more positive and hopeful attitude toward reconciliation with one's neighbor, the Matthean text reflects the negative and hardened (and no doubt later) attitude of a more structured Christian community.

[105] Already by the turn of the century Hitchcock and Brown (*Teaching*, 34-35) and Sabatier (*Didachè*, 28 n. 2, 30 nn. 1-2) had indicated the most logical parallels for consideration: "sodomy" (παιδοφθορέω) → Lev 18:22; 20:13; Rom 1:27; *Barn.* 10.6; Clem. *paed.* 2.10; 3.12; Clem. *str.* 3.36; Clem. *protr.* 10.108.5 (cf. for the verbal form *Barn.* 19.4, *AC* 7.2; Just. *dial.* 95); "philtres" (φαρμακεύς) → LXX, passim; Rev 21:8; "abortion" (φονεύσεις τέκνον ἐν φθορᾷ) → *Barn.* 19.5; Clem. *paed.* 2.194; "perjury" (ἐπιορκέω) → Zech 8:17; Wis 14:28; 1 Tim 1:10; "malice" (μνησικακέω) → Prov 21:24; Zech 7:10; 8:17; *Barn.* 2.8; *Herm. Vis.* 2.3.1; *Herm. Man.* 8.3; 9.3; *Herm. Sim.* 9.23.4; 1 *Clem. 2.5*; Clem. *str.* 7.14.

[106] Cf. Clem. *protr.* 10.108.5 versus Clem. *str.* 2.7.3 and 4.3.10. Harnack argues from the presence of the term in the initial reference that Clement here is dependent upon the Didache's listing of the decalogue, versus the listing that is found in *Barn.* 19 (*Lehre*, 9). Of course, it was not uncommon for patristic authors to use their source texts in varying forms.

[107] Cf. also Ps 18:5; Eccl 5:1-7; Wis 1:11; Tob 14:10; Pirqe Aboth 1.15.

[108] See Warfield, "Texts," 144; Funk, *Patres Apostolici*, 8; Oxford Society, *New Testament*, 25; Knopf, *Lehre*, 12; Vokes, *Riddle*, 19; Lilje, *Lehre*, 50-51; Lake, *Apostolic Fathers*, 313 n. 1.

exhortations, however, admonitions toward prayer (cf. 1.3 above) and "love of neighbor," which are not paralleled in Jude's salvation by "fire and fear." Thus, while the two texts reveal a certain similarity in structure and in theme, these elements might well be attributed to a common literary source or oral tradition that was widely recognized during the early Christian period.

Most importantly in our brief review of early Christian literature are those parallels that are offered by the text of Barnabas. Both *Did.* 2 and 3 reveal some special unity with *Barn.* 19, as is indicated by those verses which traditionally were attributed to the Two Ways source. While *Barn.* 19.4 reveals a much abbreviated version of the decalogue (οὐ πορνεύσεις, οὐ μοιχεύσεις, οὐ παιδοφθορήσεις) the chapter contains many other elements that are paralleled in *Did.* 2.[109] One must be careful, however, to recognize the incorporation of several sources within *Did.* 2, i.e., a form of the decalogue which is more readily paralleled both by the Matthean Gospel and by the OT than it is by Barnabas, and some form of the Two Ways source. Further, one must take into account that the text of the Didache was molded by several redactors, some of whom combined chap. 2 with chap. 3 and others of whom installed the redactional insertion of 1.3b-2.1. Finally, vv 3-5 may in fact indicate an additional element of commentary or elaboration that was interlaced within the framework of the chapter, so as to complicate even further the web of influences that have shaped the text.

Conclusions

As will be supported further in the discussion below, the framework of the decalogue serves as the structure upon which much of chaps. 2-3 are constructed. The particular literary texts that most accurately reflect that form of the decalogue which is found in *Did.* 2 include the materials of Exod 20 MT and Codex Alexandrinus, as well as the texts at Matt 5 and 19.[110] While arguments have been made by scholars to support the opinion that the Didachist was dependent upon either a specific OT or NT version of the decalogue, no study has been conclusive. In point of fact, any of the canonical sources for the decalogue easily could have been incorporated into the framework of *Did.* 2. Since no specific influence from the narrative frameworks that surround the Matthean versions of the decalogue is apparent in the Didache, however, it is suggested here that the Didachist relied upon an OT source. By the same token, the Matthean redactor likewise may have been

[109] Cf. *Did.* 2.4 = *Barn.* 19.7a, 8c-d; *Did.* 2.5 = *Barn.* 19.4d, 5; *Did.* 6 = *Barn.* 19.6b, 3d; *Did.* 2.7 = *Barn.* 19.11, 5c.

[110] The murder → adultery order of the prohibitions in H is supported over against the L reading by the Church Ordinances, the Apostolic Constitutions and Clem. *protr.* 109.

dependent upon this same OT source (i.e., the source that was used by the Didachist) for the basis of the Matthean construction that appears at Matt 5:21-48. Further, the Matthean redactor may have implemented this source again at Matt 19:16-22 as a standard by which to correct the Marcan and the Lucan forms of the pericope about the "Rich Young Man."[111]

The final element of the decalogue that appears in *Did.* 2.3 ("false witness") has become the thematic basis for vv 3-5. It is impossible to determine whether the Didachist has incorporated this collection of exhortations from a separate source, or whether s/he simply composed the segment him/herself. In either case, the framework that is formed by the motif of "covetousness" which surrounds the segment can probably be attributed to the redactor.

Finally, vv 6b-7 serve two functions within the framework of chaps. 1-2. On the one hand, these verses repeat the "love of neighbor" motif that was found originally in 1.2b, and therefore, form a thematic *inclusio* around the text of chap. 2 (and by the time of the final redaction of the text, they were used to form an *inclusio* around 1.3-2.1 as well).[112] On the other hand, vv 6-7 form a carefully-tailored set of exhortations that are based upon the framework and the considerations of Lev 19:17-18. The manner in which the closing admonitions to "reprove/convince, pray and love" are structured suggests that one finds here a reflection of some well-established system for the confrontation of dissenters within the community – a system which stems from an idealized vision of the early Christian movement, unlike the more legalistic and negative criteria for judging wrongdoers which appears in the later texts of the Matthean Gospel and of Jude.[113]

---

[111] I thus would disagree with Warfield's analysis that *Did.* 2.4-6 "expands" upon Matt 19:19, but instead, I would assert that both the Matthean redactor and the Didachist are dependent upon the same source.

[112] Warfield ("Texts," 144-45) notes here that "the final clause of the chapter is apparently again due to Matt xix. 19; as the one closes the list of commandments with the command to love our neighbors, so does the other bring his list to an end with a somewhat strengthened reminiscence of the same." As is argued above, this observation is consistent with that tradition concerning "love of God" and "love of neighbor" sayings that is shared both by the Matthean redactor and by the Didachist.

[113] Thus Frend notes: "The ethical teaching of both writers [Didache and 1 Clement] seems also to owe less to the Sermon on the Mount, though the *Didache* was familiar with this, than to ideas drawn from the Two Ways combined with the wisdom of Job, Proverbs, and Ecclesiastes" (*Christianity*, 137).

Didache 3: A Fence to the Law (Part 1)

Introduction

From the outset there appears to be little question that chaps. 3-4 form a concatenation of hortatory instructions whose Jewish literary sources and ethical principles have been interwoven with early Christian concerns. In this respect chap. 3 serves as a more specific complement to chap. 2[114] as the text now stands. Thus, in association with chap. 4, chap. 3 was labeled by many early scholars who were conversant with the rabbinic tradition as a "fence to the Law," i.e., a legalistic "safeguard" with respect to the exhortations of 2.2-7.[115]

Two distinctive literary units appear within the third chapter of the Didache: vv 1-6, a structurally unified list of negative admonitions, and vv 8-10, additional admonitions with parallels in the text of *Barn.* 19. V 7, which is a positive response to the exhortations of 3.1-6, will be examined in a separate discussion below.

Analysis of 3.1-6[116]

Vv 2-6 have been recognized for many years as a distinctive literary unit that was incorporated from an independent source by the Didachist, who probably also inserted 3.1 to accompany the text as an introductory statement for the entire unit.[117] The unit is that portion of the chapter which most closely

---

[114] Sabatier notes that chap. 3 must be a secondary reading that was inserted and was arranged by the Didachist (*Didachè*, 33 n. 2). He believes that chaps. 3-4 are a thematic elaboration, which is based upon that form of the decalogue which is provided in chap. 2 (34-35 n. 1).

[115] Taylor, *Teaching*, 23; Harris, *Teaching*, 80; Vokes, *Riddle*, 76. Taylor places special emphasis upon the nature of 3.1, which parallels in both theme and wording the texts of *b. Ḥul* 44b (הרחק מן הכיעור ומן הדומה לו ["Keep far from the base and from that which resembles it."]) and *'Aboth R. Nat.* 2 הרחק מן הכיעור ומן הדומה לכיעור ["Keep far from the repulsive and from that which resembles the repulsive."]). In opposition to Taylor's views, Audet argues that one does not in fact find a "fence" motif here, since the text does not legalistically protect the specificities of Torah via elaborate discussion, as in traditional rabbinic style (*Didachè*, 301-302). While Audet's point carries some validity with respect to discussions of the elaborately-developed rabbinic methodology which served to mold the parameters of an oral Torah, the failure of the Didachist to reproduce precisely such an exacting methodological format need not indicate that the Didachist did not desire to create such a fence. It merely implies that the Didachist either was not steeped in such rabbinic tradition, or more likely, that s/he chose not to incorporate such a format of rhetorical discourse into the tractate. Interestingly, Audet appears to reverse himself later by his notation that Taylor's comparison of 3.1 with *b. Ḥul.* 44b in fact represents a justified analysis of the argumentative context of 3.1-6, which accurately reflects the sages! Funk (*Patres Apostolici*, xvi) even argues that 3.1-6 is merely a commentary upon the sins that are illustrated in 2.2-3.

[116] For critical apparati to the text, see Wohleb, *Übersetzung*, 25-28, and Rordorf and Tuilier, *Doctrine*, 152-54.

[117] McGiffert, "Relations," 436; Harnack, *Lehre*, 11, 52 (the redactor took a more active role

reflects the themes of chap. 2 that are derived from the decalogue. The section is characterized by a tightly-knit strophic pattern that is not revealed elsewhere in the Didache. It does not present any materials that are paralleled in Barnabas. This lack of association with Barnabas is atypical of the Two Ways source that is used by both documents, i.e., by Barnabas and by the Didache, and in this respect vv 2-6 diverge from vv 9-10, a section that is aligned closely with *Barn.* 19.4-6.

With respect to structure, 3.2-6 presents five negative admonitions on "murder" (φόνος), "adultery" (μοιχεία), "idolatry" (εἰδωλολατρία), "theft" (κλοπή) and "blasphemy" (βλασφημία) respectively. Each in its turn is accompanied by a coterie of lesser sins, participation in any one of which leads to these five more contemptable vices. Unlike the list of vices that is given in chap. 2, which appears to be merely an abbreviated form of the decalogue that has been elaborated by contemporary (Christian?) writers without any particular stylistic flair, 3.2-6 is structured according to a distinctive, repetitive pattern that uses the catchword μηδέ ("nor") as a mnemonic device.[118]

With respect to possible source texts behind vv 2-6, scholars have offered numerous parallels from the OT, NT and Intertestamental literature for the individual verses.[119] As might be expected by the close adherence of the text to elements in the decalogue, however, the primary sources to be suggested have been Exod 20, Deut 5 and Matt 5.

A cursory glance at *Did.* 3.2-6 immediately reveals a dependence upon the terminology that is found in commandments 6-9 of the decalogue (cf. Exod

---

in composing the segment based upon OT sayings [67]); Robinson, *Barnabas*, 61-62 (borrowed from some "apocryphal book"); Muilenberg, *Relations*, 34, 74 (following Harnack and Robinson, "derived from a *Jewish* apocryphal work" with revision by the redactor [emphasis mine]); Vokes, *Riddle*, 39, 63, 120-25; Audet, *Didachè*, 156-57; Kraft, *Barnabas*, 63 ("perhaps pre-Christian addition"; notes that the term for "blasphemy" (βλασφημία), while common in ancient vice-lists in general, appears only at this point in the Didache [146]). Vögtle (*Lasterkataloge*, 197-98) attributes the composition of 3.1-6 to "Christian authors," but does not "in a word" reject the supposition that the segment derives from a separate source.

As is observed by Connolly ("Fragments," 152), the author of the Greek fragment of *Did.* 2-3 (i.e., POxy 1782), seems to have noted on purpose that there was to be some significant separation between chaps. 2-3, as is indicated within the text "by a row of wedge-shaped signs below which there are 'horizontal dashes.'" It is conceivable, therefore, that this scribe also recognized a distinctive change of style (= new source?) beginning with chap. 3.

[118] Harnack, *Lehre*, 52; Kraft, *Barnabas*, 146; cf. the opposite opinion of Warfield, "Texts," 147. For a detailed analysis of the structure, see the discussion that is provided by Audet (*Didachè*, 297-98), who notes that minor distortions in the pattern have resulted from the transmission of the tradition. So too, Schlecht (*Apostellehre*, 50) argues that 3.3-4a, which is missing in L, is probably original to the pattern, since it also appears in the Church Ordinances, *AC* 7 and Pseudo-Athanasius.

[119] Suggested parallels include the following: for 3.1, *T. Dan* 6.8, Gal 5:21, and 1 Thes 5:22; for 3.2, Gal 5:20; for 3.4, *T. 12 Patr.* 4.19, *Sib. Or.* 3.22ff., Lev 19:26, 31, and Deut 18:10-11; for 3.5, Prov 21:6; for 3.6, Wis 1:11, 1 Cor 10:10, Phil 2:14, Titus 1:7, 1 Pet 4:19, 2 Pet 2:10.

20:13-17; Deut 5:17-21).[120] These elements, with the addition of the concluding admonition concerning "covetousness," in effect form the "second tablet" of laws within the corpus of the decalogue (as that tablet of laws was conceived by the early rabbis).[121] Attempts to make strict associations between the individual elements of *Did.* 3.2-6 and the latter laws of the decalogue are at best strained.[122] It indeed may be that 3.2-6 was designed simply to offer sufficient parallels with the decalogues of the OT so as to suggest the latter half of the corpus (i.e., the commandments that are related to human interaction) to the hearer/reader or to the catechumen. In this respect, vv 2-6 never actually were intended to be a rigorous reflection of each individual element in the decalogue.[123] Thus, 3.2-6 readily leads the reader's mind to an association with the decalogue even today, yet places this basic body of ancient law into a structure that was incorporated easily by the Didachist for use in the contemporary situation.

The second primary set of materials to consider as a source for *Did.* 3.2-6 is that of Matt 5:21-37. While scholars have argued with good evidence that this section of the Matthean Gospel shows close affinities to 3.2-6,[124] one

---

Drews ("Untersuchungen," 56-59) has in fact demonstrated the unique verbal and thematic parallels that exist betweeen *Did.* 3, Col 3:5-12 and Eph 4:2, 26-32. Each of these sources most assurably reflects a knowledge of a standardized virtue- and vice-catalogue of the contemporary Greco-Roman world. This is to be expected for the texts of Colossians and Ephesians, but would be an interesting "forerunner" if it indeed was shared as well by *Did.* 3.2-6. Drews, unfortunately, does not speak to the unique structural aspects of vv 2-6. These structural peculiarities in fact argue that a different textual tradition was used in the Didache.

Of course, many of those elements that are found in 3.2-6 are paralleled in varying order throughout the post-apostolic texts (cf. Seeberg, *Katechismus*, 23-30. Just. *dial.* 93.1 lists the elements as adultery, fornication and murder, and associates these with a theme that is found in *Did.* 1.2ab, that of the "Great Commandment.") and other Greco-Roman writings (cf. Cic. *tusc.* 4.7, and its source texts, Diogenes Laertius 7.111, 113). Yet, as has been well demonstrated by Hitchcock and Brown (*Teaching* 36-38), a number of terms in this unit appear either infrequently within the NT and the LXX, or are *hapax legomena* of that literature.

[120] The order of elements 1 (murder), 2 (adultery) and 4 (theft), again reflects that of Codex Alexandrinus (see the discussion of 2.2-3 above).

[121] Harnack, *Lehre*, 52. See *Mek. Bah.* 8, where the order of the elements that is provided on the tablets is given as 1-5 (= tablet 1) and 6-10 (= tablet 2), according to Rabbi Hananiah ben Gamaliel. Cf. Philo. *decal.* 29-33.

[122] Cf. Taylor (*Teaching*, 25-26), who argues that *Did.* 3.2 served as a "fence" to decalogue commandment 6; 3.3-4 to commandment 7; 3.5 to commandment 8; and, 3.6 to commandment 9. He further notes that commandment 10 did not receive comment in the Didache because "it is itself of the nature of a fence."

[123] As such, a certain adaptation to "wisdom categories" may have been of primary concern to the Didachist here, in keeping with the nature of *Did.* 3-4 in general; so Audet, *Didachè*, 301. Cf. Klevinghaus, *Stellung*, 147. (See the discussion of *Did.* 3.7 below.) The use of wisdom texts and categories throughout chaps. 3-4, the repetition of the phrase τέκνον μου (["my child"] a common stylistic feature of wisdom literature throughout ancient Greece, Persia, Egypt and Israel; see Festugière, *La révélation*, 1.332-36) and the absence of any early Christian kerygmatic emphasis, all serve to support this argument.

[124] Cf. Funk, *Doctrina*, 12-14; Greyvenstein, "'Teaching,'" 111; Goppelt, *Christentum*, 187,

must, of course, recognize that the Matthean redactor likewise is dependent upon the decalogue here as one of several literary sources (including M and Q) which were available for the construction of the Matthean redactor's version of the decalogue pattern.[125] Close associations in structure and theme between *Did.* 3.2-6 and Matt 5:20-37, which are based upon the elements of murder, adultery and lying/false-swearing, likewise reflect parallels in the decalogue.

One notes, despite those elements that were shared with the decalogue both by Matt 5:21-37 and by *Did.* 3.2-6, that a strong bond of additional concerns also appears to link the Didache with the Matthean text. Firstly, structural elements are shared in the construction of both arguments, as is illustrated by the following outline:

Didache 3 argument	**Matthew 5 argument**
Concern for murder	Concern for murder
	Murder draws judgment
	Anger draws judgment
Anger yields murder	(Anger equals murder)
Concern for adultery	Concern for adultery
Lust yields adultery	Lust equals adultery

Secondly, while both *Did.* 3.5 and Matt 5:33 focus upon the ninth commandment of the decalogue, they further conclude in related discussions that are based upon a second OT passage. At Matt 5:34-35 one finds a response to the commandment of 5:33 which is attributed to the historical Jesus, though it is formulated upon the text of Isa 66:1. Remarkably, *Did.* 3.8 is structured upon Isa 66:2, which thus reveals that each redactor has utilized a similar pattern of illustration from Isa 66 to serve as a commentary statement upon this particular commandment of the decalogue. This suggests that some common element of interpretive tradition may perhaps have been shared between the Didache and the Matthean Gospel.[126]

---

who argues that 3.2-6 represents the manner in which the Didachist restricts the momentous theological shifts of the Sermon on the Mount to "good sense rules" for living; Lilje, *Lehre*, 51.

[125] For contrasting positions, see Bultmann (*History*, 135-36), who believes that Matt 5:21f., 27f. and 33-37 formed the older association of elements upon which the six Antitheses of the redactor were constructed, versus Strecker ("Antithesen," 39-43), who argues that Matt 5:21f., 27f. and 31f. formed the original pattern.

[126] Though v 5 and v 8 in fact are separated in the Didache by the text of vv 6-7, the effect of the separation is minimized by the recognition that v 7 does not belong truly to either 3.2-6 or 3.8-10 in terms of the sources that were utilized by the redactor; cf. discussion of 3.7 below. The association between v 5 and v 8, as is suggested by Matt 5:33-37, need not lead one to the conclusion that *Did.* 3.2-6 and 3.8-10 derive from the same source, since the Didachist could have chosen to insert 3.2-6 here in order to complement 3.8 as a completion of the thematic parallel that is offered by the Matthean text. It would seem more likely, however, that these two units originally stemmed from the same source. It is most interesting that Matt 5:33-37 commonly is characterized by scholars as M material.

Further, a predominant concern for the significance of "land" in the Didache, as is demonstrated by the important role of the promise that "the meek shall inherit the earth" (οἱ πραεῖς κληρονομήσουσι τὴν γῆν) in *Did.* 3.7, appears as well throughout the subtle strain of supporting texts that are used by the Matthean redactor at Matt 5:21-32.[127] At Matt 5:22 one discovers a reflection of an OT pattern of community judgment that is modeled upon the text of Deut 16:18-20, a pericope which concludes with

> δικαίως τὸ δίκαιον διώξῃ, ἵνα ζῆτε καὶ εἰσελθόντες κληρονομήσητε τὴν γῆν, ἣν κύριος ὁ θεός σου δίδωσίν σοι.
>
> ("Justice, and only justice, you shall follow, that you may live and inherit the land which the LORD your God gives you.")

Subsequently, in Matt 5:32 one finds a reflection of admonitions concerning marriage that is based upon Deut 24:1-4, a pericope which concludes with the notation that the former husband of an ousted wife shall not take her again so as to

> οὐ μιανεῖτε τὴν γῆν, ἣν κύριος ὁ θεός ὑμῶν δίδωσιν ὑμῖν ἐν κλήρῳ.
>
> ("not bring guilt upon the land which the LORD your God gives you for an inheritance.")

While it is difficult to establish definitive connections between the text of the Matthean Gospel and the Didache based simply upon this "inheritance of the land" motif, there can be little question that each redactor again is familiar with some tradition that unites these various OT pericopae: each redactor is governed by a concern for the land, and each chooses to unite the exhortations against murder and adultery that are found in the decalogue with that particular "land motif."

Finally, it is somewhat interesting that both the Matthean redactor and the Didachist have chosen to focus upon the decalogue here in the first place. As a text that was considered for discussion by later Jewish writers, the decalogue appears to have received only limited consideration, and both texts in question here, i.e., the Matthean Gospel and the Didache, are highly dependent upon Jewish sources and traditions.[128] In point of fact, the decalogue had a singular appeal both to the Matthean redactor and to the Didachist. The nature of that appeal is characterized by the ready applicability of the decalogue for the ethical instruction within the early Christian congregation. As we have seen in the use of the decalogue by the respective redactors, however, the ways in

---

[127] See discussion of *Did.* 3.7 below.

[128] In his extensive analysis of the tradition, Berger finds only three discussions of the text in late-Judaism – Philo *decal.* passim; Jos. *AJ* 3.91-93 and Pseudo-Philo (*Liber Antiquitatum*) – though use of the decalogue was widely attested among Christian authors by the end of the second century (*Gesetzesauslegung*, 258).

which the text was used to structure the social parameters of each redactor's community represents two distinctly different perspectives upon religious instruction and its role in the "community of faith."[129]

In conclusion, the following points seem relevant with respect to 3.2-6. These verses appear to stem from an early source that was incorporated by the Didachist and most certainly was composed of materials that were originally independent of the Two Ways tradition.[130] The way in which this segment is self-contained in terms of structure and theme, and the way in which it has maintained the identifiable nature of "wisdom instruction,"[131] indicates that it is one of those sections in the Didache which may not have been affected significantly by later attempts to align the text with the Matthean Gospel. Thus, it probably was constructed to function in the original Jewish milieu of the document and not in response to the rise of "Gentile concerns."[132] This is supported further by the fact that 3.2-6 reflects elements of wisdom rhetoric and a concern for the decalogue, but does not include the list of sins that commonly are associated with more traditional Christian lists of virtues and vices (cf. *Did.* 2.2-3). In keeping with chaps. 1-5 of the Didache in general, 3.2-6

---

[129] Thus, Harnack observes from the onset of modern examinations into the text of the Didache what has become the scholarly consensus, that *Did.* 3.1-6 may represent the modification of the decalogue by the early church for its use in the instruction of new members, most probably at baptism (*Lehre*, 52-53). On the other hand, the way in which the Matthean redactor used the decalogue in the construction of the Sermon on the Mount does not necessarily suggest a similar employment of the text for the instruction of new members at baptism. Interestingly, Clem. *paed.* 3.12 presents an outline of instructions that apparently combines the general order of elements in the texts of the Didache and the Matthean texts: 1) Golden Rule; 2) Great Commandment; 3) decalogue (adultery, idolatry, corruption of youth, theft, honoring of parents); 4) prayer; 5) fasting; etc. Later authors also incorporated elements of *Did.* 3.1-6 into the recognized stream of the Two Ways tradition that is found in post-apostolic writings (Schlecht, *Doctrina*, 77-94); cf. Boniface (*Ammonitio sive predicatio sancti, Epistulae de Abrenuntiatione in Baptistate*), St. Benedict (*Benedicti Regula*[4]) and Severin (*Doctrina Severini Epistulae de Sapientia*). Of these four examples, only that of Severin includes any material that is reflective of OT texts, which thus suggests that later Christian authors may have known some form of the 3.1-6 pericope apart from any thematic or structural associations with other OT texts.

[130] McGiffert ("Relations," 436) dates the "incorporation" of 3.2-6 into the Didache by the end of the first century, but Audet (*Didachè*, 115, 301) more correctly attributes it to the original compiler of the text, since these materials appear in all subsequent versions of the Didache, e.g., the Church Ordinances and L, but not Barnabas. Cf. Greyvenstein, "'Teaching,'" 73-79; Kraft, *Barnabas*, 62.

[131] Giet, "L'énigme," 88.

[132] Audet, *Didachè*, 301. This would be in keeping with traditional views of *Did.* 1-6, which attribute the bulk of these materials to a Jewish or Judeo-Christian setting; cf. Vögtle (*Lasterkataloge*, 197-98), who emphasizes that the μηδὲ ζηλωτὴς μηδὲ ἐπιστικὸς μηδὲ θυμικός ("nor zealous, nor contentious, nor passionate") of 3.2 represents more of a Jewish understanding than it represents a verification of an early Christian catalogue. Audet, however, does offer an interesting discussion of various elements in the section, which may be a response to the dangers of contemporary cults and "mysteries" (306-308).

no doubt was employed in some communal setting,[133] where its value as a mnemonic text for catechumens would have been appreciated most fully.[134]

Analysis of 3.8-10

These three verses are unquestionably from the Two Ways source of materials that was incorporated into both the Didache and Barnabas. Scriptural parallels have been offered for each verse, as with 3.1-6 above,[135] but it seems more likely (in comparison with parallel materials that are found at *Barn.* 19.3-6) that the authors of each writing derived these verses from a common source document, instead of from scattered sayings. A comparison of the two texts by individual verse immediately reveals the close relationship of the segments:

Did. 3.8 – γίνου μακρόθυμος καὶ ἐλεήμων καὶ ἄκακος καὶ ἡσύχιος καὶ ἀγαθὸς καὶ τρέμων τοὺς λόγους διὰ παντός, οὓς ἤκουσας.

("Be longsuffering, merciful, guileless, quiet, good and ever-fearing of the words that you have heard.")

Barn. 19.4d – ἔσῃ, ἡσύχιος, ἔσῃ τρέμων τοὺς λόγους οὓς ἤκουσας.

("Be quiet; fear the words that you have heard.")

Did. 3.9 – οὐχ ὑψώσεις σεαυτὸν οὐδὲ δώσεις τῇ ψυχῇ σου θράσος. οὐ κολληθήσεται ἡ ψυχή σου μετὰ ὑψηλῶν, ἀλλὰ μετὰ δικαίων καὶ ταπεινῶν ἀναστραφήσῃ.

("You shall not exalt yourself, nor let your soul be presumptuous. Your soul shall not consort with the lofty, but you shall walk with righteous and humble men.")

Barn. 19.3ac, 6c – οὐχ ὑψώσεις σεαυτόν . . οὐ δώσεις τῇ ψυχῇ σου θράσος . . . οὐδὲ κολληθήσῃ ἐκ ψυχῆς σου μετὰ ὑψηλῶν, ἀλλὰ μετὰ ταπεινῶν καὶ δικαίων ἀναστραφήσῃ.

("You shall not exalt yourself . . . you shall not let your soul be presumptuous . . . nor shall you consort with the lofty, but you shall consort with humble and righteous men.")

---

[133] Suggs ("Two Ways," 71-72) further notes that "the positive admonition to seek the companionship of the saints in 4.2 may represent a muted concern for community consciousness appropriate to a movement which is more established and self-confident." While this is no doubt true, this need not signify that the community of the Didache is a *late* Christian community, but only one that is firmly-rooted in a communal structure, and thus, presumably, is Jewish in origin (synagogue or synagogue-church?).

[134] Audet emphasizes that the use and construction of 3.1-6 is designed for catechetical purposes at baptism, and hence, that this section does not reflect a use that was original to the Two Ways source (*Didachè*, 303). As he further notes here, those who would have read 3.2-6 as instruction for the catechumens in a baptismal context would have been the "older" members of the community, who were established in the heritage. Cf. the comments of Suggs in n. 130 above.

[135] Cf. 3.8 (=Isa 66:2); 3.9 (=Prov 28:26; Sir 6:2a; Matt 18:4; Rom 12:16); and, 3.10 (=Ps 34:35; Matt 10:29-30; Sir 2.1, 4).

Did. 3.10 – τὰ συμβαίνοντά σοι ἐνεργήματα ὡς ἀγαθὰ προσδέξῃ, εἰδὼς ὅτι ἄτερ θεοῦ οὐδὲν γίνεται.

("Receive the accidents that come your way as good, knowing that nothing happens without God.")

Barn. 19.6d – τὰ συμβαίνοντά σοι ἐνεργήματα ὡς ἀγαθὰ προσδέξῃ, εἰδώς, ὅτι ἄνευ θεοῦ οὐδέν γίνεται.

("Receive the accidents that come your way as good, knowing that nothing happens without God.")

In contrast to 3.1-6, vv 8-10 (as they are introduced by 3.7) represent various positive exhortations.[136] This positive approach to the text continues through 4.1-4 until negative exhortations are resumed with 4.5. At 3.8-10, however, the wisdom motif of "my child," which is found earlier in 3.1-6 and later in 4.1-4, is not present. In all respects, then, this segment appears to be representative of the Two Ways source as it is found elsewhere in the Didache.

Conclusions

From the above analysis it appears that 3.2-6 and 3.8-10 come from two different sources. The latter reflects the Two Ways source, which is incorporated throughout *Did.* 1-6 and paralleled in *Barn.* 18-20. The former is from an independent source that is not paralleled elsewhere in apostolic or post-apostolic literature. Yet, while the source of the 3.2-6 segment is not attested as a structural unit in other known literature, it indeed does reflect themes and materials that are found in the OT and in the Matthean Gospel.

While v 1 has been provided by the Didachist as an introduction to 3.2-6, v 7 has been introduced both as a conclusion to these same materials and as a link to vv 8-10. The reflection of Isa 66:2 that is found in 3.8 may have suggested to the Didachist the appropriateness of the current position in the text for 3.2-6, since Isa 66:1 likewise serves as a conclusion to similar themes and arguments in Matt 5:21-37.

Individual elements in chap. 3 indicate that the text or its sources were known to later authors. Hence, one notes with interest three specific texts that appear in the writings of Clement, Origen and Dorotheus Abbas:

---

[136] Audet suggests that vv 9-10 are in fact based upon vv 7-8, which represent a consideration for the concerns of "self," "community" and "outsiders." Thus, the first temptation of "poverty" (or "meekness") would be "self-exaltation" (*Didachè*, 324-26)! Cf. Warfield ("Texts," 120), who sees a more overarching structure represented in chaps. 3-4, i.e., 3.1-6 (the "forbidden elements" of 2.2-7), 3.7-10 ("duties to self"), 4.1-4 ("duties to church"), 4.5-8 ("duties to poor") and 4.9-11 ("duties to household").

Clem. *str.* 1.20.100.4 (cf. *Did.* 3.6) – It is such a person that is by Scripture called a "thief." It is therefore said, "Son, be not a liar; for lying leads to theft."[137]

Orig. *prin.* 3.2.7 (cf. *Did.* 3.10) – And therefore Holy Scripture teaches us to receive all that happens as sent by God, knowing that without Him no event occurs.

Dor. *ep.* 3 (cf. *Did.* 3.10) – I exhort you, child, to endure and be thankful for what happens (σῦμβαίνουσιν) in the course of calamity, in accordance with what was said: "Receive as good (ὡς ἀγαθὰ προσδέχου) everything that comes to you . . .[138]

The texts that are provided by Clement and Origin are indeed interesting in that they reveal an early use of the Didache material, in both cases in Egypt. Of course, it is in Egypt that the Didache found a home within specific liturgical texts, and to that extent one should not be surprised that use of the material would appear within an Egyptian milieu, nor that the material would be associated with "scripture" in an atmosphere where no fixed canon had been established by the end of the third century C.E.

Some opposition has been offered against the belief that either Clement or Origen equates "scripture" here with a text that was derived from the Didache itself.[139] But one may note several observations to argue in favor of this view, or at least, that Clement and Origen refer to those sources which the Didachist incorporated.

With respect to Clement, there is little question that the logic of the wisdom tradition and the Jewish principles of ethics normally would argue that "theft" leads to "lying," which is quite the opposite view of *Did.* 3.6, where "lying" is believed to lead to "theft."[140] Hence, the order that is posed by the Didachist is somewhat unique. But the source that is used by the Didachist in fact may be based upon the same order as that which is found in Prov 30:6-9, where there is a further connection between lying, stealing and denying God.[141] Admittedly, Prov 30:6-9 and *Did.* 3.5 reveal at best a similarity of

[137] The text in Greek: οὗτος κλέτης ὑπὸ τῆς γραφῆς εἴρηται φησὶ γοῦν υἱέ, μὴ γίνου ψεύστης· ὁδηγεῖ γὰρ τὸ ψεῦσμα πρὸς τὴν κλοπήν.

[138] Translation by Greyvenstein, "'Teaching,'" 10; cf. also Dor. *doct.* 13.1: ὀφείλει γὰρ ὁ μοναχὸς ὁ μετὰ ἀληθείας προσερχόμενος τῷ κυρίῳ δουλεῦσαι, ἑτοιμάσαι κατὰ τὴν ψυχὴν αὐτοῦ εἰς πειρασμούς, ἵνα μὴ ξενίζηταί ποτε μηδὲ ταράσσηται ἐν τοῖς συμβαίνουσι· πιστεύων ὅτι οὐδὲν ἄνευ τῆς προνοίας τοῦ θεοῦ γίνεται.

[139] Cf. on Clement, Vokes, *Riddle*, 74-76; Rordorf and Tuilier, *Doctrine*, 124-25, 125 n. 1, 155 n. 3; and on Origen, Harris, *Teaching*, 47; Vokes, *Riddle*, 76-77. Both Harris and Vokes prefer *Barn.* 19.6 as the source text for Origen here. Vokes notes that the probable source for Barnabas was Rom 8:28, and he indicates further that Tert. *virg. vel.* 2 probably also uses Barnabas at this point. For an argument in support of the Didache as the source here, see Creed, "Didache," 373-74.

[140] Taylor, *Teaching*, 30; cf. Jer 7:9; Hos 4:2; *Mek. Bah.* 8. Taylor notes that *Herm. Man.* 3.2 also reflects the order of the Didache, but believes that *Did.* 3.6 is the earlier version.

[141] Vokes (*Riddle*, 76 n. 1) comments that in Clement this is a quotation from memory of a

patterns with respect to terminology and theme. But the attention that has been given to wisdom themes in *Did.* 1-5 could well have qualified this OT text (taken from wisdom literature) for use by either the Didachist or by the Didachist's source at 3.2-6. One thus discovers here that a further OT source has managed to influence the composition of vv 2-6, though the unit is structured primarily upon the concerns of the decalogue.

The text that is quoted by Origen, of course, could be attributed to *Barn.* 19.6, which is an extremely close parallel to *Did.* 3.10.[142] Earlier in Orig. *prin.* 3.2 there does indeed seem to be some knowledge of Barnabas, but it may in fact be fortuitous to remind ourselves that Origen probably was dependent upon the Two Ways source itself, which became a tradition that was used commonly by early Christian authors in Egypt.

---

passage occurring not only in the Didache, but also in the *Epitome of Rules*, and was assigned "the authority of Scripture because the statement is based upon Prov. xxx.6-9 . . ." I am unable, however, to find this in the *Epitome of Rules*.

[142] Harris (*Teaching*, 47), with a focus upon the Latin text of Origen (Propterea docet nos Scriptura Divina omnia quae accidunt nobis tanquam a Deo illata suscipere, scientes quod sine Deo nihil fit ["Therefore divine scripture teaches us that we should receive whatever comes to us as sent from God, knowing that nothing happens without God."), believes that the reference here is to Barnabas. While Origen's text indeed is only roughly parallel to that of L 3.10 (quae tibi contraria contingunt, pro bonis excipies sciens nihil sine deo fieri ["Whatever adversities you receive, receive them as good knowing that nothing happens without God."), his syntax uniquely follows that of H 3.10/*Barn.* 19.6 (τὰ συμβαίνοντά σοι ἐνεργήματα ὡς ἀγαθὰ προσδέξῃ, εἰδὼς ὅτι ἄτερ/ἄνευ θεοῦ οὐδὲν γίνεται)! The only difference between the Didache and Barnabas is in the Didachist's use of ἄτερ, which also is found in Origen. Spence (*Teaching*, 18 n. 8) likewise argues that *Did.* 3.10 was known and taught by Clement of Alexandria, which thus lends credence to its subsequent use by Origen.

Didache 3.7: The Meek

Comparison of Sources

H 3.7[143]	**Ps 36.11a**[144]	**Matt 5:5**	***Barn.* 19.4**
ἴσθι		μακάριοι	ἔσῃ
δὲ			
		οἱ	
πραΰς		πραεῖς,	πραΰς,
ἐπεὶ		ὅτι	. . .
οἱ	οἱ		
	δὲ		
πραεῖς	πραεῖς	αὐτοὶ	
κληρονομή-σουσι	κληρονομή-σουσιν	κληρονομή-σουσιν	
τὴν		τὴν	
γῆν.	γὴν	γῆν	

Ps 37:11a

It is difficult to determine a formative tradition behind Ps 37 (LXX 36), though certain features of the text in many ways suggest a late historical milieu. Internal evidence, i.e., a recognition of socio-economic injustice, an emphasis upon individual responsibility, the incorporation of wisdom motifs and the presence of theological inconsistencies, belies a late setting. So too, the manner in which the psalm has been introduced into the corpus proper characterizes it as a redactional intrusion.[145]

---

[143] L reads *esto autem mansuetus, quia mansueti possidebunt sanctam terram* ("Be you mild, for the mild shall possess the holy earth"). Schlecht (*Apostellehre*, 52) views *sanctam* as a redactional clarification. Audet, however, argues that the phrase *sanctam terram* instead reflects a Jewish concern for piety and hope (cf. 1 *Enoch* 27:1; 2 *Apoc. Bar.* 29.2), which ultimately develops into a prominent motif in early Christian literature (*Didachè*, 132-33; cf. Bonnard, *Matthieu*, 56-57). Consider also the explicit attempt to connect this saying with authoritative Jewish tradition in *AC* 7.7: ἴσθι δὲ πρᾶος ὡς Μωσῆς καὶ Δαβίδ ἐπεὶ οἱ πραεῖς κληρονομήσουσι τὴν γήν ("But be meek as Moses and David, for the meek shall inherit the earth"). This motif, according to Audet, appears in that recension of the Two Ways which was used by L, but which was not used by H.

A third perspective is offered by Wohleb (*Übersetzung*, 26-28), who considers τὴν γῆν τὴν ἀγαθὴν ("the good earth") to be a common typology of the intertestamental and apostolic periods (cf. the paraphrase of Exod 33:1-3 in *Barn.* 6.8; Deut 1:25; Josh 5:15 and its citation in Acts 7:33; Luke 8:8; Jos. *AJ* 5.178; Clem. *paed.* 1.6.34, 1.10.91; Clem. *str.* 1.7.37, 5.10.63). The pervasiveness of this typology easily could have led to an unconscious alteration of the text by an early Latin translator.

[144] Cf. Ps 37:11a MT: וענוים יירשו ארץ ("and the meek shall possess land"). The present discussion makes consistent reference to "Ps 37" with the understanding that the MT and the LXX each must be considered to be a possible source.

[145] While Pss 36 and 37 are joined thematically by discussions of "the wicked," Ps 37 is for-

Ps 37 is dominated by two complementary themes: the certainties of retribution for the wicked[146] and of reward for the righteous. For the author, "the wicked" are equated with "the apostate," i.e., those who have abandoned the Law of Yahweh and the customs of Israel; "the righteous" are equated with "the faithful," i.e., those who have clung to the divine promises. A theological dilemma arises with the recognition that "the wicked" have gained worldly power and prosperity (vv 7, 33, 35), while "the righteous" are sublimated and humbled (v 16). The author thus queries whether a "covenant" can indeed be maintained in a world whose moral order is not sustained by Yahweh's power.[147]

The psalmist answers this crisis in two ways. Firstly, the threat of divine retribution is reiterated through the mixing of "the ancient concept of disaster as the mechanically inevitable 'fruit' . . . with the more rationalistic idea of the chastising interference of Yahweh."[148] Secondly, the author offers a renewed eschatological hope that is derived from the promise of a homeland for the wandering/homeless Israel. This appeal to "land as symbol" is based upon a central Pentateuchal motif by which early Israel identified itself.[149] The psalmist emphasizes that Israel's "elite" have forgotten that the land of promise is a gift from God.[150] Thus, Ps 37 contains the vision of a day when the "promised land" will be redistributed to the righteous as a reward for faithfulness – the *future* realization of an ancient promise.

Those who are to receive the divine redistribution of the land are characterized by the psalmist (who is a wisdom teacher)[151] in accordance with the standards of OT wisdom and according to four primary motifs (cf. vv 9, 11, 22, 34), i.e., קוה (they "wait for" the Lord), ענו (they are "the poor" of the Lord), ברך (they "are blessed" by the Lord) and שמר (they "guard" the Lord's way).[152] Ps 37:11a appears as the second motif within this series. It

---

mulated around an acrostic structure, which thereby suggests that it originally stood as an independent unit. This structure has not been duplicated in the LXX. Mowinckel (*Psalms*, 2.114), who emphasized the cultic background of the Psalms, further argued that Ps 37 was among those texts which were "deposited as a votive and memorial gift to Yahweh and a testimony to future generations, and *on a later occasion* . . . included in the treasury of psalms" (emphasis mine).

[146] For a general reading, see Koch, "Vergeltungsdogma," 1-42.

[147] In this respect Kraus (*Psalmen*, 1.440) notes that "the zeal for security by the pious was not simply from moral indignation, but stemmed instead from the difficult questions of whether Yahweh truly was an active participant in history and whether His power had dominion in this world (cf. Prov 24:19)" (translation mine).

[148] Mowinckel, *Psalms*, 1.212-13.

[149] E.g., Israel is consistently recognized as the עם הארץ ("people of the land"). Cf. Gen 18:13-15; 35:12; 47:29-30; Deut 6:10-12; 8:7-10; 11:8-22; etc. See Brueggemann, *Land*, passim; Davies, *Gospel*, 3-48; Kraus, *Psalmen*, 1.440-41.

[150] Cf. Isa 5:8; Amos 4:1-3; 7:17; 8:4-6; Mic 2:1-3. While Rife ("Beatitudes," 107) suggests that the threat to the righteous stems from "foreign conquerors and oppressors," the overall context of the psalm indicates otherwise, that the wicked are within the fold of Israel itself.

[151] Kraus, *Psalmen*, 1.440.

[152] The LXX reads: ὑπομένω, πραεῖς, εὐλογέω and φυλάσσω respectively.

bears no special distinction from the other three elements. Indeed, the same reward is promised to the hearer/reader with the achievement of each element – the "inheritance of the land." The central focus for each characteristic, however, is the realization that wicked injustice is suffered by those who share in earthly poverty, and that this class of persons is "the meek." It is the promised reconciliation for this injustice that consequently serves as the basis of hope for those who are impoverished.[153]

Matt 5:5

Immediately obvious with respect to the Matthean form of the text is the purposeful alteration of structure. There is little question that the redactor is dependent upon some form of Ps 37:11, which has been cast here into the form of a macarism.[154] Whether this alteration of genre should be attributed to the redactor or to the redactor's source is problematic. But since the stylistic alteration enables the text to adhere to the format of Matt 5:3-12 through its structural association with the remaining materials, one might argue that the changes were provided by the redactor and were not incorporated from a separate source.[155]

---

[153] A recognition of the "congregation of the Poor" as those who will be ultimately delivered from evil is the crux of the interpretation that is provided for Ps 37:11 by the Qumran community in 4QpPs 37.2.8-11 (see the text of Allegro, "Fragment," 69-75). Perrin (*Kingdom*, 182-83) notes that both the Matthean redactor and the Qumran community have cast the text into a decidedly eschatological perspective, and thus he suggests that there is a common link between the communities which is hinged upon this association. (Craigie notes that the interpretation of the text at Qumran indicates a neglect of "its primarily educational function" [*Psalms 1-50*, 300]. I would hold this also to be true with regard to the Matthean Gospel, though such an emphasis indeed is maintained in the Didache.) Cross (*Library*, 62 n. 53, 67 n. 81) further emphasizes this view. He notes a perspective that is shared between the Qumran and the Matthean communities, i.e., that the poor will inherit the "Kingdom of the New Age," an age which is associated with the eschatological banquet, as is further suggested by parallels that are found in Luke 6:20-21 (cf. Friedlander, *Sources*, 20. Notice that in 1 *Enoch* 5-7 it is the elect who will inherit the earth.) The obvious connections between these texts lead Kloppenborg to suggest that such a text as that which is found at Qumran may have served as a source for the Didachist as easily as could have Ps 37 itself ("Sayings," 80).

While one must always respect the complexity of a text's history of tradition, there is no particular reason to consider the Qumran text as a more desirable source than the OT itself for the reconstruction of the saying that lies behind *Did.* 3.7. Indeed, while 3.7 continues the eschatological associations that already were inherent in Ps 37:11, it lacks the association with the eschatological banquet that is apparent in the Matthean, Lucan and Qumran versions of the text. Instead, the Didachist appeals to a much simpler understanding that is based upon themes from OT wisdom literature, which apparently predates the eschatological emphasis that is associated with the saying in the Matthean Gospel.

[154] Kloppenborg, "Sayings," 78; Strecker, *Weg*, 23. Note that the minor alteration of the saying proper comes as a result of the incorporation of the introductory phrase.

[155] This verse, from the M source (though Gundry [*Use*, 132, 132 n. 4] suggests that the form alone is Matthean, with Luke 6:21b offering a Q parallel in somewhat different phraseology), appears variously in the manuscripts in either the second or the third position of the beatitudes (see

With respect to theme, however, there is little deviation here from the primary emphasis that is found in Ps 37,[156] i.e., a concern for the "poor of Israel" and their claim upon the earth. Indeed, this claim has been reinforced in the Matthean text by the authoritative figure of the historical Jesus.[157]

The incorporation of this motif of poverty here symbolizes a new self-consciousness within the early Christian community, which was a community that was infused with a messianic spirit – a spirit which only is implied in Ps 37.[158] The motifs of socio-economic injustice, the homeless covenant people and the projection of an eschatological promise to the faithful are all in evidence here. Thus, one finds reflected in the Matthean text those emphases which were of primary importance to the original intent of the psalmist. Indeed, it is the concluding motif, i.e., the eschatological promise, which dominates the core of the beatitudes through its characterization of the beatitudes as a "greatly abbreviated apocalyptic vision of the world to come."[159] Hence, the primary

---

Dupont, *Beatitudes*, 1.252-53; Gundry, following M. Black [*An Aramaic Approach to the Gospels* (3rd ed.; Oxford: Clarendon, 1967) 156], emphasizes that the relationship between 5:3 and 5:5 may have been that of a "doublet" rather than of a "couplet," with which I agree.) Spicq ("Benignite," 328-29) emphasizes that the Matthean redactor perhaps incorporated Ps 37:11 as an interpretation of 5:3 (also Grundmann, *Matthäus*, 124; Dupont, *Beatitudes*, 1.257). Cf. the position of Beare, *Matthew*, 130; Soiron, *Bergpredigt*, 161; Eichholz, *Auslegung*, 36. Davies (*Gospel*, 360) suggests that 5:5 may have been included by the redactor to assist in bringing the number of beatitudes in the Sermon on the Mount to seven.

[156] This original understanding of πραῢς as "the impoverished" in both Ps 37 and Matt 5:5 is elsewhere exemplified in the writings of the various early Jewish and Christian authors. Cf. Jas 2:5, where a parallel rendering of the saying incorporates the term πτωχός ("beggar") as a reinforcement of the association of *meek* with *poor*.

[157] An appeal to the authority of Jesus appears once again in *Gos. Thom.* 54, where one reads ⲡⲉϫⲉ ⲓ̅ⲥ̅ ϫⲉ ϩⲛ̄ⲙⲁⲕⲁⲣⲓⲟⲥ ⲛⲉ ⲛϩⲏⲕⲉ ϫⲉ ⲧⲱⲧⲛ̄ ⲧⲉ ⲧⲙⲛ̄ⲧⲉⲣⲟ ⲛ̄ⲙ̄ⲡⲏⲩⲉ ("Jesus said, Blessed are the poor, for yours is the Kingdom of Heaven"). It is interesting to note the use here of "Kingdom of Heaven" ("Kingdom of God" in Luke), which thus suggests some parallel with Matt 5:3/Luke 6:20. It appears that the Gospel of Thomas indeed has preserved some early features of this beatitude from which one may determine evidence of Matthean alteration, i.e., "poor in spirit" and "Kingdom of Heaven." If the Matthean redactor has incorporated 5:3 from the Sayings Gospel Q, such alterations may indicate both theological considerations and the desire to preserve variant versions of the same saying. (Note that for the Matthean redactor, πραῢς and ταπεινός indeed contain an equivalent ethical meaning [Strecker, *Weg*, 174; also Soiron, *Bergpredigt*, 160; cf. Sir 3:17, 20 and 10:14, 15].) Thus the redactor, having both the Q saying in 5:3 and the slightly divergent saying of the Matthean community in 5:5 (= M), may have consciously altered the former in order to accommodate the insertion of the latter into the structure of the text. This would offer further evidence for the priority of the Lucan form of the Q saying here, since it varies from the M parallel in 5:5 (Schulz, *Q*, 76-84; Polag, *Fragmenta Q*, 32-33).

[158] Audet, *Didachè*, 320-21. Rife ("Beatitudes," 107) notes a tone of proselytism that develops with the association of this early thematic emphasis: "the Christian reader understands that the poor persecuted Christians of the Roman Empire were founding a religion that would eventually convert the whole world."

[159] Betz, *Essays*, 24. See Matt 5:4-9. Gaechter notes that the *inheritance* here is that of a "future earth" as is indicated in Matt 25:34 (*Evangelium*, 148-49); cf. Wellhausen, *Evangelium Matthaei*, 14; Lohmeyer and Schmauch, *Matthäus*, 85-86; Zumstein, *Condition*, 290; Soiron, *Bergpredigt*, 161.

emphasis of Ps 37:11 that the poor indeed will inherit the promised land is not only maintained by the Matthean redactor, but is reified for a living community through an association with the authoritative figure of Jesus. Furthermore, this "promised land" is recast into the promised inheritance of an eschatological kingdom.

Barn. 19.4

Like Matt 5:5, and ultimately like H 3.7,[160] *Barn.* 19.4 is characterized by a specific introductory phrase, i.e., ἔσῃ πραΰς. Unlike the others, however, the structure upon which *Barn.* 19.4 is modeled is not that of Ps 37:11, but instead, is that of Isa 66:2.[161] This becomes evident in a simple comparison between the texts:

> Isa 66:2b – καὶ ἐπὶ τίνα ἐπιβλέψω ἀλλ' ἢ ἐπὶ τὸν ταπεινὸν καὶ ἡσύχιον καὶ τρέμοντα τοὺς λόγους μου.
>
> ("and this is the one upon whom I will look, one who is humble and quiet and who trembles at my word.")
>
> *Barn.* 19.4 – ἔσῃ πραΰς, ἔσῃ ἡσύχιος, ἔσῃ τρέμων τοὺς λόγους οὓς ἤκουσας.
>
> ("Be meek, be quiet, fear the words that you have heard.")
>
> *Barn.* 19.6 – οὐδὲ καλληθήσῃ ἐκ ψυχῆς σου μετὰ ὑψηλῶν, ἀλλὰ μετὰ ταπεινῶν καὶ δικαίων ἀναστραφήσῃ
>
> ("You shall not be joined in soul with the haughty, but shall converse with humble and righteous men.")[162]

Interestingly, there remains some parallel with the text of *Did.* 3.8, which itself serves as an exposition to 3.7:

> *Did.* 3.8 – γίνου μακρόθυμος καὶ ἐλεήμων καὶ ἄκακος καὶ ἡσύχιος καὶ ἀγαθὸς καὶ τρέμων τοὺς λόγους διὰ παντός, οὓς ἤκουσας.
>
> ("Be longsuffering, merciful, guileless, quiet, good, and ever-fearing the words that you have heard.")
>
> *Barn.* 19.4 – ἔσῃ πραΰς, ἔσῃ ἡσύχιος, ἔσῃ τρέμων τοὺς λόγους οὓς ἤκουσας.
>
> ("Be meek, be quiet, fear the words that you have heard.")

---

[160] See the discussion below.

[161] Robinson, *Barnabas*, 62-63, and "Didache," 242.

[162] Both πραΰς and πτωχός are used to translate the Hebrew ענו in the LXX (hence, Aquila's use of πτωχός in his translation of Isa 66:2; cf. Ziegler, *Isaias*, 364-65), which thus argues that the authors of the Didache and Barnabas use the same, or parallel, sources. Curiously, while πραΰς and πτωχός occur nowhere together in the LXX, ἡσύχιος ("quiet"; *Did.* 3.8; *Barn.* 9.4) and ταπεινός ("humble"; *Barn.* 19.6) occur together at only one juncture, i.e., Isa 66:2, which thereby strengthens the probability that both authors are using a common LXX source tradition.

For further parallels, see KO 11 and the *Acts of Paul and Thecla* 6.

While one readily might choose to conjecture that there are different sources for *Barn.* 19.4 and for *Did.* 3.7, this does not appear to be the case with respect to the relationship between *Barn.* 19.4 and *Did.* 3.8. Indeed, modern scholarship has focused here in an attempt to determine whether one text is dependent upon the other, or whether the two have incorporated a common source.[163]

While it indeed may be that *Did.* 3.8 is also dependent upon Isa 66:2 at this point and that the Didachist probably has incorporated additional terminology that was not available to the author of Barnabas, the traditions are too elusive for a clear explication.

Did. 3.7

Here, as elsewhere, scholarly opinion concerning the source upon which the Didachist has derived the text of *Did.* 3.7 is divided.[164] One readily notes the confusion encountered by earlier studies, since *Did.* 3.7 reflects both similarities and divergencies with regard to the texts of Ps 37:11a and Matt 5:5. At the core of all three sources, however, is the central aphorism that "the meek/poor will inherit the earth."[165]

The thrust of *Did.* 3.7 no longer preserves a concern for the "meek," either as the "poor of Israel" or as the early church itself. Instead, the saying is best understood in the wisdom context of chaps. 3-4, which no doubt stems from later Jewish wisdom literature.[166] The commands of chap. 3 are indeed those

[163] Cf. Connolly ("Relation," 242) and Robinson ("Didache," 242), both of whom consider *Did.* 3.7-8 to be an expansion of *Barn.* 19.4.

[164] Those who espouse that the source is Matt 5:5 include Schaff, *Manual*, 83; Spence, *Teaching*, 18 n. 7; Funk, *Patres Apostolici*, 1.10-11; Robinson, *Barnabas*, 62-63 (though he emphasizes *Barn.* 19.4 as the probable primary source for the Didache), and "Didache," 242; Connolly, "Relation," 245; Muilenburg, "Relations," 97; and, Massaux, *Influence*, 613-14. Those who prefer Ps 37:11 are Schlecht, *Apostellehre*, 52; Oxford Society, "New Testament," 28; Knopf, *Lehre*, 16; Audet, *Didachè*, 320; Köster, *Überlieferung*, 166 n. 1; and, Köhler, *Rezeption*, 48, 48 n. 2. Kloppenborg ("Sayings," 80) believes that the introductory phrase may be from an early tradition, while the remainder may have been added later as a derivation from Ps 36:11. McGiffert (*Relations*, 433-34), on the other hand, notes that while the first phrase in *Did.* 3.7 stood in the original text as a reflection upon LXX Ps 36:11, the second phrase was inserted later under the influence of the Matthean text. Glover ("Quotations," 17) also argues that *Did.* 3.7 comes from a *variant tradition* to that of the Matthean Gospel.

[165] As is seen in the schema above, the alteration of wording in Matt 5:5 results from the redactor's recasting of the saying into a macarism through an introductory phrase, which is no doubt the result of a need to incorporate the saying into the basic structural framework of the beatitudes. *Did.* 3.7 likewise reveals a secondary introduction, though its force is that of an imperative (paralleled in the version of *Barn.* 19.4). While these divergent introductions are indeed significant, and thus reflect the concerns of the respective redactors and/or traditions of interpretation that lie behind the transmission of the saying, this does not indicate necessarily that *Did.* 3.7 circulated independently, as is suggested by Audet, *Didachè*, 320.

[166] Klevinghaus, *Stellung*, 137.

of wisdom's virtues, as is indicated by the structure of the text:

Be not proud
    for pride leads to murder
nor jealous, nor contentious, nor passionate
    for from all these murders are engendered

My child, be not lustful
    for lust leads to fornication
nor a speaker of base words, nor a lifter up of the eyes
    for from all these is adultery engendered

My child, regard not omens
    for this leads to idolatry
neither be an enchanter, nor an astrologer, nor a magician,
neither wish to see these things
    for from them all is idolatry engendered

My child, be not a liar
    for lying leads to theft
nor a lover of money, nor vain-glorious
    for from all these things are thefts engendered

My child, be not a grumbler
    for this leads to blasphemy
nor stubborn, nor a thinker of evil
    for from all these are blasphemies engendered

Be thou meek
    for the meek shall inherit the earth

There is little question that the list of categories which is presented above does not stem from the NT,[167] but instead, it has been assembled from another source. The apodosis of each specific exhortation in the list immediately identifies the substructure of the format as that of the decalogue, around which chaps. 2-3 themselves are oriented, i.e. murder, adultery, idolatry, theft and blasphemy.[168] *Did.* 3.7 is not to be considered merely as an element in this format, which is hinged upon *negative* warnings. Instead, 3.7 is to be seen as the concluding positive response to the exhortations of 3.1-6. The warnings themselves are most notably not a repetition of the decalogue so much as a consideration of those specific elements which lead to a renunciation of the decalogue's standards. Thus, these elements form a core association of wisdom catchwords that are reflected elsewhere in the Psalms, Proverbs and Sirach.

---

[167] Kloppenborg, "Sayings," 79-80. Yet note that the concept of "meekness" itself passed early "into the instruction of the church," and appeared as a category in virtue- and vice-lists among early Christian writings, e.g. Gal 5:23, Eph 4:2, Col 3:12 and 1 Tim 6:11 (Best, "Tradition," 108).

[168] Once again, the order of elements 1, 2 and 4 reflects that of Codex Alexandrinus.

Conclusions

Both Matt 5:5 and *Did.* 3.7 are dependent upon Ps 37:11 as their source text.[169] The verbal similarities between the MT and LXX offer no distinctive traits by which one may determine whether either the Didachist or the Matthean redactor found their original source in Hebrew or Greek. In addition, the primary differences between the Didache and the Matthean Gospel here are those which are necessitated by the association of varying introductory phrases. The Didachist molds the text into a conclusion for the structure of gnomic exhortations that are consistent with *Did.* 3-4, while the Matthean redactor constructs a macarism that is in character with the structure of Matt 5:3-12.

Further, the association of πραεῖς with the "impoverished," in the light of the theological ramifications that were associated with that term in the early church, is a theme that was common to both early Jewish and Christian texts.[170] The same motif appears within the context of the Didache, though the "poor" are justified according to the standards of ancient wisdom and not according to the promise of an eschatological reward, in opposition to the view that is offered in the Matthean text. That the Didachist is concerned with wisdom *per se* indicates an early incorporation of the saying within the text of the Didache – which is perhaps indicative of the early Jewish nature of the redactor and/or of his/her community. Such an emphasis may add support for 3.7 as a forerunner to that form of the saying which appears from the hand of the Matthean redactor in the Sermon on the Mount.[171]

From a consideration of its minor role in Ps 37, the function of 37.11 offers no inherent evidence as to why it should have been of any special appeal to either the Didachist or the Matthean redactor. As is indicated by the incorporation of the verse both here and in Matt 5:5, however, it would seem that the early Christian community, or at least that community which I suggest preserved a core source of sayings materials that were used in both the Didache and in the Matthean Gospel, did indeed find a special affinity for the saying. We note, however, that while each text uses the same source, i.e., Ps 37:11, that source is used within differing contexts: Matt 5:5 incorporates the saying

---

[169] While Gundry argues for Matthean dependence upon the Targums at this point, the evidence is certainly not conclusive (*Use*, 133, 150; cf. Jeremias, *Matthaeus*, 10).

[170] Cf. also Clem. *str.* 4.6 and KO 6.2. In *b. Sukk.* 29b one finds an interpretation that is based more upon an association of the term with "virtues," while *Herm. Man.* 11.8 reflects *both* the perspectives of *poverty* and of *virtue.*

[171] Köster suggests that the Matthean redactor may have taken the text from an early source that is found in the Didache and did not take it from Ps 37 itself (*Überlieferung*, 167). It would seem more probable, however, that the two redactors shared a source which was interpreted similarly within a common early Jewish-Christian community.

into a discussion of poverty; *Did.* 3.7 incorporates it into a discussion of wisdom.[172]

These divergent emphases need not indicate that the two discussions originated within separate communities. Indeed, the roles of the "poor" and of the "wise" in early Jewish-Christian theology are the same, i.e., they are the representatives of that facet of society which will receive divine blessing. It is the means to that blessing which is in fact divergent between these texts: the Didachist appeals to a practical ethic, while the Matthean redactor appeals to the rewards of faith.

In result, *Did.* 3.7 reveals traits of a pre-Matthean construction (i.e., a dependence upon the OT), no influence from the Matthean Gospel and an association with early wisdom thought. With respect to the Matthean tradition, the parallel in Matt 5:5 shows only the alteration of an introductory clause that was added to make the verse consistent with the redactional context of the beatitudes. So too, the edition of the verse from the Saying Gospel Q that is found in Matt 5:3 has been altered both for theological reasons and for the accommodation of 5:5 into the text. The presence within the Matthean text of both 5:3 and 5:5, which themselves are in essence simply parallel readings of the same saying,[173] argues for the preservation of parallel sources that were extracted from variant traditions. Since the Matthean text and the text of the Didache preserve a theological motif that is centered upon the desire for "land," however, one must assume that both redactors shared an early source that emphasized this theme as an integral aspect of God's promise both to Israel and to the church of the first century.

Didache 4-5: A Fence to the Law (Part 2)

As was observed above, chap. 3 has been constructed as a restatement of the exhortations that appear in the decalogue (*Did.* 2.2-3), the prohibitions of which now are set in a distinctly rhetorical framework. This is to say that

[172] The use of Ps 37:11 both in rabbinic sources and in the writings of the early Church Fathers does not seem to offer any subsequent trend of interpretation that results from this "poor/wisdom" distinction; cf. Iren. *haer.* 5.9.4, 5.32.2; Clem. *str.* 4.36.1; *AC* 7.7; *KO* 6.2; *b. Sukk.* 29b. For other rabbinic references see Str-B, 1.197-220 and Hyman, *Torah*, 3.27.

[173] The alternate readings for "poor" and "meek" in fact indicate by necessity the same group; see Gaechter, *Evangelium*, 148; Schmid, *Matthäus*, 79; Zahn, *Matthäus*, 186-87.

Beare notes with respect to 5:5 that while the clause may have been formed by the Matthean redactor, "it is in substance a paraphrase of the first beatitude"; and immediately thereafter, "the beatitude is a doublet of the first" (*Matthew*, 130). While I agree with Beare's analysis of the situation to the extent that the similarities between verses reveal some relationship between the texts as they are understood by the Matthean redactor, I believe that this is better explained as the redactor's attempt to preserve variant versions of the same saying, not an attempt to reemphasize a point by means of textual duplication. Beare's perspective does little to explain the rationale for the divergencies between the two verses.

those sins of day-to-day activity which will lead the catechumen toward the greater sins against which the decalogue warns are explicated in a uniform pattern (3.1-6). In chap. 4 the Way of Life concludes with additional, specific charges that are related to the expectations of the catechumen by the religious community.[174] In chap. 5 the final warning is provided for the catechumen in the form of a Way of Death, the primary components of which reflect the life that results when the Way of Life is rejected.[175]

On the one hand, the Didachist has not included materials from his/her special sayings source in chaps. 4-5. Therefore, there are no texts here that reflect specific sayings or aphorisms which are paralleled in the Synoptic Gospels. On the other hand, these chapters reveal the most obvious point at which the Didachist is dependent upon the Two Ways source (cf. *Barn.* 19-20), a source whose structure has been used throughout chaps. 1-3 as the framework into which the Didachist has inserted individual sayings from his/her sayings materials.

The use of the Two Ways source varies between chap. 4 and chap. 5.[176] In the former chapter there is a wide divergence from the ordering of elements that appears in *Barn.* 19. In the latter chapter the ordering of elements is almost precisely that of *Barn.* 20. The ordering of these elements appears as follows:

Did.	*Barn.*	*Did.*	*Barn.*
4.1a	19.9b	*5.1*	20.1
4.1b	19.10a	5.2	20.2
4.2a	19.10b		
4.3a	19.12a		
4.3b	19.12b		
4.3c	19.11f		
4.4	19.5a		
4.5	19.9a		
4.6	19.10d		
4.7	19.11a-c		
4.8b-d	19.8a-c		
4.9	19.5e-f		
4.10	19.7c-f		
4.12a	19.2g		
4.12b	b19.2f		
4.13b-c	19.11d-e		
4.14a-b	19.12c-d		

[174] As is suggested by Klevinghaus (*Stellung*, 137-39), the section perhaps is understood best as "ethical duties" (4.1-8), *Haustafel* (4.9-11) and "counsel" (4.12-14). In v 12 and v 14 the phrases ἀρεστὸν τῷ κυρίῳ ("pleasing to the Lord") and αὕτη ἐστὶν ἡ ὁδὸς τῆς ζωῆς ("This is the Way of Life") also would seem to suggest that the discussion of chap. 4 is to be understood in close connection with the sayings that appear in chaps. 1-3.

[175] An excellent discussion of the relationship of the elements in chaps. 4-5 is offered by Knopf, *Lehre*, 16-20. With Poschmann (*Paenitentia*, 88-89) we must agree that the concerns of baptism, authority and sin naturally occur together!

[176] See the discussion on order that is offered here by Warfield, "Text," 134-36, 145-46.

In chap. 4 the Didachist further reveals a propensity for the inclusion of redactional comments.[177] Most often these insertions are provided as qualifiers for specific instructions and exhortations that appear in the Two Ways source itself. Oftentimes, they are derived from OT foundations:

4.1a(1) – "My child"; from the redactor in the stylistic form of chap. 3
4.1c – "you shall honor him as the Lord"; from the redactor (cf. 15.2)
4.1d – "where the Lord is mentioned, he is present"; Exod 20:24 (cf. Matt 18:20)
4.2b – "that you may find rest in his words"; from the redactor[178]
4.3d – "do not favor a man's person in reproving transgression"; 1 Sam 16:7 (cf. John 4:24)
4.8a – "Do not turn away the needy"; from the redactor
4.11 – "Slaves be subject to your masters as representatives of God, in reverence and fear"; from the redactor
4.14c – "This is the Way of Life"; from the redactor

It seems that the Didachist feels a certain freedom to manipulate the Two Ways source as needed, which thereby suggests that the source has entered the construction of the Didache as an authoritative text whose value is derived from its framework, within which practical exhortations could be organized. If the Didachist indeed has constructed chaps. 1-6 to serve as the words of instruction for catechumens (and most probably as the prelude for a ceremony of baptism, as is indicated by chap. 7), it is interesting to find that the Didachist also has chosen to maintain the short *Haustafel* segment of 4.9-10 that apparently was a part of the Two Ways source. The Didachist, as with other authors of the apostolic and post-apostolic tradition, recognized the value of "household exhortations" for the development of ecclesiastical authority and community obedience within the early Christian congregation.

A comparison of chap. 5 with *Barn.* 20 reveals that the Didachist has been much more faithful to the ordering of elements in the Two Ways source here than s/he may have been in chap. 4. Chap. 5 (the Way of Death), which provides a lengthy list of characterizations about the nature of a wicked existence, opens with twenty-three elements in the form of a vice-list (*Lasterkatalog*).[179] The majority of these elements derive directly from the Two Ways source, at least as that source is confirmed from the witness of Barnabas. But six

---

[177] See the analysis of 2.6-7 and 3.8-10 above.

[178] Rordorf and Tuilier (*La doctrine*, 29) find this "superficial Christianization" of the Two Ways source throughout chaps. 4-6 (see pp. 29-34).

[179] Köster (*Überlieferung*, 164) and Kloppenborg (*Sayings*, 87-88) note among the many representatives of this genre in early Jewish-Christian texts the lists of Wis 14:25-26; 3 *Apoc. Bar.* 4.17, 8.5, 13.4; *T. Ash.* 2.1-10; Rom 1:29-31; 1 Tim 1:9-10; *Herm. Man.* 8.3.5; and, 1QS 4.9-11. Harris (*Teaching*, 82-86) argued early in the history of research upon the Didache that the catalog of vices in chap. 5 was dependent upon an early Jewish source which was known to the Didachist. Such a source indeed may have been used in the construction of the Two Ways source at this point in the text.

elements are unique to the Didache. Each of these elements is reflected elsewhere in chap. 3: ἐπιθυμία ("desire"; *Did.* 3.3); πορνεία ("fornication"; *Did.* 3.3); κλοπή ("theft"; *Did.* 3.5); ψευδομαρτυρία ("false witness"; *Did.* 3.5 [ψεύστης]); αἰσχρολογία ("evil speech"; *Did.* 3.3); and, ζηλοτυπία ("jealousy"; *Did.* 3.2).

In Mark 7:21-22 one finds a list of thirteen sins that stem from the "evil heart," many of which parallel those elements in *Did.* 5.1 that are unique to the Didachist's version of the Way of Death. In the same context as the Marcan account, and no doubt dependent upon the Marcan Gospel, Matt 15:19 lists only six sins that stem from the "evil heart." The Matthean list (φόνοι, μοιχεῖαι, πορνεῖαι, κλοπαί, ψευδομαρτυρίαι, βλασφημί) is almost exactly the same as those elements which are special to the Didachist's list. But while scholars often have argued from this connection that the Didachist must have been dependent upon the listing in the Matthean Gospel,[180] which in theory is a reduction of the Marcan list, it cannot be ignored that this collection of elements (both in the Didache and in the Matthean Gospel) is constructed around specific items that have been borrowed from the decalogue. Because the Didachist has listed these elements previously in chap. 3,[181] and because the early chapters of the Didache are focused upon the decalogue, it must be assumed that the Didachist has drawn this special group of sins from the OT and not from the list of the Matthean Gospel.[182] So too, it is obvious that the Matthean redactor in fact has constructed his/her list of elements from the terminology of the decalogue, instead of merely reducing the Marcan listing.[183]

The addition of elements from the decalogue to the Way of Death by the Didachist probably derives from the desire of the Didachist to "flesh out" this portion of the Two Ways source with items that were inserted independently in chap. 3. Since the remainder of the Way of Death segment appears almost exactly as that which is found in *Barn.* 20.2, it must be assumed that the Didachist was satisfied with either the format or with the tradition from which this portion of the Two Ways source was derived.

---

[180] See Connolly ("Relation," 237-53), who argues for a dependency upon the Matthean Gospel here as an explanation for the "run of plurals" which begins the Didachist's list.

[181] Even Connolly notes this earlier use of elements ("Relation," 241-42); so too Creed ("Didache," 377) and Kraft (*Barnabas*, 158).

[182] Köster (*Überlieferung*, 163) admits that the catalogs of the Marcan and the Matthean traditions are closer to that of the Didache than are the Pauline (Rom 1:29-31; Gal 5:19-21; 1 Cor 5:10-11, 6:9-10; 2 Cor 12:20-21) and Deutero-Pauline (Eph 5:3-5; 1 Tim 1:9-10; 2 Tim 3:2-5) lists that appear elsewhere in the NT. He also agrees, however, that the Didachist is dependent upon the OT and Judaism for the list of elements in *Did.* 5 (p. 260).

[183] Thus, since the Matthean list of sins both follows the ordering of the decalogue (unlike the Marcan account) and includes the additional term ψευδομαρτυρία that is derived from the language of the decalogue (which also is omitted by the Marcan text), this conclusion seems the most plausible.

Didache 16: The Little Apocalypse

Unlike the sayings that appear in chaps. 1-5, whose sources can be traced with some assurance either to OT/Jewish foundations or to early Christian traditions, the same cannot be said with respect to chap. 16. Apart from the eschatological statements of *Did.* 10.5 (which are most likely an insertion by the second redactor, or possibly the final redactor), chap. 16 alone preserves any true emphasis upon eschatology in the Didache. The restriction of these materials to a single segment of the text does not leave the modern exegete with a secure basis upon which to evaluate the relationship of the chapter to the remainder of the text. To be sure, the materials in *Did.* 16 probably derive from some early collection of apocalyptically-oriented sayings that was widely popular within the primitive church. The roots of that collection, however, are not particularly distinct.[184]

On the one hand, this obscurity with respect to the origin of the materials results from the essential nature of early Jewish-Christian "apocalyptic" literature in general, whose terms and phrases are short, emphatic and readily conveyed through oral tradition.[185] On the other hand, many of the sayings that are preserved in these materials have numerous parallels in the canonical witness: primarily within the Synoptic Gospels (especially in the Marcan/Matthean tradition); secondarily within the later writings of the LXX.[186] The difficulty in any attempt to indicate exact textual parallels between the text of *Did.* 16 and the biblical witness becomes apparent when one compares these texts:

H 16 **(v 1)**	**Synoptic Parallels** **(Matt 24:42; Mark 13:35)**
Γρηγορεῖτε	*Γρηγορεῖτε . . .*
ὑπερ τῆς ζωῆς ὑμῶν·	
	(Luke 12:35)
οἱ λύχνοι ὑμῶν μὴ σβεσβήωσαν *καὶ αἱ ὀσφύες ὑμῶν* μὴ ἐκλυέσθωσαν,	. . . *ὑμῶν αἱ ὀσφύες* περιεζωσμέναι *καὶ οἱ λύχνοι* καιόμενοι
	(Matt 24:44; Luke 12:40)
ἀλλὰ *γίνεσθε ἕτοιμοι·*	. . . καὶ ὑμεῖς *γίνεσθε* *ἕτοιμοι,*

---

[184] Ladd's efforts to date the Didache from an analysis of the eschatological elements in *Did.* 16 have proven conclusively that such attempts are of a tenuous nature at best (he "narrows" the date for the text to the years c. 75-150! ["Eschatology," 175]).

[185] See the discussion of Bammel, "Schema," 253-62.

[186] With respect to the LXX, see for example Mal 3:2-4 (cf. *Did.* 16.5); Isa 11:10 (cf. *Did.* 16.6); and, Dan 7:13 (cf. *Did.* 16.8).

	(Matt 24:42b; 24:44b; 25:13b)
οὐ γὰρ οἴδατε τὴν ὥραν, ἐν *ᾗ ὁ κύριος* ἡμῶν *ἔρχεται.*	ὅτι *οὐκ οἴδατε* ποίᾳ ἡμέρᾳ *ὁ κύριος* ὑμῶν *ἔρχεται.* . . . ὅτι *ᾗ οὐ δοκεῖτε ὥρᾳ ὁ* υἱὸς τοῦ ἀνθρώπου *ἔρχεται* . . . ὅτι *οὐκ οἴδατε τὴν* ἡμέραν οὐδὲ *τὴν ὥραν.*
	(Mark 13:33b; 13:35b)
	οὐκ οἴδατε γὰρ πότε *ὁ* καιρός ἐστιν. *οὐκ οἴδατε γὰρ* πότε *κύριος* τῆς οἰκίας *ἔρχεται,*
	(Luke 12:40b)
	ὅτι *ᾗ ὥρᾳ οὐ δοκεῖτε ὁ* υἱὸς τοῦ ἀνθρώπου *ἔρχεται.*
(v 2)	**(*Barn.* 4.9b)**
	. . . ἐν ταῖς *ἐσχάτ*αις ἡμέραις·
. . . οὐ *γὰρ ὠφελήσει ὑμᾶς ὁ* *πᾶς χρόνος τῆς πίστεως* *ὑμῶν, ἐὰν μὴ ἐν τῷ* *ἐσχάτῳ* καιρῷ τελειωθῆτε.	οὐδὲν *γὰρ ὠφελήσει* ἡ*μᾶς ὁ* *πᾶς χρόνος τῆς πίστεως* ἡ*μῶν, ἐὰν μὴ* νῦν *ἐν τῷ* ἀνόμῳ καιρῷ . . .
(vv 3-5)	**(Matt 24:10b-12)**
	καὶ τότε σκανδαλισθήσον- ται πολλοὶ καὶ ἀλλήλους παραδώσουσιν
ἐν γὰρ ταῖς ἐσχάταις ἡμέραις *πληθυνθή*σονται οἱ *ψευδοπροφῆται καὶ οἱ* φθορεῖς,	καὶ *μισήσουσιν ἀλλήλους·*
καὶ στραφήσονται τὰ πρόβατα εἰς λύκους, καὶ ἡ ἀγάπη στραφήσεται εἰς μῖσος. αὐξανούσης γὰρ τῆς ἀνομίας *μισήσουσιν ἀλλήλους* καὶ διώξουσι καὶ παραδώσουσι, καὶ τότε φανήσεται ὁ κοσμο- πλανὴς ὡς υἱὸς θεοῦ, καὶ ποιήσει σημεῖα καὶ τέρατα, καὶ ἡ γῆ παραδοθήσεται εἰς χεῖρας αὐτοῦ, καὶ ποιήσει ἀθέμιτα, ἃ οὐδέποτε γέγονεν ἐξ αἰῶνος. τότε ἥξει ἡ κτίσις τῶν ἀνθρώπων	καὶ πολλοὶ *ψευδοπροφῆται* ἐγερθήσονται καὶ πλανήσουσιν πολλούς· καὶ διὰ τὸ *πληθυνθῆ*ναι τὴν ἀνομίαν ψυγήσεται ἡ ἀγάπη τῶν πολλῶν.

εἰς τὴν πύρωσιν τῆς	
δοκιμασίας, καὶ σκανδαλισ-	
θήσονται πολλοὶ καὶ	**(Matt 24:13; Mark 13:13)**
ἀπολοῦνται, *οἱ δὲ*	*ὁ δὲ*
*ὑπομείνα*ντες ἐν τῇ πίστει	*ὑπομείνας* εἰς τέλος
αὐτων *σωθήσ*ονται ὑπ' αὐτοῦ	οὗτος *σωθήσεται.*
τοῦ καταθέματος.	
(v 6)[187]	**(Matt 24:30-31)**
καὶ τότε	*καὶ τότε*
φανήσεται τὰ σημεῖα	*φανήσεται τὸ σημεῖον*
τῆς ἀληθείας· πρῶτον σημεῖον	τοῦ υἱοῦ τοῦ ἀνθρώπου
ἐκπετάσεως *ἐν οὐρανῷ*	*ἐν οὐρανῷ* . . .
εἶτα σημεῖον	καὶ ἀποστελεῖ τοὺς
	ἀγγέλους αὐτοῦ μετὰ
φωνῆς σάλπιγγος,	*σάλπιγγος φωνῆς* μεγάλης. . .
καὶ τὸ τρίτον ἀωάστασις	
νεκρῶν.	
(v 7)	**(Matt 25:31)**
οὐ πάντων δέ, ἀλλ' ὡς ἐρρέθη·	ὅταν δὲ ἔλθῃ ὁ υἱὸς τοῦ
Ἥξει ὁ κύριος	ἀνθρώπου ἐν τῇ δόξῃ
	αὐτοῦ
καὶ πάντες οἱ ἅγιοι	*καὶ πάντες οἱ* ἄγγελοι
μετ' αὐτοῦ.	*μετ αὐτοῦ,*
(v 8)	**(Matt 24:30b; Mark 13:26; Luke 21:27)**
τότε *ὄψεται* ὁ κόσμος	. . . (καὶ = Matt) *ὄψονται*
τὸν κύριον	τὸν υἱὸν τοῦ ἀνθρώπου
ἐρχόμενον ἐπάνω	*ἐρχόμενον* (επὶ = Matt;
	ἐν = Mark, Luke)
τῶν νεφελῶν	(*τῶν νεφελῶν* = Matt;
	νεφέλαις = Mark;
	νεφέλῃ = Luke)
τοῦ οὐρανοῦ.	(*τοῦ οὐρανοῦ* = Matt) . . .

Even in this simple comparison of texts one immediately perceives the problem that is associated with the corpus of early Christian "apocalyptic literature." The Didachist (or perhaps a later redactor?) reflects words, phrases and motifs that are shared with the Synoptic Gospels. In most cases the correspondence is with the Matthean text; in fewer cases the correspondence is also with the Marcan text; and in at least one instance, the correspondence is with the Lucan text alone. Most notably, the parallels are generally with those portions of the Synoptic Gospels that fall within the parameters of the so-called "little apocalpyse" (i.e., Matt 24 and Mark 13), though the Lucan

---

[187] The parallels for vv 6-8 are based upon the formulation of Kloppenborg, "Didache," 55-56.

parallels occur primarily in another section of the Lucan Gospel (chap. 12). They are not within the broader range of the Synoptic writings.

Since an extremely large portion of the Synoptic apocalyptic material is *not* included in *Did.* 16, one correctly may question whether the text of the Didache is not dependent upon some common source that also was used in the NT accounts. Such a source most probably would have been shared by the Matthean redactor, since the majority of parallels between the NT and *Did.* 16 are with the Matthean text.[188] But a level of caution is necessary in this presupposition, since the Matthean text is dependent primarily upon the Marcan framework that is subsumed by the Matthean version of the apocalyptic materials (i.e., Matt 24).[189] One also must remember that the influence of the Lucan text (as with *Did.* 1.3b-4 above) may imply that portions of chap. 16 (if indeed not all of the chapter) were composed under the influence of some later tradition.[190] From the above analysis of chaps. 1-5, we have argued that Lucan influence probably is restricted to a later tradition, and thus, such an influence was not inherent within the earliest compilation of the Didache's materials.

There is also the possibility that chap. 16 has been influenced by Pauline materials,[191] as for example:

> 1 Cor 15:52b – σαλπίσει γὰρ καὶ οἱ νεκροὶ ἐγερθήσονται ἄφυαρτοι καὶ ἡμεῖς ἀλλαγησόμεθα.
>
> ("For the trumpet will sound, and the dead will rise immortal and we will be changed.")

---

[188] Seeberg (*Didache*, 45) attributes the materials to common apocalyptic materials within early Judaism (so too Oxford Society [*New Testament*, 32-33 (on 16.3-5): "There are several points of connexion with Matt. 24:10-13, but this may not represent more than a common oral basis containing a good many conventional Apocalyptic ideas." (on 16.6): "use of our Synoptic tradition is highly probable, [though] the verdict in relation to the individual gospels must remain doubtful"]). Also, Köster, *Überlieferung*, 188-89. Kloppenborg ("Didache," 63-67) argues specifically that 16.6-8 is based upon texts from the special Matthean source of M, which itself is under the influence of Dan 7:13.

[189] So, one finds the argument of Drews ("Untersuchungen," 68-79), who argues for a common source that is shared by the Didache and by the Marcan text. He notes, however, that this source was also familiar to the Matthean redactor, who contributed additional materials that were incorporated into the Didache. Thus, one finds that this foundational source was widespread within early Christian circles.

[190] Butler seems to have no difficulty in distinguishing materials in chap. 16 that he ascribes to a source which he calls "M(g)" (which is in effect our M source, and which he eventually admits became the Matthean Gospel proper), while at the same time he finds materials from either the Lucan Gospel or proto-Luke ("Relations," 265-83). I would concur with his findings in this regard, but based upon the above analysis of *Did.* 1-5 (which he obviously has not attempted) and with respect to the resulting observations of that analysis that the earliest form of the Didache was dependent upon an M-type of sayings collection with no evidence of influence by the Lucan Gospel, it is difficult to make any firm statement concerning the date of chap. 16 based upon the sources which he identifies.

[191] So Oxford Society, *New Testament*, 33.

1 Thes 4:16 – ὅτι αυτός ὁ κύριος ἐν κελεύσματι, ἐν φωνῇ ἀρχαγγέλου καὶ ἐν σάλπιγγι θεοῦ, καταβήσεται ἀπ' οὐρανοῦ καὶ ὁ νεκροὶ ἐν Χριστῷ ἀναστήσονται πρῶτον,

("For the Lord himself will descend from heaven in a commanding voice of authority and with the trumpet sound of God, and the dead in Christ will rise first.")

But even here one perceives the presence of motifs that are typical of apocalyptic materials in general. There need not be any specific influence from the Pauline texts proper. Indeed, if one should choose to argue that the materials in chap. 16 are original to the earliest layer of the Didache, the influence of the Pauline letters would not be expected, since no such influence is predominant in *Did.* 1-5.

It is also true that some materials that are preserved in chap. 16 derive directly from the LXX. Thus, one finds

Did. 16.7 – οὐ πάντων δέ, ἀλλ' ὡς ἐρρέθη· Ἥξει ὁ κύριος καὶ πάντες ὁ ἅγιοι μετ' αὐτοῦ.

("but not all of the dead [shall rise], but as it was said, "The Lord will come and all of the holy ones with him.")

Zech 14:5 – καὶ ἥξει κύριος ὁ θεός μου καὶ πάντες οἱ ἅγιοι μετ' αὐτοῦ.

("and the Lord God will come and all of the holy ones with him.")

This reference is marked with the introductory phrase ὡς ἐρρέθη ("as it was said"), however, so that the reader is alerted immediately to the use of a specific citation from scripture. Unfortunately, one cannot determine with confidence those places at which the Didachist has used OT phrases and allusions that are not direct citations elsewhere within his/her construction of chap. 16.

Finally, certain portions of chap. 16 indicate specific concerns and interests that probably are better attributed to one of the later redactors of the Didache. Thus, one discovers in 16.1 the phrase ὑπερ τῆς ζωῆς ὑμῶν ("[Watch] over your life"), which is a theme that obviously reflects upon the Way of Life motif which appears throughout chaps. 1-5. In other materials, such as with vv 4b-5a, there is no way to determine for certain whether the redactor has contributed original sayings (whether from contemporary Christian prophets or from popular non-canonical literature), or whether s/he has drawn upon some sayings materials that were available from the developing corpus of apocalyptic tradition in Jewish and Christian communities of the first century.

From the broad mixture of sayings and apocalyptic materials that are found in chap. 16, one must admit that it is difficult, if not impossible, to make conclusive and convincing statements concerning the background texts that were incorporated into the chapter. Evidence of traditions that were used by the

Marcan, the Matthean and the Lucan traditions appears. A source that was common to Barnabas also is evident, as is a dependence upon OT texts. So too, the hand of a redactor is apparent throughout chap. 16. Oral traditions from the larger sphere of the apocalyptic tradition also probably are present here. Furthermore, since Barnabas does not include an apocalyptic chapter at the end of the Two Ways source, it is not possible (apart from mere speculation) to argue whether any of the materials in chap. 16 can ,be attributed to that early source.[192]

In the final analysis, the situation of the chapter with respect to its sources and with respect to the historical framework of the development of the Didache must remain without certain answers.

Summary of Conclusions

An analysis of chaps. 1-5 and 16, i.e., an examination of those chapters of the Didache that most commonly are assumed to be among the earliest portions of the text, reveal several notable findings concerning the sources upon which those materials may have been constructed.

As is evident from a comparison of the Didache and with Barnabas, these early chapters of the Didache are patterned upon a structural and thematic framework that generally is consistent with the pattern that appears in *Barn.* 18-20. While early scholars struggled to see one of these two writings as the literary source for the other, such opinions no longer hold the majority view among recent students of early patristic literature. Instead, one now can assume that both the Didache and Barnabas are dependent upon a common collection of materials that currently is designated by the label of the "Two Ways source." The close parallels between these materials in the Didache and in Barnabas argue that this Two Ways source was a written document, the knowledge of which (in one form or another) was widespread among early Jewish and Christian circles.

In addition to the Two Ways source, whose boundaries and basic characteristics for the Didache may be discerned in general from the attestation of Barnabas, the materials of *Did.* 1-5 and 16 present other specific sayings that are paralleled very closely in the biblical materials. The sources from which these sayings were incorporated may be divided into three distinct categories: 1) materials that are exclusively derived from an early Jewish milieu and/or from OT texts; 2) materials that reveal a direct knowledge of the Lucan Gospel; and, 3) other New Testament materials that do not indicate an awareness of the Lucan Gospel. The low incidence of sayings that fall within the second category (i.e., materials that specifically reflect some knowledge of the Lucan

---

[192] Though see the discussion of Draper, "Tradition," 280-83.

Gospel) and the tendency among modern exegetes to assign this category to a level of redaction that arose after the occurrence of the original collection of materials in the Didache, traditionally have led scholars to suspect a strong connection between the sayings of the Didache and the sayings of the Matthean Gospel. The close affinity between the sayings of the Didache and those of the Matthean Gospel has been acknowledged widely among those scholars who have undertaken a comparison of the two writings.

Though scholars typically have attempted to view the sayings of the Didache as the successors of an "earlier" Matthean tradition, this perspective has met with limited success at best. Instead, one finds that in most cases the relationship between the sayings collection in the Didache and the collection in the Matthew Gospel is best explained by the hypothesis that the Didachist and the Matthean redactor have shared a common sayings source. It appears reasonable to believe that the Didachist had at close hand a collection of early sayings materials (possibly in a written format) that was known to the Matthean redactor in a comparable form. In the composition of the Matthean Gospel, however, the Matthean redactor chose to depend primarily upon other early sayings traditions instead of upon that collection of materials which was used by the Didachist. These "other early sayings traditions" (i.e., the Sayings Gospel Q and the Marcan tradition) were more complete collections of texts than was the tradition which the Didachist used. They reflected many of the same materials that were preserved in the sayings source upon which the Didachist was dependent, but in a slightly different form. While this choice for other traditions is an obvious feature of the Matthean text, there are scattered signs throughout the Matthean Gospel which indicate that the redactor was familiar with the tradition from which the sayings of the Didache were derived.

The majority of sayings that have been included by the Didachist are dependent to some extent upon early Jewish ethical instruction or wisdom materials. Further, many of these sayings have been included within a literary and structural framework that is modeled upon the decalogue. Since, as we have seen above, the Didachist has chosen to structure these chapters around the same Two Ways source that also appears in Barnabas, one must assume that the further incorporation of a decalogue framework into the Two Ways source must indicate that the Didachist bore a serious concern for the decalogue, in particular, and OT/Jewish tradition, in general. The Didachist, therefore, knew and respected the Jewish religious tradition, a tradition from which the Didachist had collected numerous sayings (that now may be applied to the new Christian faith in some satisfactory manner) and the basic framework of the decalogue. The decalogue framework and the collected sayings then were inserted into the structure of the Two Ways source, which served as the guiding pattern for the presentation of chaps. 1-5, and perhaps for chap. 16 as well.

As we shall see below, *Did.* 6 (with the probable exception of 6.1a) does not reveal a dependence upon the Two Ways source. Instead, this chapter, in keeping with *Did.* 7-15, focuses upon specific issues of ecclesial polity that were directed toward the concerns of a specific Christian *community*. The insertion of this chapter may have been dependent upon the need either to orient chaps. 1-5 to a catechetical purpose or to assimilate chaps. 1-5 to chaps. 7-15. In either case, these materials have been included by a later redactor who was inspired to use the collected sayings of chaps. 1-5 in a setting that was of practical value to an early Christian community.

The situation of *Did.* 16 also differs slightly from that of *Did.* 1-5 in that there does not appear to be any dependence upon the framework of the Two Ways source in this concluding chapter. Instead, these materials appear to be dependent upon the "apocalypse tradition (source?)" that is reflected as well in the Synoptic Gospels. The origin of these materials *may* be very early, but it is impossible to determine the original association of these texts with the sayings that were incorporated by the Didachist in chaps. 1-5. As we have seen above, various exhortations in chap. 16 probably stem from an early M source (though this source most likely was not a single literary document). One must note, however, that some of the materials in this chapter reveal a knowledge of the Lucan Gospel, which makes the entire collection of sayings in *Did.* 16 immediately suspect with respect to attempts to date the composition.

With this perspective now in view, the remainder of the study will be devoted to a consideration of the nature of the issues that are confronted in chaps. 7-15. Specifically, it must be determined why these chapters were considered to be of a suitable nature for attachment to chaps. 1-5(6, 16?). We will suggest a larger historical framework in which these materials assist the modern reader to understand the ultimate relationship of the Didache to the Matthean Gospel. As will be demonstrated below, the key to this association may be found in the evolutionary history of an early Christian community, a community that progressed from a predominantly Jewish mindset to a more non-Jewish (Hellenistic?) and therefore non-Torah-oriented view of religion. The elements of such an evolution readily surface throughout the Matthean Gospel. The same shift of emphases can be seen in the concerns of the Didache.

CHAPTER THREE

RELATED INVESTIGATIONS

The Witness from Pauline Tradition

The Text of Didache 6

Discussions of the opening chapters of the Didache traditionally have divided concerning the need to include chap. 6 within the corpus of the Two Ways materials that appear in chaps. 1-5. To be sure, there is no indication of the Two Ways source in this chapter;[1] however, in many respects, neither does chap. 6 reflect the formal liturgical and ecclesial concerns of chaps. 7-15. A more accurate consideration of chap. 6 must recognize its role within the developing corpus of the Didache, i.e., chap. 6 serves as a transitional section between the previous chapters and the subsequent materials. While this necessarily suggests that some redactor other than the Didachist has been at work in the formulation of chap. 6 (and a redactional hand is evident throughout), there is strong evidence that the materials within the chapter are constructed upon the inspiration of a separate source – a source that is related in some way to Paul. An analysis of the chapter suggests, in fact, that the text is primarily a compilation of materials that were available to a secondary redactor, but materials which were not used by the Didachist proper.

In 6.1 a warning appears from the redactor in which the hearer/reader is exhorted ὅρα, μή τίς σε πλανήσῃ ("see that no one mislead you") "from this Way of teaching . . ." Similar warnings already appear in the NT, and scholars often have indicated one or another of these biblical parallels to be the source of the specific phrase in *Did.* 6.1a.[2] Because of the close verbal parallels with the Marcan and the Matthean (par. Lucan) versions of the exhortation (i.e., βλέπετε μή τις ὑμᾶς πλανήσῃ ["Take heed that no one lead you astray"]), it perhaps is true that the Didache's version is related to this particular strain of the tradition. On the other hand, the Marcan tradition places the exhortation within the "little apocalypse" of the Marcan and Matthean texts, while the Didachist reveals no knowledge of any eschatological setting.

---

[1] Muilenburg's notation (*Relations*, 74) that *Did.* 6.1 is dependent upon *Barn.* 18.1 and 21.6a is somewhat strained at this point.

[2] So, 2 Pet 2:21 (Sabatier, *Didachè*, 50); Rom 1:17 (Funk, *Patres*, 16); 1 John 3:7, 2 Pet 2:15 and Matt 24:4 (Vokes, *Riddle*, 95-96); 2 Pet 2:15 (Rordorf and Tuilier, *La doctrine*, 168 n. 4); Kloppenborg ("Sayings," 93) also lists as additional parallels the texts of Mark 13:5b (upon which Matt 24:4 and Luke 21:8 are based), *T. Gad* 3.1, 1 Cor 6:9, Jas 6:9 and *Apoc. Pet.* 1.

Once again, the redactor appears to know materials that also were known by the Matthean redactor, but whose content in the Matthean Gospel was not known by the Didachist.

As we have seen above, this set of conditions (i.e., a saying which is paralleled in the Didache and in the Matthean Gospel, but whose context in the Matthean text is not reflected in the Didache) is found consistently throughout chaps. 1-5. The reemergence of these conditions here suggests that the hand which provided this warning concerning the Two Ways teaching is indeed the same as that which constructed chaps. 1-5, i.e., the Didachist proper. Because such warnings appear throughout the early Jewish/Christian materials, where a common eschatological setting exhorts the faithful to be wary of the appearance of false teachers and false teaching during the final days, the particular warning in *Did.* 6.1a need not have been drawn either from the Matthean or from the Marcan Gospels.[3]

Though it is difficult to determine the level of redaction from which 6.1 was derived, an entirely different situation is suggested in the case of 6.2-3.[4] In these latter verses the motifs of "bearing the yoke (ζύγος) of the Lord" (6.2) and "not eating food offered to idols" (6.3) reflect issues that were of contention within the early Christian community. Presumably, the "discovery" of a source for these verses will lend a more definitive understanding to the circumstances that led to the insertion of 6.1.

Because Matt 11:28-30 retains a saying that is based upon the motif of the "yoke of the Lord" (from the special Matthean source M), many exegetes of *Did.* 6.2 have indicated that the Didache may be dependent here upon the Matthean Gospel.[5] The evidence for this is buttressed by the observations that 1) only here in the NT Gospels is the word ζύγος used, and 2) the theme of τέλειος ("perfection"), which is used in *Did.* 6.2., is a significant motif in the Matthean Sermon on the Mount as well (Matt 5:48; cf. also Matt 19:21).[6] On

[3] Kloppenborg, "Sayings," 94-95. It is my contention that this phrase of warning in 6.1a-b in fact derives from the hand of the Didachist, though the concluding rationale for its presence, which appears in the text at 6.1c, as well as the subsequent materials that appear in vss 2-3, derive from a later hand.

[4] Thus Rordorf and Tuilier (*La doctrine*, 32) and Knopf (*Lehre*, 20-21) believe that 6.2-3 is some form of appendix to the Two Ways tradition.

[5] So, Funk, *Patres Apostolici*, 61; Massaux, *Influence*, 615; Lilje, *Lehre*, 56; and, Rordorf and Tuilier, *La doctrine*, 168.

[6] Robinson (*Barnabas*, 88-90; so too Johnson, "Motive," 112) observes that questions of retaliation and giving in *Did.* 1.4 (which are concerned with τέλειος and are based upon the Sermon on the Mount) and the issue of "bearing the yoke" in *Did.* 6.2 (which is concerned with τέλειος and may be based upon the function of the Sermon on the Mount within the early Christian community [Matt 5:48]), expresses a doctrine of a "higher and lower observance" that is espoused by the redactor of 1.3b-2.1 and 6.2-3. This is to say that a later redactor of the Didache was influenced by the ethic that appears in the Sermon on the Mount. S/he then sought to reflect the double standard of participation within the community that had arisen among the early Christians, i.e., between those who could "bear the yoke" fully and those who could "bear the yoke"

the other hand, the materials in Matt 11:28-30, as in 1 John 5:3, do not preserve the same saying as that which appears in *Did.* 6.2. They instead serve to assure the reader that the "yoke of the Lord" is not burdensome and, in fact, that it is light.[7] This need for assurance concerning the nature of the yoke probably stems from a concern within the developing Christian community that the ways and the teachings of Jesus, like those of the Torah, might be more than the early Christian could bear. For the new convert, particularly one who already was unfamiliar with the tenets and the practices of Judaism, this would have been seen as a concern of unknown proportion.

The Didache, however, perceives no such concern for the nature of the yoke's burden. Instead, the "yoke of the Lord" is offered with the stipulation that "good" Christians will attempt to bear its burden as they are able.[8] While the texts of the Matthean Gospel and 1 John probably reveal some extensive theological reflection upon a historical moment in late first-century Christianity, a period in which the developing Christian community was in the process of becoming widely infused with Gentiles, the Didache shows no awareness of such a historical need to explain the easy nature of the "yoke of the Lord." This divergence between the Didache and the Johannine/Matthean Gospels suggests two points with respect to the Didache account: 1) the use of the "yoke of the Lord" motif in the Didache may have occurred prior to the use of the same motif in the Matthean and the Johannine texts (though this certainly does not speak to the antiquity of the motif in any of these traditions); and, 2) the text of the Didache may be a direct and swift response to the establishment of the "yoke of the Lord" motif within the community in which the Didache was used, whereas the Matthean and the Johannine texts obviously develop the theme through the guidelines of extended theological reflection upon community problems. We will consider these implications below.

In 6.3 the issue of "sacrificed food" is broached. The style of this verse, with its opening περὶ δὲ ("and concerning"), is consistent with the style in which the materials of chaps. 7-11 (on immersion ritual, table fellowship and ecclesial leaders) appear.[9] Unlike 6.2, however, there does not seem to be any immediate parallel to these "table" concerns within the Matthean Gospel.

---

only in part. While I find this understanding to be strained, others have agreed that the materials of 1.3b-2.1 and 6.2-3 may derive from the same redactional hand; cf. Rordorf and Tuilier, *La doctrine*, 92; and by implication, Schlecht, *Apostellehre*, 64, and Drews, "Einleitung," 183.

[7] Lilje, *Lehre*, 53-57.

[8] I would argue against Rordorf and Tuilier (*La doctrine*, 169 n. 8), who see a "concessive spirit" in the phrases "if you can bear" (εἰ μὲν γὰρ δύνασαι βασάσαι) and "do what you can" (ὃ δύνῃ, τοῦτο ποίει) in 6.2 (and 6.3). If this were the attitude of the redactor, an approach like that of the Matthean and Johannine texts would have been more appropriate to the situation. Instead, the "yoke of the Lord" is offered without compromise, and the hearer/reader is challenged to accept it to whatever degree they are able.

[9] Kraft, *Barnabas*, 161.

One's first consideration is for the discussion that arises in the Pauline letters: Rom 14:1-3; 1 Cor 8:4 and 10:25-28. There is no question that the issue of idol worship and "sacrificed food" was a paramount consideration within early Christianity. There also is little debate that the Didache reflects the wide parameters of this discussion, as does the correspondence of Paul.[10] But since the Didache does not continue in pursuit of this issue, one must assume, as is the case with 6.2, that some widely recognized statement upon this "table" issue lay behind the authoritative exhortation of 6.3. This is to say that while Paul must speak at greath length on the issue of "sacrificed food" in order to meet the immediate ethical and theological concerns of his readers, the Didache seems merely to reconfirm an understanding with respect to "sacrificed food" that does not necessitate any further elaboration within the community which is addressed by the text. Our question, therefore, must be concerned with the specific nature of this ruling which addressed such early Christian concerns as the "yoke of the Lord" and "food sacrificed to idols."

The Apostolic Decree of Acts 15

A number of those scholars who have commented upon *Did.* 6 have noted the possible association of this chapter with the Apostolic Decree of Acts 15.[11] In the Decree (Acts 15:23-29) several pertinent issues with respect to *Did.* 6.2-3 are elucidated. Firstly, the reason for the Decree is stated in its opening lines – "we have heard that some persons from us have troubled you with words, unsettling your minds" (τινὲς ἐξ ἡμῶν ἐξελθόντες ἐτάραξαν ὑμᾶς λόγοις ἀνασκευάζοντες τὰς ψυχὰς ὑμῶν οἷς οὐ διεστειλάμεθα; Acts 15:24). Secondly, the figure of Peter is depicted as one who argues against the necessity to place the ζύγος of the Mosaic Law around the necks of those who follow the teachings of Jesus (15:8). It is to this ζύγος that the term βάρος ("weight") makes reference in the Decree itself (15:28). Finally, the issue of "eating sacrificed food" is resolved ("in theory," that is; 15:29). Thus, Acts 15:23-29 sets forth three elements that serve as the foundational structure for the Decree in the exact order as the elements that are under contention in *Did.* 6.1-3: the threat of false teaching; the desire for freedom from an unnecessary yoke/burden; and, the resolution of the question of "sacrificed foods." As is noted above, the style of the Didache as it reflects upon these three themes is by no means polemical or emphatic, but it is merely a brief comment upon what presumably is authoritative for the readers of the text. It is not difficult

[10] Harris, *Teaching*, 87; Knopf, *Lehre*, 21.

[11] Thus, Taylor, *Teaching*, 46-48; Funk, *Patres Apostolici*, 16-17; Vokes, *Riddle*, 95-96; Kraft, *Barnabas*, 163; Rordorf and Tuilier, *La doctrine*, 32, 168-69.

to envision that the Apostolic Decree served as that community standard upon which *Did.* 6 was composed.[12]

If some early form of the Apostolic Decree that is mentioned here by the witness of Acts can be considered to be the source behind *Did.* 6, other aspects of the relationship of the Didache to Paul may be deduced quite readily.[13] Since the Decree purportedly was sent from Jerusalem to Antioch, it is possible that the redactor of *Did.* 6 used the text in Antioch itself. This might well explain the similarity of various materials within the Didache that are paralleled in the Pauline letters. For example, as is noted above, the question of "eating sacrificed food" was of primary concern to the communities to which Paul wrote.[14] Likewise, Paul (and the Deutero-Pauline author) makes constant use of virtue- and vice-lists that are similar to those that are found in *Did.* 5. Finally, while the Didachist has attached a concern for the decalogue in chap. 2 to the "love of God"/"love of neighbor"/Golden Rule sayings of 1.2, Paul also seems to know this tradition in which the decalogue serves as a more detailed explication of the "love of neighbor"/Golden Rule (Rom 13:8-10).[15]

Since Paul is listed by tradition and in the witness of Acts as one who accompanied the transmission of the Apostolic Decree to Antioch (Acts 15:25), and since he appears to have considered the city to be an important axis during his missionary journies, it is conceivable that much material that appears in the Pauline letters was drawn from Antiochene sources which were known to

---

[12] Kraft (*Barnabas*, 163) also argues that 6.3 "represents a larger, older source that listed the various relevant food laws which Christianity had adopted from the Jewish "Noachic Laws for sympathetic Gentiles." He too looks to Acts 15 as a representative example, though he does not indicate that the Apostolic Decree of Acts was the direct source of the Didache. See the discussion of Telfer ("*Didache*," 133-46, 259-71) in reaction to the challenge of Creed ("Didache," 387). The assumption that the Didache here has used a source for the Apostolic Decree that also was used by the redactor of Acts does not by implication mean that these verses in the Didache were composed after the composition of the text of Acts. Instead, one can assume only that the redactor of the Didache had a knowledge of some form of the Decree as it was known and circulated in early Christian communities (pre-70 C.E.?).

[13] The questions of historical validity behind the report of the Decree in Acts 15 are well-known; cf. the reviews of Haenchen, *Acts*, 468-72, and Conzelmann, *Acts*, 114-22. The following remarks in no way are intended to claim that *Did.* 6 can be traced to some historical moment such as that which is reported by the author of Acts. Instead, as is noted by Conzelmann (p. 119): "It is at least correct that the decree certainly arose in mixed congregations." Whatever the circumstances of the origination of the "Apostolic Decree," the text of *Did.* 6 would seem to indicate that the primary issues of the decree were widely known in the early church. The redactor of the Didache apparently has some knowledge of those issues. S/he has chosen to address them in a brief statement here.

[14] The theological position of the Didache here, however, appears to conflict in part with the Pauline position. As is noted by Johnson ("Motive," 114-15), the Didache represents the case of the "'weak,' *i.e.* strict party, as Paul calls it."

[15] See the discussion of Kretschmar, "Askese," 44-45. Massaux (*Influence*, 643-46) finds additional parallels with the Pauline literature at *Did.* 3.8 (1 Thes 4:11); 3.9 (Rom 12:16); etc.

the community of the Didache. In this case, one need not argue that the Didache itself reflects a knowlege of the Pauline letters, but only that the Didache and the Pauline letters draw from a common source of early Christian materials. The thesis that the community which produced the Didache in fact did reside in the sphere of Antioch will receive attention in the discussion that follows.

A New Construction: The Role of World-View

Introduction

In order to transcend the limitations that are inherent in traditional religio-historical approaches to early Christian literature and in our effort to categorize the development of a specific community tradition from which the text of the Didache may have derived, it should be of valuable assistance to undertake an analysis of the shift in emphasis that is evident among the various redactors of the Didache. The sociological approach of Bryan R. Wilson already has demonstrated convincingly that any early religious community may be classified according to the reaction of that community toward society ("the World").[16] The Didache indeed does exemplify a reaction toward society, and it does so on at least two different redactional levels: 1) in chaps. 1-5 one finds that the community understands itself within the guidelines of an established religion (i.e., Judaism); 2) in chaps. 7-15 one finds that the community reevaluates itself in the light of an encroaching Hellenistic Christianity. As has been demonstrated above, the most obvious reaction that is exhibited in the text of the Didache is that which appears in the need of the community to adopt, to preserve, to canonize and to maintain a "credal/liturgical" body of doctrine, i.e., the decalogue. We also have noted that a focus upon the decalogue is not extensive among early Jewish and Christian authors. Therefore, the fact that this authoritative corpus of literature serves such an axial role in the Didache may provide us with an important key in our characterization of the community that produced the text.

While the Didache is the product of several different redactional hands, the core of the text, which centers around the structure of the decalogue as it is provided in chaps. 1-5, has been preserved in a prominent role for the Didachist, and for each subsequent redactor as well. It is most important,

[16] Wilson, *Magic and the Millenium*, especially 18-30, where Wilson outlines basic responses to the world in seven categories: "revolutionist" (overturning of the world); "introversionist" (abandonment of the world); "reformist" (amendment of the world); "utopianist" (reconstruction of the world); "conversionist" (changing of the world); "manipulationist" (changing of one's perception of the world); and, "thaumaturgist" (dispensation and miracles within the world). See also Smith, "Description," 17-25

however, to understand the specific way in which these chapters have been perceived on each redactional level, since those individual perceptions widely diverge from each other as they appear throughout the text. It must be assumed that this transition in perception among the redactors is itself indicative of a similar transition within the communities within which the redactors compiled and recorded their materials. According to Wilson, our success in the characterization of the developing world-view of the community as it shifts from its original allegiance to a textual *credo* (i.e., the decalogue, which serves as the core of chaps. 1-5) toward an entirely different concern, i.e., an allegiance to the authority of the religious *institution*, should enable us to perceive more accurately the nature and the function of this core material as it is maintained and utilitzed within the community. With this achieved, we should have more to say concerning the character of the community tradition from which the Didache is derived.

Previous attempts to understand both the redactors and the communities that those redactors represented have failed to notice such developments. Here one must recognize that the consideration of texts by means of the classical approach of historians, which serves to eliminate the individuality of those texts "and so extract for use as historical evidence those elements which are not the creation of the author,"[17] appears to offer little new information concerning the milieu of the Didache, regardless of whatever level of redaction that one chooses to examine. A sociological analysis of the Didache with a particular attention given to evidence that implicates responses to the early world of Christianity as they appear throughout the text, however, should aid in either the alteration or in the support of the conclusions that have been reached by previous researchers of the text.

Analysis of 1-5(6)

As we have concluded above, the initial chapters of the Didache traditionally are viewed as the materials that are dominated by a prominent Two Ways motif, such as that which commonly is found among various religious groups during the early centuries of Christianity's existence.[18] While the rigid dualism that is exhibited by the Two Ways theme hardly can be restricted to early Christian thought, this element in the world-view of the Didache's community is precisely that characteristic which should aid us in the formulation of a definition for the tradition from which the core materials of the Didache are

---

[17] H. Cherniss, "The Biographical Fashion in Literary Criticism" (*University of California Publications in Classical Philology* 12/15; eds. J. T. Allen, W. H. Alexander, G. M. Calhoun) 279-80, as it is quoted by Neusner, "Weber Revisited," 63.

[18] See Suggs, "Two Ways," 176 n. 23.

derived. The concerns of dualism were manifested in most forms of first-century Christian thought, regardless of whether those forms eventually were judged either to be *orthodox* or *heretical*. Consequently, one can learn much about a community from this "perspectival element" that contributes to a community's own particular view of the world.

Admittedly, one cannot define the community of the Didache simply according to the dualistic perspective that is exhibited by the text. A second guideline is necessary. Thus, the presence of the decalogue in the text becomes crucial, since this material represents an axis of canonical authority that is significant for the community. Here one discovers a *mixed* decalogue, which obviously is based upon Exod 20:8-17, yet has been altered significantly by the influence of early Christian concerns. The prohibitions against sodomy, fornication, magic, infanticide, etc. that are included alongside the traditional prohibitions against murder, adultery, theft, covetousness and false witness certainly indicate a reflection upon the meaning and the significance of the decalogue for the community within which the Didache was used. But further, these prohibitions suggest that the community sought to interpret the decalogue in the light of a developing threat to morality which arose from beyond the boundaries of Judaism proper.

The retreat to the canonical standard of the decalogue by a community which found itself in the face of adversity suggests that the community was initially under extensive influence by Judaism. Similar reactions against outside threats appear in the rising tide of "isolationism" and "self-absorbtion within the study of the Torah" that came to characterize the rabbinic tradition in general.[19] Indeed, if one accepts the conclusion that *Did.* 2.2 originally existed in isolation and became a core text around which the remainder of chaps. 1-5 later was constructed, there would be little need to attribute the earliest materials of the Didache to anything other than a strictly orthodox circle of devout first-century Jews. In this event, one could recognize here the possibility of an "introversionist response"[20] to the world (i.e., a retreat from the pressures of a hostile society) by the author of the Didache, who seeks to maintain a "canonical authority" and to expand its applicability in the face of an ever-encroaching world.

It is the remainder of chaps. 1-5 that alters such an interpretation. The

---

[19] This position, which provides some rationale for the rise and the development of the rabbinic tradition into an atmosphere of isolation from the world of Hellenistic Judaism, first was suggested to me by Louis M. Barth. It seems probable that the concern to preserve a tradition of beliefs and thought under the threat of persecution could have forced an "introversionist response" to the world (in the words of Wilson) among the orthodox theologians of Judaism, a response that was strangely both akin to and divergent from the manner in which the core of the decalogue has been preserved in *Did.* 2.

[20] This is how one must understand Wilson, *Magic*, 23-24.

"first and second commandments" of *Did.* 1.2, while they also are focused upon the Torah of Hebrew tradition, are based quite obviously upon a further reflection of circulating *logia* from within the Jesus tradition.[21] So too, chaps. 4-5 consistently construct a perception of morality within nascent Christianity that was developed from an explicit focus upon the decalogue as it appears in chaps. 2-3.

Thus, one finds that chaps. 1-5 open with a statement concerning the Two Ways, i.e., a saying that is inherently dualistic in nature. The redactor then chose to develop and to explicate this Two Ways motif with the incorporation of materials that are an accepted tradition of the community, i.e., the decalogue. This tradition has been expanded sufficiently to encounter the contemporary needs of a community whose moral ethic has been challenged by society at large. In addition, the tradition has been established as the basis upon which more Christian-oriented materials have been formulated as a moral guide for the community. The community that would adhere to such a use of these materials would be one that had maintained an allegiance to the tenets of Judaism as a core of ethical beliefs. Yet this community has accepted an inclination toward Christian values apparently without having incorporated any explicit apocalypticism.[22] While the members of such a community indeed may be considered to be Christian Jews, the world-view of that community could have remained quite easily within the parameters of the numerous contemporary lines of Jewish thought as they existed early in the first century.[23]

Prior to the fall of the Temple in C.E. 70, the world of Judaism, though under seige, was still somewhat stable. Jewish theology was able to maintain the belief that the temporal world was under the reign of the eternal God, who was symbolized by the Temple at Jerusalem and by the religious cultus that was oriented around that institution. Here, even under the rule of Rome and in the face of a widespread Diaspora, there was no "loss of world"[24] for Judaism, but only the need to reclassify the value structure by which the world was interpreted – a world whose hostile intentions toward Judaism were at worst temporal and certainly were under the eternal guidance of a divine plan. Such a reclassification of world-view holds true both for contemporary Judaism and for the perspective of *Did.* 1-5. And while this reclassification represents a considerable shift in theological focus, it was itself ultimately superseded by the world-view of the Matthean Gospel, which sought to exchange a larger portion of its Jewish heritage for a more radical understanding

---

[21] Giet, *L'énigme*, 66.

[22] Robinson, "World," 106-107. As was indicated above, I assume here that chap. 16 and its attendant apocalyptic elements cannot be argued to be an original part of the Didache.

[23] See Malina, "Christianity," 46-57, esp. the chart on 57.

[24] See the use of this phrase by Robinson, "World," 103.

of the world. It is certainly true that the ultimate rejection of Judaism *per se* by late first-century Christianity, or at least the rejection of that form of Judaism which became radically ensconsed in a formal adherence to the Torah, is renounced both in the Matthean Gospel and in the later chapters of the Didache.[25] In the core materials of chaps. 1-5, however, the tradition of the decalogue is preserved in agreement with Judaism, and thereby does not reveal the tension between Judaism and Hellenistic Christianity that is so evident in the Matthean Gospel.

The witness of chaps. 1-5 clearly indicates that the Didachist's adjustment from a Jewish perspective to a perspective which could accommodate the needs of an emerging Christian world-view did not seek to replace the "yoke of the Torah" with the "yoke of Jesus" (cf. *Did.* 6.2), but instead, that the Didachist was anxious to weld the two yokes into a single system. Once more, the goal of these chapters reflects to a certain extent the focus that is sought subsequently in the Matthean Gospel.[26] In the Matthean text, Jesus embodies the figure of Sophia as the expression of a wisdom that attempts to replace the Pharisaic Torah with the true Torah of Wisdom.[27] In the Didache, the thread of traditional Jewish wisdom appears in the formulaic introduction of "my child" (3.1, 3-6; 4.1),[28] which presumably should be associated with the figure of the historical Jesus. *Did.* 1-5 incorporates a much more gentle union of the Jewish Law and the Christian gospel through its use of wisdom, however, than does the Matthean Gospel. While one might expect a harsh condemnation of Judaism in the post-apostolic church, as is reflected in the catholic epistles and in the final stage of redaction in the Matthean Gospel, one would expect a softer reconcilation in those earlier forms of Christianity which had not yet parted from their Jewish roots, such as with the Sayings Gospel Q and, as is suggested here, with the Didache.

Both the incorporation of the decalogue from Jewish tradition and the apparent attempt to link the Jewish Torah with the person and the teaching of Jesus speak initially to the immediate characterization of the community that produced *Did.* 1-5. The presence of the Jewish roots upon which this com-

---

[25] For example, see the use of "hypocrite" as a reference to Jews in *Did.* 8.1-2. Goppelt (*Times*, 120) makes this same observation, though he places the rationale for the ultimate rejection of Judaism by the Didachist to a third-century provenance.

[26] Suggs, *Wisdom*, 106.

[27] Suggs, *Wisdom*, 107.

[28] A subtle distinction must be made here in opposition to the suggestion by Schoedel that the Christian catechetical tradition typically incorporated such formulations from the Hebrew wisdom tradition of the OT without any further association with contemporary Judaism ("Wisdom," 175-76). Only two examples are offered by Schoedel, Clem. *str.* 1.29.2 and this section of the Didache. This hardly seems to be a sufficient basis upon which Schoedel can deny that the community of the Didache was in strong communion with contemporary Judaism, and not just in communion with the "scriptures" of Judaism.

munity evolved suggests that the community probably arose within the stable religious environment that would have been offered by a religion which was accepted under the law of the Roman empire and within the psychological/emotional security of a well-developed religious tradition. As far as any early Christian community can be extrapolated from the roots of Jewish tradition, there is no way to assert a specific geographical milieu for this community. This is to suggest that the community which produced *Did.* 1-5 may just as easily have come either from within Palestine or from outside of it. So too, the doctrines of Judaism serve admirably in the Didachist's attempts in chaps. 1-5 to establish an ethic that is able to meet the demands of an environment which seemed to defy any considerations of ethical morality. Such doctrines provide the social control that is necessary to regulate the community.[29]

While the core of materials in chaps. 1-5 appears to preserve the values that are associated with the "sacred" (here, the decalogue) as the basis for the existence of the community, this is achieved with a certain preconception. This preconception revolves around the realization that even though the "sacred" (i.e., the decalogue and its ethical implications as they appear in the Way of Life) clearly must be differentiated from the "profane" (i.e., the daily activities of the believer), the latter is not to be despised, but is to be subordinated to the former.[30] This view, which is obscured to a certain extent by the more "Christianized" portions of chaps. 1-5 (especially 1.3b-2.1), is deleted completely in the subsequent chapters.

Analysis of 7-10

The next segment of the Didache shows an immediate shift in interest from the "decalogue as *credo*" motif of chaps. 1-5. While the initial chapters emphasize both the preservation of a recognized standard of tradition, i.e., the decalogue, and the need to adhere to that tradition, chaps. 7-10 are concerned instead with the correct observation of ritual. In itself, the association of appropriate ritual practice with a correctly-observed community rule should not be considered so much as a complete shift in emphasis by the redactor as it should be considered a transition to another aspect of the community's religious life. It follows naturally that where there is a concern to preserve the foundation upon which correct decisions and actions are made, that a concern for the correct method of executing those actions should develop.

One may appeal to the historical development of early church dogma as

---

[29] O'Dea, *Sociology*, 227.

[30] Seguy, "Revolution," 105. Seguy continues to note that a specific characteristic of Judaism (and Islam) is its drive to regulate the relations of mankind "with the two worlds that solicit him" through "divinely revealed law." This certainly is true of *Did.* 1-5 as well.

support for this observation. As the early church gradually alienated itself from its Jewish background, a distinct loss of structure and tradition occurred which led to the need for a systematized liturgy and dogma within the ἐκκλησία ("congregation"). One finds evidence for this pattern in the interpretation of liturgical traditions that were received by Paul (see 1 Cor 11:23-26), in the manipulation of *logia* throughout the Synoptic Gospels in order to accommodate a fading strain of Jewish ethics (see Matt 5:32b) and in the post-apostolic drive to standardize both theology and ecclesiastical polity around developing centers of orthodox perspective – Rome, Jerusalem, Antioch and Alexandria.

The concerns of chaps. 7-10 are no longer oriented around the preservation of Jewish tradition, but are intimately more concerned with the structuring of developing Christian institutions. The first of these institutions as they are addressed in the Didache, i.e., "baptism," reflects a trend of development that is similar to that which is found in the NT, though with a noticable emphasis upon the *words* of institution rather than upon the *practice* of the ritual itself. The ritual is staged as a secondary element to chaps. 1-5. Thus baptism comes only after the catechumen understands the correct form of preservation and the appropriate practice of the Torah: "Having first rehearsed all these things . . ." (ταῦτα πάντα προειπόντες; *Did.* 7.1). In a certain respect, the "activity" of baptism consciously is molded upon the foundation of Torah – it is the imperative response to the indicative. Such an emphasis is paralleled throughout 1 Peter, where the understanding of baptismal liturgy is associated quite closely with a consistent exhortation toward moral order, as well as with a close adherence to OT ethics. The ordering of this baptismal ritual in accordance with the authority of Jewish faith and practice reveals, both here and in 1 Peter, a concern for an acceptable basis upon which the evolving liturgy of Christianity could be rooted. It is significant that in *Did.* 7, unlike *Did.* 1-5 and 1 Peter, the association of the ritual with the authority of the risen Christ is not preserved in the various *logia* of the historical Jesus, but is preserved instead in the maintenance of "the words of institution," i.e., "of the Father and of the Son and of the Holy Spirit" (7.1, 3). The ritual itself is aligned according to one of the early purity laws of rabbinic tradition (i.e., the use of "running water").

The second institution that appears in this section is that of "the meal" (chaps. 8-10). Again one finds the concerns of "the meal" to be oriented around the contemporary practices of Jewish table fellowship. Thus, in *Did.* 8.1 the period that is required for fasting consciously is altered from those periods that were approved within Judaism – Mondays and Thursdays – to alternative days of the week – Wednesdays and Fridays. The ritual of the meal itself, however, appears to be dependent upon the traditional Passover format. In this respect our redactor reveals the intuited need to formulate some authoritative basis for the liturgical ritual that has developed concerning "the meal" and that has been selected for inclusion here. The authority of *logia* that are attributed to the historical Jesus is implemented in these chapters (though no such appeal to the teachings of Jesus are made in the materials on baptism that appear in chap. 7), as is demonstrated by the presence of the Lord's Prayer in 8.2-3. Yet here the prayer does not make a smooth transition into the text, unlike the ready context in which the prayer is discovered in Matt 6:9-13. The insertion of the prayer into *Did.* 8 instead seems to reflect the desire of the redactor to incorporate new materials into the authoritative tradition of the community, regardless of the violence to the flow of the text that results from this intrusion. For the redactor, it is the incorporation of authoritative pericopae that is important in these chapters, not a concern for the actual flow of the text.

As with the baptism ritual in *Did.* 7, the meal is oriented around the authority of the words of institution. The text in no way is concerned with the ordering or praxis of the ritual itself. The same observation hardly can be made with respect to the meals that are portrayed in Matt 26:26-29, Mark 14:22-25, Luke 22:14-20 and 1 Cor 11:23-26.[31]

Finally, the central figure in this liturgy of "the meal" is the object of the attendant prayers themselves, viz., God as "Father." It is not the more theologically refined view of the historical Jesus as the figure of the Messiah that eventually dominates throughout Christian tradition.

Another development in chaps. 7-10 is the recognition of an evolving community consciousness, which is not reflected in chaps. 1-5. While chaps. 1-5 seek to incorporate Jewish Law as the undisputed foundation for the structure of Christian institutions, chaps. 7-10 seek to associate these institutions with the historical Jesus and with the Christian Trinity, both of which appear in the document for the first time in this section. Here too, the church as ἐκκλησία first is mentioned as a common body of believers that is aware of its individual existence either apart from the authority of tradition that is found in chaps. 1-5 or from the words of ritual that appear in chaps. 7-10. The existence and salvation of this body of believers is the focus of the petition on behalf of the church that appears in *Did.* 10.5.

As has been mentioned above, the most striking elements that seem to be absent from the ritual structures in this section are a cross/resurrection theology and a well-developed form of Christology. If one were to attribute these chapters to a date near the end of the first century or to the beginning of the second century, it seems incredible that such elements should be absent.

---

[31] Thus I disagree with the observation of Peters (*Harvest*, 492), who tends to see this eucharistic liturgy in the Didache as already "fairly sophisticated." Indeed, the perspective of the Didache is quite divergent from the "Christ cult" idea of eucharist that is found both in the Pauline and in the Synoptic traditions.

A ready alternative to such a date for chaps. 7-10 may come through the recognition that these chapters represent a change of attitude toward the original portion of the document (i.e., chaps. 1-5) within the community from which the Didache is derived. One must assume that the materials of *Did.* 1-5 were collected originally because they were the core of a living tradition within the community. The addition of *Did.* 7-10 to these materials serves to displace the primary status of this tradition to a secondary "supporting role," the purpose of which is to justify the development of the ritual institutions that are presented in chaps. 7-10. This is to say that the basis for chaps. 7-10 was found in the materials that were preserved in chaps. 1-5, and that this perception, while it provided some purpose and justification for the addition of community liturgy and ritual, sublimated the original role of chaps. 1-5 to a set of formalized rules and regulations for use in the community.

All of this served to fossilize the code of ethics that had been set for the community,[32] without permitting any access for the rise of that charismatic spirit which eventually came to characterize the form of Christianity that swept the Mediterranean world. This formalization of an ethical code is well-represented in the simple command of *Did.* 8.3 to pray the Lord's Prayer "three times a day" (τρὶς τῆς ἡμέρας). Such an exhortation is designed to contradict the contemporary practices of daily Jewish prayers, and may represent a formalistic hardening within the community against the perceived threat of a Judaizing influence (versus the perceived threat of a Gentile influence that dominates chaps. 1-5, the earliest stage of the tradition).[33] While the influence of Jewish Law would not have been perceived as a threat to the structure or to the thought of the earliest community of the Didache, it certainly would have required some reinterpretation within the later form of the community. This later community was devoted to an attempt to consolidate theology and ethics into a self-contained agenda either apart from the influence of "the old faith," i.e., Judaism,[34] or from the new "destabilizing pressure" of wandering charismatic preachers.

---

[32] O'Dea, *Sociology*, 249.

[33] Goppelt, *Times*, 48. While I would agree with Goppelt that the legalistic hardening of the Didache is foreign to the thought of the Matthean redactor, this does not indicate necessarily that the two documents stem from different communities. Indeed, the Didache simply may represent within the community the theology of a more conservative Jewish element whose religious stance is based upon a legalistic view of Torah. The Matthean Gospel, on the other hand, may represent that element of the community which was open to a theology of cross/resurrection, the parameters of which permitted this latter group to accept more readily an open relationship with society outside of the community proper.

[34] The tact taken by the community of the Didache in chaps. 7-10 thus may reflect a polemical counter to the form of Judaism that was evident in Syria, the locale in which the Didache ultimately was subordinated under the wave of a more charismatic Christianity such as that which is represented in the NT. This form of Judaism seems to have remained a persistent problem for the developing churches of Syria, as is evidenced by the Church Fathers and synods of both Asia Minor and Syria that fought it into the fifth century (Goppelt, *Times*, 127-28).

The establishment in chaps. 7-10 of a stable ritual within the midst of a vivid rejection of Jewish formalism, however, reveals some specific and central concern for a "pure community" that perceived itself to be segregated in a hostile world. Thus, the world-view of the Didache here is not so alien from many aspects of the Pauline vision, e.g., that this world is transitory and is temporarily ruled by darkness, though ultimately the rule of Christ will be made known to those who are faithful.[35] The primary difference in this perception, though, is the way in which these two representatives of a limited dualism (i.e., Paul and the redactors of *Did.* 7-10) incorporated this perspective into practice. While the Pauline emphasis places a prominent value upon the believer's faith in a resurrection Christology, the emphasis in the Didache is upon the maintenance of a correct ritual within the religious community. Both for Paul and for the later redactors of the Didache, however, there is the recognition that "the night is retreating and the morning approaches."[36]

While chaps. 1-5 rest upon the authority of an established *tradition*, i.e., the Torah, chaps. 7-10 probably receive their authority from *individuals* who are associated with the institutional structure of the congregation itself.[37] This is to say that these latter chapters do not appeal to scripture for their justification, but instead, that they themselves are words which are spoken from an ecclesiastical office that is assumed to be authoritative. It is significant that such persons within the structure of the community are in established positions by the time that chaps. 11-15 are affixed to the Didache, since the individual who transmits the "rules of the community" (i.e., the tradent) appears to bear authority for the evaluation of wandering charismatics and of traveling preachers.[38] This was extremely important, since such charismatic figures often were viewed as the bearers of divine power.[39] At this stage in the development of this specific community, a bureaucratic authority structure, which was "bound to intellectually analyzable rules," had taken precedence over the movement of charismatic authority in the extended church, a movement which was "foreign to all rules."[40]

---

[35] Bornkamm, *Experience*, 22-23. Cf. *Did.* 16.5.

[36] Bornkamm, *Experience*, 24.

[37] Weber, *Organization*, 341. Weber contends that such authority within a community need not come from any particular figure who is associated with an established institution. Instead, such power or authority more accurately may be attributed to that person who shows the most faithful, personal loyalty to the immediate (or to the most immediately practical) cause. This would certainly hold true for the authority of Paul. Weber does recognize that the legitimation for such personal authority comes through some association with pre-established authority, as I argue here.

[38] As has been stated above, while chaps. 7-10 probably were added to the core of materials in 1.1-6.1a prior to the addition of chaps. 11-15, there is no specific reason to think that the whole of chaps. 7-15 derives from the same redactor (i.e., the second redactor).

[39] Boring, *Sayings*, 88.

[40] Weber, *Organization*, 361. Weber later states that "in its pure form charismatic authority

The presence of such a bureaucratic dominance in the Didache is intriguing, since the majority of extant evidence from the first century suggests that the more popular form of early Christianity was demonstrated in the authority of spiritual charisma. The temporing of such charisma, however, seems to have been a necessary component of survival for nascent Christian communities, as is attested by the failure of the Jesus revolution (itself a renewal movement) within the framework of Judaism.[41] It is important to observe that the earliest community of Christians in Jerusalem established a basic structure soon after the death of Jesus primarily through an acknowledgment of familial kinship, as is represented in the figure of James, the brother of Jesus.[42] This naturally lends some support to the argument against early, restricted sociological theories which claimed that community and ecclesial *structure* were simply the product of a charismatically-dying faith. Ultimately, however, one cannot deny that those forms of legitimation which were dependent upon charisma, as is evidenced in the figure of Paul, had a substantial influence upon the development of ecclesial structures and liturgical formulas. Indeed, it would appear that a lack of adherence to such charismatic authority ultimately may have led to a certain disdain for the use of the Didache within its own community liturgical tradition, since the Didache was a document that soon was lost to the Christian tradition.

Analysis of 11-15

Chaps. 11-15 reveal yet another turn in the developing perspective of the Didache. In these chapters the reader/hearer is instructed concerning the need for an awareness of those persons who come into the community from outside, i.e., the "wandering apostles" and the "wandering prophets" (chaps. 11-12). As ancillary to this instruction, a brief statement is made concerning the structure and the hierarchy of those persons who are within the folds of the community, i.e., the "bishops," the "deacons," the "resident prophets" and the "teachers" (chap. 15). It is probably not by accident that this development of a community self-identity does not appear immediately after the close of chaps. 1-5, which are tied so closely to OT Law (since the earliest form of the community would have continued to structure its authoritative offices ac-

---

may be said to exist only in the process of originating" (p. 364). While one certainly is not free to conclude from this observation that the existence of a "bureaucratic authority" necessarily implies the presence of a fixed tradition within a community, such a conclusion would seem to be suggested. In the case of the Didache, where the community ultimately adheres to a non-charismatic authority in the midst of lesser charismatic authorities, one is reminded of the situation both of Jesus and Paul, whose "charismatic roles stood firmly within a line of *tradition*" (Gager, *Community*, 70 [emphasis Gager's]).

[41] Theissen, *Sociology*, 112.

[42] Gager, *Community*, 69.

cording to the guidelines of the Jewish tradition), but instead, that this community self-characterization appears in the text only after the intrusion of various "anti-Judaic" tendencies in chaps. 7-10.

The problems and the concerns that were associated with traveling prophets have been demonstrated to reflect a situation that was immediately relevant to the earliest Christian communities.[43] In the rise and expansion both of Christian missions and of Christian theology, it seems that the wandering preacher/evangelist, e.g., Paul, Barnabas and Apollos, took early precedence in the development of non-Palestinian churches. While this has been recognized as a factor that may have led to the expansion of the earliest Christian message among various towns and villages of the Roman empire,[44] it must be observed that the eventual backlash of these evangelistic efforts into the early strongholds of Jewish-Christian communities led to an imminent threat to those Christians whose internal organizational and theological structures were organized so tightly around their early Jewish roots. This is evidenced both in the Pauline-Petrine confrontations of Acts and Galatians and in the anti-Pauline bias of the Matthean Gospel. No doubt, the recognition of such a backlash lends much in terms of an explanation for the rationale behind the composition of chaps. 11-12.

The actual response of the Didache to wandering preachers seems confused in its own right, which perhaps suggests that in addition to the work of the second redactor, chaps. 11-15 may have been altered by an even later hand. For example, nothing that is spoken by a prophet is to be questioned if it is spoken "in a spirit" (ἐν πνεύματι; *Did.* 11.7); however, some things that are spoken "in a spirit" cannot be tolerated (11.12).[45]

With the threat of such wandering preachers, the community of the Didache, which originally understood itself within a developing Jewish tradition, was forced to define more rigidly its perspective of Christian principles. The determination of true and false teaching became necessary. It is interesting to note that the criteria for such determinations in the Didache primarily reflect those criteria that appear in the Matthean Gospel as well. It has been argued elsewhere that the Matthean community, as it is attested by the witness of the Matthean Gospel, also was forced to respond to the expanding form of non-Jewish Christianity that was espoused by Pauline supporters.[46] The judgmental attitude of the Didache at this point, however, seems to be more pronounced and harsher than that of the Matthean Gospel, since the Didache concludes with the recognition that the "outsider" is not to be accepted at the expense of the community's good (chap. 12).

---

[43] See Boring, *Sayings*, passim, and Cothenet, "Les prophètes chrétiens," 281-308.
[44] Theissen, "Wanderradikalismus," 245-71.
[45] Boring, *Sayings*, 48.
[46] Betz, "Episode," 1-30.

In chaps. 13-15 the value of the true prophet is recognized. The community receives specific instructions with regard to the way in which such a person is to be honored (13.3-7). The example of dispute that is offered in chap. 14 serves to reinforce further the need to establish a hierarchy of leadership within the community, both to preserve authority and to settle questions of community practice. In chap. 15 one finds evidence of a developing list of ethical and moral criteria by which such leaders are to be chosen and treated. These criteria are standard within early Christian texts, though they are enumerated only briefly: "meekness" (πραΰτης), "unselfish with respect to money" (ἀφιλάργυπος), "truthful" (ἀληθής) and "approved" (δόκιμος) – cf. 15.1b. All of these criteria, which are understood to be authoritative within the community, are subsumed under the category of "worthy of the Lord" (ἀξίους τοῦ κυρίου; 15.1b).[47] In support of such criteria, and unquestionably the ultimate basis of authority by which further determinations are to be made within the community, a short exhortation follows in 15.4:

> τὰς δὲ εὐχὰς ὑμῶν καὶ τὰς ἐλεημοσύνας καὶ πάσας τὰς πράξεις οὕτω ποιήσατε, ὡς ἔχετε ἐν τῷ εὐαγγελίῳ τοῦ κυρίου ἡμῶν.
>
> ("But your prayers and alms and all your acts perform as you find in the Gospel of the Lord.")

Three observations now should be made concerning chaps. 11-15. Firstly, these materials represent a community mindset that had developed extensively from the predominantly Jewish orientation that is represented in chaps. 1-5. The primary concern here is the need of the community to develop an ecclesial orientation, a concern that is attested in the response of the congregation to the problem that is posed by itinerant preachers and prophets. The focus upon "wisdom" that appears in chaps. 3-4 (see above discussion) is not evident in chaps. 11-15. While it certainly may no longer be stated as unequivocable that the role of wisdom as a living religious tradition perished in the early Christian era, and was replaced by the image of the *exalted prophet*,[48] it must be recognized that within the confines of early Jewish Christianity, and hence within the structure of the community which produced the Didache, the temptation of a developing Gnosticism (i.e., the arena into which much of early wisdom thought ultimately was funneled both in the Jewish and the Christian traditions) primarily was oriented away from the mainstream of formal Judaism. Hence, the lack of concern for the message of wisdom in chaps. 11-15 and the more immediately-perceived need to engage the current situation,

[47] Even here the formal guidelines of the community, and presumably the authority upon which the redactor makes his/her exhortations, is based upon the Jewish Torah; see Grant, *Christianity*, 41: "The sentence echoes the words of Deuteronomy on the appointment of judges, including even the requirement that the judges must not take bribes."

[48] Schoedel, "Wisdom," 169-70.

i.e., the wandering prophets, seems to be indicative of a milieu that had changed radically from the milieu of chaps. 1-5.

Secondly, while it is possible that an extended period of time is represented here, this is not required. Indeed, the role of wandering prophets/preachers seems to be among the earliest functions that were attested in nascent Christianity, as is demonstrated by the Sayings Gospel Q and by the writings of Paul. The influence of such wandering charismatics continued unabated in the early days of the Jesus movement,[49] and took advantage of the early hospitality that was offered toward Jewish-Christian travelers by early house-churches (see Luke 10), since Jews "for obvious reasons, avoided the inns."[50] This open attitude toward Jewish travelers and strangers by the early churches may have served only to establish quite early the need to defend against abuse by those travelers.[51] It would not be surprising, therefore, to see a community – such as that which produced the Didache – shift from its original concerns (i.e., the establishment of a system of ethics for the community) to concerns that were oriented around the practical needs of community regulation and structure.

The motif of wandering prophet/preacher also returns one to the question of the community's character, a discussion that first arose with respect to chaps. 1-5. An important characteristic of a developed ἐκκλησία is the structured system for the determination of true and false prophets that is found here. This is no longer a "sect community" whose priorities remain unexamined. Instead, the community of the Didache may be classified as a *church* instead of a *sect*, because of a central realization that is recognized by the congregation: it perceives itself as a religious institution that is in "objective possession of grace."[52] In other words, chaps. 11-15 depict the community of the Didache as a community that understands itself as the bearer of salvation within, yet apart from, the "outside world." This might once again be attributed to a strong association with a firmly-rooted Jewish tradition. In fact, it is this element of "distinctiveness within the world" that has led so many scholars to date the text of the Didache to a period after the first century. On the other hand, a certain "sect-like" quality appears throughout chaps. 7-15 that is not at all evident in the core materials of chaps. 1-5. This quality is quite apparent in the Christian universalism that is resident in the eschatological perspective of these chapters.[53] It is ultimately true, however,

---

[49] Theissen, *Sociology*, 21.

[50] Malherbe, *Aspects*, 66.

[51] Malherbe, *Aspects*, 66-70, 92-112.

[52] Troeltsch, "Relationship," 124.

[53] Troeltsch, "Relationship," 125. This eschatological perspective, while not explicitly stated apart from the materials of *Did.* 10.5 (as has been noted above), is implicit in the nature of those materials that are preserved in chaps. 7-15.

that the primary focus of these chapters is upon church structure, and is not upon eschatology.[54] It also is quite likely that such eschatological elements are the remnants of an earlier perspective of the world that has remained within the community tradition.

Finally, in chaps. 11-15, as with chaps. 1-5, there is a primary concern for the maintenance of a central social system. In chaps. 1-5 this pattern is focused presumably upon the social world that was offered by Judaism. By the time of chaps. 11-15, however, this pattern seems to have shifted to a new set of criteria that are associated with the radical alteration of the community as it experienced the shift in the early Christian situation. This shift in social patterns is perhaps best illustrated in the definitions of ritual that appear in chaps. 7-10 and in the establishment of ecclesiastical offices in chaps. 11-15. Indeed, one must agree that "institutional patterns are the 'backbone' of the social system."[55] This radical shift in patterns no doubt became necessary in the community that produced the Didache as the old institutional patterns of Judaism began to weaken under the new circumstances and the growing threats of the "traveling kerygma."

It has become quite evident throughout our reading of the Didache that the text is focused upon the development of the "institution." The perceived weaknesses of the old institution, which is represented in chaps. 1-5 and which receives correctives in two phases (chaps. 7-10; chaps. 11-15) both by a second and by a later redactor, indicates that the old institutional religion of Judaism was no longer adequate for the changing world-view of the Christian religion as it grew and was nurtured in the community. This is not to deny the motivations of the old world-view, but it is to affirm that these motivations would no longer be achieved through the old institution. While the community that lay behind the composition of the Didache found it necessary to continue to adhere to a self-identity within Judaism, it gradually was forced to engage a form of Christianity 1) that quickly developed apart from Judaism and 2) that no longer wished to see either its own existence or the message of the risen Christ within the framework of Jewish theological structures. The concern for the "world that lay outside," then, became a concern for the larger "Chris-

---

[54] Troeltsch makes an observation about the nature of *church* versus *sect* that seems most pertinent to our consideration of the community of the Didache and its relationship to the world: "The Church has its priests and its sacraments; it dominates the world and is therefore also dominated by the world" ("Relationship," 127). The first half of Troeltsch's statement is obviously evident in the loosely-woven pattern of clerical offices that are represented in chap. 15 and by the emphasis upon baptism and eucharist that is evident in chaps. 7 and 9. The second half may be derived from the comfort that the community no doubt derived from the preservation of a religious tradition (chaps. 1-5) as the stable element around which it constructed an ordered economic, political and moral vision of the world. On this basis, the community should definitely be classified within the parameters of a *church* structure.

[55] Parsons, *Essays*, 239.

tian community that lay outside." The text of chaps. 11-15 reveals a world-view that primarily is concerned for this engagement with other forms of Christianity.

Analysis of 16 and 1.3b-2.1

While there is no certainty that these two sections of the Didache should be attributed to the same redactional layer, they reveal several elements in common, and hence will be discussed together at this juncture.

Firstly, both sections show influence from the Lucan Gospel. To be certain, several scholars have argued for alternative source theories whereby the Didache is considered to be a document that is directly dependent either upon the Sayings Gospel Q[56] or upon some form of the Lucan Gospel.[57] From our analysis of the sayings materials above, however, it now seems more reasonable to consider these sections to have been influenced by a later literary tradition that was incorporated into the Didache and that displayed Lucan influence: 1.3b-2.1 shares specifically Lucan elements, which are coupled with materials from the fifth and sixth Antitheses of the Matthean Gospel; 16.1 displays a knowledge of Luke 12:35-40.

Secondly, both *Did.* 16 and 1.3b-2.1 reveal a high concentration around specific NT themes. This is not to say, of course, that the remainder of the Didache does not engage various NT *logia*, especially those sayings that appear in the Synoptic Gospels. In these two sections, however, nearly all of the materials form a concatenation of repeated phrases, sayings and exhortations that are paralleled almost precisely by the Synoptics. In 1.3b-2.1 this emphasis is centered within the Matthean Antitheses, as was mentioned above. The apocalyptic orientation of chap. 16 also reveals the warnings and exhortations concerning eschatological themes that are paralleled in the Synoptic Gospels.

Finally, there is the consideration of textual orientation. The verses of 1.3b-2.1 serve as the explanation of the "love of God," the "love of neighbor" and the Golden Rule motifs that are found in chap. 1. The concluding statement of this section, which appears at 2.1, forms the introduction to the remainder of chaps. 2-6, and denotes these chapters as the content of the "second commandment" (δευτέρα ἐντολή). Both of these elements seem to suggest that some redactional concern is evident, and especially here, a concern to introduce specifically NT sayings into a collection of materials that were originally Jewish in orientation. With respect to chap. 16, there can be little question that one finds here a typical, early Jewish-Christian tendency

[56] See Glover, "Quotations," 12-29.

[57] This presupposition is evidenced throughout the works of Giet (*L'énigme*), Harnack (*Lehre*), the Oxford Society (*New Testament*) and Vokes (*Riddle*).

to conclude important writings with the promise and threat of an eschatological warning. While these materials at one time may have formed a conclusion to chaps. 1-5(6.1a), their present location probably is the work of a later redactor.

The insertion of specifically Christian materials (1.3b-2.1) and the addition of an eschatological conclusion (chap. 16) seem to indicate the presence of a community that has shifted in its perception of the world. The religious structure of Judaic institutions that were tempered by the teaching of the historical Jesus, as is found in chaps. 1-5, had lost either its validity or its usefulness for the community. One assumes that with the addition of chap. 16, and subsequently with the promise of a "future eschatology" (a world beyond this world), the presence of a living community tradition was no longer of central concern.[58]

These two sections often have been the bane of modern attempts to determine the sources behind the Didache. The most viable solution probably is represented in the arguments of Köster, who indicates the significance of oral sources behind the text. But even here there is no confirmation of the community's milieu or of its historical setting, since there does not appear to be any consensus of understanding among early Christian communities that *logia* should be transmitted in any fixed form.[59]

Finally, these sections are specifically oriented toward a "language of separation,"[60] which becomes especially prevalent in chap. 16. For example, in this concluding chapter one finds an apocalyptic emphasis upon "the wolves" (ὁ λύκος; 16.3) and "the world deceiver" (ὁ κοσμοπλανής; 16.4) that is reminiscent of apocalyptic motifs which are found in the Synoptic Gospels and in 2 Thessalonians. Such "language of separation" appears exclusively in chaps. 7-16 and in the interpolation of 1.3b-2.1.[61] It reaches its climax in the concluding admonition concerning *the world* in 16.8:

---

[58] One sees this rising trend toward an eschatological perception of the world in previous chapters, but one does not find the sort of apocalyptic imagery that appears in chap. 16.

[59] This is a major focus of Kelber, *Gospel*, 1-43. The significance of the *oral tradition*, however, is the very element which Streeter suggests in his view that the Didache is a collection of memorized materials from Q that were preserved by the older members of the Matthean community (*Gospels*, 511): ". . . for some years after Matthew was written certain sayings would still be remembered in their Q form. A work like the Didache would certainly be composed by senior members of the Church in whose recollection turns of phrase in the older document would be likely to be deeply embedded, and all the quotations in the Didache are clearly made from memory."

[60] Meeks, *Christians*, 94-96.

[61] Other examples of "separation" language in the Didache appear as follow: "Gentiles" ([ἔθνος] in the redactional title and three times in 1.3); "hypocrites" ([ὑποκριτής] 8.1, 2); "dogs" ([κύων] 9.5); and, "this world" ([ὁ κόσμος οὗτος] 10.6). In addition, a number of passages are concerned to distinguish between "true and false prophets."

Of particular interest, on the other hand, are the numerous examples of "language of belonging" (see Meeks, *Christians*, 85-94) in the earliest portions of chaps. 1-5: "neighbor" ([πλησίον]

τότε ὄψεται ὁ κόσμος τὸν κύριον ἐρχόμενον ἐπάνω τῶν νεφελῶν τοῦ οὐρανου. ("Then shall the world see the Lord coming on the clouds of heaven.")

Because this language was considered by the community to be appropriate for use in the conclusion to the text, one must conclude that the world-view of the community was transformed into one which held a hostile perception of those forces and influences that originated from outside the ἐκκλησία. Such a world-view is far from that which was represented originally in the materials of chaps. 1-5. Indeed, there is no "language of separation" in those particular chapters, which would suggest that the community did not perceive a need to establish any specific "we/they" boundaries around which to organize the community structure. Evidently this security, which probably came from a close association with the Jewish religious tradition, seems to have been shaken violently by outside influences and to have been dismissed ultimately by the community.

Conclusions

Because the Didache is a document that originated under the influence of a substantial core of Jewish Law and tradition and because it became a document that served as a manual of ritual and ethical practice in the early Christian community, it is apparent that much material that reflects the world-view of the community itself should remain within the document. This perspective of the community's world-view, however, only can be determined through the eyes of the document's redactors at each stage of the developing tradition as that tradition is represented within the text. This implies that the ever-changing world-view of the community occurred within a particular historical timespan in which basic attitudes and theological views arose both among the redactors and among the communities that the redactors represented. Thus, we may conclude as well that some recognition of this changing world-view can help define the historical milieu of the document and of its community.

It is noted here that the role of Jewish thought and ritual is perceived throughout the structure of the Didache, though it is difficult to know to what extent that structure became infused with Hellenistic ideas. The "sayings source," which has been woven into the text of the Two Ways source, represents a collection of important materials that first was used as the theological crux for the work in chaps. 1-5. Since these materials do not bear signs of any

1.2; 2.2, 6); "child" ([τέκνον] in the sense of wisdom exhortation = 3.1, 3, 4, 5, 6); "saint" ([ἅγιος] 4.2); "brother" ([ἀδελφός] 4.8); and, "church" ([ἐκκλησία] 4.12). While "language of belonging" indeed appears in chaps. 7-16, it does so in a most intense and exclusionary form: "church" (9.4; 10.5); "worldly mystery of the church" ([μυστήριον κοσμικὸν ἐκκλησίας] 11.11); "Christian" ([Χριστιανός] 12.4); and, "neighbor" (15.3).

specific Hellenistic influence, this "sayings source" must be considered to stem from a very ancient tradition within the Jewish-Christian community.

As is demonstrated above, the most immediate example of "eschatological awareness," which itself appears in chap. 16, is not an integral portion of the initial core of materials. This is not to say that early Christianity did not operate within the parameters of a churning eschatological perspective, nor that an eschatological orientation was not an operant element at the root of the evolving thought of the Didache's redactors. On the other hand, it is also not to be argued here that the decline of a concern for eschatology *per se* is indicative only of the later phases of Christianity that appeared in the second-fourth centuries C.E.[62] The self-examination of the community which produced the Didache became an important part of that community's existence, as is exhibited in chaps. 7-16. This self-examination led to an existential tension that arose as the community reoriented itself toward an allegiance to eschatological concerns. Indeed, the community eventually took upon itself a "*worldly* perspective," which upon first examination appears to reflect the nature of a "manipulationist response" to the use of OT materials (as also is attested in the later Church Fathers). In fact, this "worldly perspective" was actually the product of a developing Christian community that was separating from its Jewish heritage.

The Didache reflects a community whose roots are established in a solidly established tradition and which develops only to reshape itself around those roots. There is no evidence here that the community perceives the need to "justify its religious existence within the world" such as one finds with Paul in the Pauline epistles, but which gradually is lost in the later Pastorals. The world-view that is established by Paul in his confrontations with various communities reveals his constant experience of the *sacred* or the *holy*, but such an experience certainly is not evident in the Didache. Instead, the Didache offers a community that seems to shelter itself against this existentialist encounter through the very milieu of institutional religion – a form of religion against which Paul struggled to free himself in reshaping his theological doctrine.

Most characteristic of the Didache, and that element which has lent much support for the modern label of "manual of discipline" to the text (a label that automatically conjures the image of "old and dry" with respect to religious life), is the lack of any specific "charismatic moment," i.e., the absence of a "period of the original religious experience and its corresponding vitality and enthusiasm."[63] There is little engagement with the "beyond."

---

[62] Robinson, "World," 101-102. Robinson emphasizes the view of Bultmann here that the "understanding of existence for Paul and John . . . peters out in the Apostolic Fathers." If this is to be maintained, one must ultimately date the Didache as very late or as the product of an early Christian strain that existed apart from Pauline and Johannine Christianity, and probably was opposed to these forms of Christianity.

[63] O'Dea, *Sociology*, 243.

The absence of this charisma, once again, is not to be attributed to the institutionalization of Christianity into a sphere of motivational forces that were no longer associated with the charismatic motivation of pre-institutional religion, a religion which depends upon values that are embodied in a charismatic leader.[64] Instead, the absence of this charisma reflects the gradual denial of Judaism as a valid support for the development of Christianity.

The world-views of the Didache and of the Matthean Gospel are for the most part disparate. This is not unexpected, since those persons in the community who supported the respective documents – if in fact the two documents are derived from the same community tradition – would themselves have shared divergent world-views. That portion of the community which maintained a self-identity within Judaism was attached to the doctrines and *logia* that are preserved in chaps. 1-5. That portion of the community which produced the Matthean Gospel to serve as the primary witness for its religious experience, represented a charismatic, kerygmatic fervor that was associated with a restricted version of resurrection theology. The typical response of a community to some social threat generally falls into one of two categories: 1) a reaction of such intensity so as to be able to eliminate the change; 2) "a permanent state of malintegration and tension which will prevent stable institutionalization of the new patterns."[65] It seems that the latter option was taken by that portion of the community which produced the Didache. The world-view of this group either was never aligned adequately with that of the remainder of the community or eventually was subordinated by it. In either case, the presence of *logia* material that closely paralleled other sayings materials that are found in the Matthean Gospel might be explained by such a rift within the community.

The world-view of the Didache is similar to that of later Christian authors. This does not imply, however, that the Didache should be dated similarly. Instead, one must recognize that any community's theology, doctrine and attitude toward the world must reflect that community's current social and institutional circumstances.

In conclusion, the final version of the Didache reflects a mixture of world-views that ultimately were deemed to be useless by later religious communities. In its abandonment of Judaism and in its rejection of kerygmatic

---

[64] O'Dea, *Sociology*, 244. Much of how O'Dea characterizes the forces of motivation that are found in institutional religion seem to report directly upon the nature of the Didache: "With the emergence of a stable institutional matrix, there arises a structure of offices – of statuses and roles – capable of eliciting another kind of motivation, *involving needs for prestige, expression of teaching and leadership abilities, drives for power, aesthetic needs, and the quite prosaic wish for the security of a respectable position in the professional structure of the society*" (italics mine).

[65] Parsons, *Essays*, 244.

religion, the Didache was left in a unique and a disjointed position within early Christianity – a position whose uselessness in the early Christian tradition soon led to its rejection within the evolving church.

The Question of a Community Hierarchy

The Matthean Community

The text of the Matthean Gospel suggests that the Matthean redactor was forced to address a community of persons who came from divergent religious and ethical backgrounds and who were not united in perspective with respect to primitive Christian doctrines. Thus one finds within the Matthean Gospel a potpourri of traditions and theological considerations: anti-Judaism and anti-Hellenism; anti-Torah and pro-Torah attitudes; adherence to an established "disciples tradition" and devotion to the authority of wandering charismatics; etc. To be sure, the concerns of the redactor are *not* oriented toward an explication of ecclesiastical offices within the community – presumably, the readers of the Gospel already were familiar with some previously-established hierarchical structure within the community, and there remained no need to justify its existence. The historical transition from the various forms of ecclesial office that are represented in the Gospel and the forms of office that existed in the later ecclesial tradition which inherited that Gospel, i.e., presumably the letters of Ignatius, require that we reconstruct some delineation of the hierarchy of ecclesiastical offices that are assumed in the Matthean Gospel.

With respect to religious offices, a primary concern of the redactor is directed toward a denunciation of Jewish leaders. In Matt 15:14 the "Pharisees" (Φαρισαῖος), who typically are addressed in conjunction with the office of "scribe" (γραμματεύς) throughout the Gospel, are called "blind guides" (ὁδηγοὶ τυφλῶν) – persons who subsequently are associated with the sins of the decalogue.[66] As is observed by Van Tilborg:[67]

> The Pharisees represent the negative aspect of the divine salvation-economy; they have become the prototypes of the rejection. They are blind leaders. As far as the Torah is concerned they have lost their authority. Whoever clings to them, will be rooted up and will fall into the pit. A judgment more negative than this about the relationship between the synagogue and the ecclesia cannot be formulated, the more so because the people are at the same time presented as being blind. The people and their leaders are one in their blindness.

---

[66] Van Tilborg (*Leaders*, 99) notes that this version of the decalogue, while it is suggested by the Marcan tradition, in fact, has been modeled by the Matthean redactor to fit more closely with the OT format. Thus, one finds a certain degree of independence from the Marcan text here.

[67] Van Tilborg, *Leaders*, 101.

Thus one sees that the Matthean redactor has implemented the decalogue into a weapon to be turned against the ruling structure of Judaism, a structure that leads away from salvation. It is difficult to determine from Matt 15 whether the Matthean redactor seeks to remove early Christianity from the structures of Judaism[68] or whether the redactor simply wishes to redefine the place of Christianity within those structures.[69] Since the text is the product of a Christian movement that undoubtedly already had matured by the time that the Matthean Gospel was produced (in the final decades of the first century), one probably should assume that the redactor envisioned a community that no longer could exist within the theological structure of Judaism, and hence, could no longer develop to its full potential within the hierarchy of leadership that existed in that religious system. Thus we can feel certain that the Gospel stands within an ecclesiastical hierarchy of order whose roots are justified in the text of the Gospel through the argument that the structures of Judaism have been rejected with good reason. We must seek then to determine the nature of those roots of ecclesiastical hierarchy. Several such roots are aptly suggested by the text:

1) From the outset, one encounters the "disciples" (μαθητής) of Jesus. These are the persons who represent the tradents of the tradition. They are the inner circle whose association with Jesus instills upon them the authority of the new interpretation of the Torah. The role and the authority of the disciples/apostles are focused in the figure of Peter, who receives the power both to establish the foundation of the collected ἐκκλησία and to mediate the one salvation for humanity (according to Matt 16:17-19). There is little question that the figure of Peter represents the continuation of an early Christian tradition which sprouted from within the Jewish church of Palestine. Further, the figure of Peter now is announced through the revered words of the historical Jesus as the focal point from which a hierarchical structure can be derived. In Peter a certain "institutional" statement is made by the redactor.[70] The need for such structure is evidenced in the midst of more religiously charismatic figures.

2) Those persons who previously offered competitive religious authority over against the established tradition of the disciples are the "prophets" (προφήτης), who together with the "teachers" (διδάσκαλος) are envisioned as Christian functionaries in the mold of the Pharisees and scribes of Judaism. The presence of these prophets is attested variously throughout the Gospel.[71] They are among the messengers to Israel (both old and new) who are sent by Jesus (Matt 23:34):

---

[68] Strecker, *Weg*, 30-31.

[69] Hummel, *Auseinandersetzung*, 46-49.

[70] Brown and Meier, *Antioch*, 71.

[71] See Boring, *Sayings*, 43-47, and Suggs, *Wisdom*, 23-24.

> Διὰ τοῦτο ἰδοὺ ἐγὼ ἀποστέλλω πρὸς ὑμᾶς προφήτας καὶ σοφοὺς καὶ γραμματεῖς· ἐξ αὐτῶν ἀποκτενεῖτε καὶ σταυρώσετε καὶ ἐξ αὐτῶν μαστιγώσετε ἐν ταῖς συναγωγαῖς ὑμῶν καὶ διώξετε ἀπὸ πόλεως εἰς πόλιν·
> ("Therefore I send you prophets and wise men and scribes, some of whom you will kill and crucify, and some you will scourge in your synagogues and persecute from town to town . . .")

While the redactor *presupposes* the authority of this office of prophet, a warning is issued against those who misuse this authority. Thus one finds the admonition to "beware of false prophets" (προσέχετε ἀπὸ τῶν ψευδοπροφητῶν) in Matt 7:15-23. In Matt 11:9 the redactor has preserved the Q attestation (cf. Luke 7:26) that John is *more* than a prophet, and thereby, the redactor has established a community dictum by which prophets may be judged as lesser authorities to the tradition that is represented by Jesus' own disciples, i.e., the apostolic tradition. Such exhortations bespeak of a period in which the prophetic word remained a powerful interpretation of the historical tradition. They also betray a concern by the Matthean redactor (a concern which itself is probably a reflection of anxiety within the community) to harness the prophetic witness with a more readily-controlled tradition of authority, i.e., the memory of the work and of the teachings of the apostles. Thus, Bultmann writes:[72]

> The Church drew no distinction between such utterances by Christian prophets and the sayings of Jesus in the tradition, for the reason that even the dominical sayings in the tradition were not the pronouncements of a past authority, but sayings of the risen Lord, who is always a contemporary for the Church.

3) The final category to which the Matthean Gospel offers definitive attestation is that of teacher. The Matthean redactor as well was probably a product of this office, out of which derived the authority to compose the Gospel for the community.[73] Among the primary duties of the teacher within the Matthean community was that of "justification of the Torah tradition," an act that is undertaken by the redactor in Matt 5:17-20. As is noted by Meier:[74]

> If there was one element in the Jewish-Christian tradition that was especially difficult for an increasingly Gentile church to absorb into its gospel-message, it was the stringent Law material.

But apart from the task of justification for the inclusion of Jewish tradition, the Christian teacher was a primary element in the reorganization of developing community structures. For the Matthean Gospel, such organization ap-

---

[72] Bultmann, *History*, 127-28.

[73] Thus Boring (*Sayings*, 45) sees in Matt 13:52 a positive *self-portrait* by the Matthean redactor.

[74] Meier, *Law*, 23.

pears in the presentation of conflicting hermeneutical keys by which community traditions were interpreted. Thus, in Matt 18 one finds a practical, functional "catechesis" for community discipline.[75] This is the projection of a structured system in which fraternal conflicts within the church (such as those that are represented at 5:23-26) may be rectified by juridical process.[76] In tension with this perspective is the more eschatological salvation-history orientation that arises throughout the Gospel, and which perhaps is best represented in Matt 13.[77] This latter hermeneutic dominates the Gospel, yet in its appeal to the salvation of the nations (and not of Israel alone), it may reveal itself as a secondary focus of the redactor against the original and more legalistic processes of judgment that arise within Matt 18. Hence one observes with respect to this hermeneutic that the Son of Man motif, which implies the presence of a figure whose authority is both "cosmic" and eternal, has been incorporated (from the Sayings Gospel Q?) on the one hand, while the "rule of patience," which is associated with the delay of the parousia and is applicable in "this temporal age," has been incorporated on the other.[78]

The above, of course, are the initial offices of the church that were listed by Paul in 1 Cor 12:28: apostles, prophets, teachers. The latter and lesser offices of Paul's list – "miracle workers, healers, helpers, administrators, speakers in tongues" (δυνάμεις, ἔπειτα χαρίσματα ἰαμάτων, ἀντιλήμψεις, κυβερνήσεις, γένη γλωσσῶν) – are not mentioned by the Matthean redactor, no doubt because such persons were not considered to be the bearers of great authority within the community from which the Gospel derived. Yet, this triad of offices may not reflect with any significant accuracy the Matthean community's historical experience. Instead, it probably indicates the desire of the redactor to project an image of ecclesial hierarchy that would permit a manageable structure for growth within the community. As is speculated by Boring, it may be much more accurate to describe the historical development of the Matthean community in terms of the dominance of the prophetic office:[79]

> Like Schweizer,[80] Sand[81] sees prophecy as *the* category in which Matthew interpreted discipleship to Jesus as such. But the Matthean community also knows a

---

[75] Marguerat, *Le jugement*, 425. We see here that the juridical structure of the Matthean Gospel was based upon the Torah of Judaism, much in the same perspective as that which appears in the Didache.

[76] Marguerat, *Le jugement*, 430-35.

[77] Meier, *Law*, 23.

[78] Marguerat, *Le jugement*, 436-46. The Matthean community stands in the midst of a tension between two incompatible forms of ecclesiastical judgment: church discipline (cf. Matt 18:15-18) and eschatological promise/threat (cf. Matt 13:47-50).

[79] Boring, *Sayings*, 45.

[80] Schweizer, *Matthäus*, 140-47, and "Observance," 213-30.

[81] Sand, *Gesetz*, 168-77; "Propheten," 167-85.

> relatively small number of "wandering" prophets, prophets who were not independent freelancers but delegated missioners of the Matthean church. In addition, there was a larger group of congregational leaders in the church, who were not "wandering" but resident in the congregation, who recognized that discipleship to Jesus was to be practiced in prophetic terms. They performed prophetic functions in the community, including speaking in the name of the risen Lord. These are not sharply distinguished from the disciples in general but they did form a recognizably distinct group.

The office of "prophet" obviously is one that carried a primary concern for the Matthean redactor. With a system such as that which is described here by Boring, the office of prophet may well represent the true nature of the community's authority. Against Boring, however, one plainly can see the drive of the redactor to temper such prophetic authority as the church congregation matured into a community that found it necessary to await the arrival of the delayed parousia. By the time of the writings of Ignatius, this prophetic influence was subjugated almost completely to an ecclesial structure that was delineated by the offices of "bishop" (ἐπίσκοπος), "presbyter" (πρεσβύτερος) and "deacon" (διάκονος).

The Matthean Gospel is the product of a community that was in transition,[82] a community that sought to define itself not only with respect to developing theological parameters, but also with respect to fluid ecclesial offices and functions. The Gospel itself was not concerned to name or to describe such offices, but was designed simply to justify the existence of those offices within the community through an interpretation of their background in light of the words of the historical Jesus. If one may assume that the basis of these offices stems from some form of Jewish legal system, much like that system which is represented by the early testimony of Matt 18:15-20, then one may assume with justification that the Matthean community, which was confronted with the hierarchical structures of an encroaching Hellenistic model of ecclesial authority, would have required a radical shift and reorientation within its own ecclesial structure in order to meet this challenge. It is suggested here that the mode of transition from the hierarchical structures of the Jewish synagogue to the system of ecclesial offices that was offered by Hellenistic Christianity (a transition which occurred within that community from which the Matthean Gospel is derived) is reflected best in the latter chapters of another document, i.e., the Didache.

---

[82] Meier, *Law*, 22. The Matthean redactor does write, however, from the perspective of an established religious community (Luz, *Matthäus*, 65). Stanton ("Matthew," 274-77) argues that the redactor reflects a community which still is under pressure from Judaism. But I would contend that such pressure in the Matthean Gospel does not stem from Judaism itself, but instead, that it comes from that faction of the Matthean community which remains faithful to the tenets of Judaism *per se*. See the related discussion of Reicke, "Verfassung," 95-112.

The Enigma of the Didache[83]

Scholarly attempts to incorporate the Didache into a ready source of information concerning the development of nascent church communities have been frustrated by the two-tiered hierarchy of offices that seems to be attested by the text, i.e., bishops and deacons, without presbyters.[84] It therefore is imperative that one readdress the issue of whether the early Christian community that produced the text of the Didache recognized within its ecclesial hierarchy the independent office of "presbyter."

The Greek text of the Didache, which was discovered by Archbishop Bryennios in 1873, mentions several important offices that were recognized commonly within the hierarchies of early church structures – apostle (ἀπόστολος), prophet, teacher, bishop and deacon. The first three, of course, one sees featured prominently within the Matthean Gospel. From the Didache's list, however, the office of "presbyter" flagrantly seems to have been omitted. Indeed, at that point where one most might expect to see presbyters mentioned, they are absent:

> Χειροτονήσατε οὖν ἑαυτοῖς ἐπισκόπους καὶ διακόνους ἀξίους τοῦ κυρίου,
>
> ("Appoint therefore for yourselves bishops and deacons worthy of the Lord." [15.1])

The manuscript that Bryennios "discovered" presented a new piece of evidence for the ecclesial puzzle that was under assembly at the beginning of this century by Hatch[85] and by Lightfoot,[86] whose speculations concerning the formation of the Christian ministry during the first-second centuries C.E. were beginning to win the perspective of their day. Based upon biblical, patristic and classical sources, Hatch said that the administrative offices of bishop and deacon arose under the influence of contemporary Greco-Roman associations, while the office of presbyter spawned from the "council of elders" model that was attested in the internal organization of the Jewish synagogue.[87]

Lightfoot concurred with Hatch that the presbyterate derived from the constructs of Judaism, and added his view that the deaconate was an entirely new creation. The role of bishop was equivalent to that of presbyter, and it was

---

[83] The majority of the discussion that follows was presented at the "Tenth International Conference on Patristic Studies," which was held in Oxford on 24-29 August 1987. The version of the material that was presented in Oxford may be found in published form as follows: "Presbyters in the Community of the *Didache*." In *Studia Patristica* 21, pp. 122-28. Edited by Elizabeth A. Livingstone. Leuven: Peeters, 1989. Grateful appreciation is extended to Peeters Press for permission to reprint those materials here in expanded form.

[84] See for example the studies by Luz, *Matthäus*, 75, and Brown and Meier, *Antioch*, 81-84.

[85] Hatch, *Organization*, 26-111.

[86] Lightfoot, *Philippians*, 181-265.

[87] Hatch, *Organization*, 30 n. 11.

from the presbyterate that episcopacy subsequently evolved as the formulation of a higher office under which the presbyters of any given community served.[88]

As they applied to the community of the Didache, the conclusions of Hatch and Lightfoot immediately spawned three courses of argument: 1) the office of presbyter was unknown within the community; 2) the position of presbyter did not warrant mention by the Didachist; and, 3) the role of presbyter was encompassed within the office of bishop.

The first argument, viz., that the office of presbyter did not exist within the hierarchy of the community that produced the Didache, is at once the immediate response to an initial reading of the text.[89] The logic is straightforward and simple: since presbyters are not mentioned, they must not have been known. Indeed, those who argue otherwise must bear the burden of proof as to how it is known that the office of presbyter existed within the community! Yet, one must admit that it remains somewhat confusing to imagine such a community, i.e., one which was devoid of an office whose roots were both early and primary in the Judeo-Christian tradition.[90]

The second argument derives from the work of Hatch, which Harnack applied specifically to the "missing presbyters" of the Didache.[91] Harnack proposed that the early church knew of only one classification of spiritual leaders – those who were established by the Word of God as ministers of the gospel. In the case of the Didache this meant apostles, prophets and teachers.[92]

The offices of bishop and deacon, on the other hand, were *administrative* positions that were appointed for individual communities by the communities themselves. While the primary role of bishops and deacons was the *management* of community affairs, the Didachist notes that they had become in their own right "speakers of the Word of God," and thus were not to be despised.[93]

Harnack asserted that it was from the early distribution of community functions between "elders" (πρεσβύτεροι) and "youngers" (νεώτεροι) that the role of the presbyter arose. The presbyters were those aged within the community who had arisen without formal calling to positions of respect, and thus were to be "honored" for their wise counsel.[94] Since the Didachist was con-

---

[88] Lightfoot, *Philippians*, 196 notes: "The episcopate was formed not out of the apostolic order by localisation but out of the presbyterial by elevation: and the title, which originally was common to all, came at length to be appropriate to the chief among them."

[89] See for example, Schweizer, *Order*, 142-43; Von Campenhausen, *Authority*, 70-71.

[90] See Andresen, *Kirchen*, 50; Von Campenhausen, *Authority*, 76.

[91] Harnack, "Analecten," passim; and *Lehre*, 88-94, 140-68.

[92] See for example, 1 Cor 12:28 and Acts 13:1.

[93] Thus *Did.* 15.2 – μὴ οὖν ὑπερίδητε αὐτούς·

[94] Harnack notes that the concept of "appropriate honor" (τιμὴ καυήκουσα) became a *terminus technicus* in the early church. See 1 *Clem.* 1.3; 21.6 and Clem. *str.* 7.1.2.

cerned primarily to identify the established offices of the apostolic order, however, the function of presbyter purposefully was omitted from the Didache. Presbyters had a role within the community, but they had no association with its order. They neither were instilled by God "to speak the divine word," nor were they *appointed* by the community.[95]

The third argument, which is held widely in current circles, derives from the observation that the office of presbyter certainly was not distinctive in every primitive Christian community. Lightfoot, who capitalized upon a growing inclination of the nineteenth century,[96] asserted that the term "bishop" often was used synonymously with that of "presbyter" in many churches, since episcopacy (mono-episcopacy?[97]) had not gained universality by the time of the composition of the Didache.[98] One thus discovers early texts where so-called "presbyter-bishops" ruled with deacons, such as in Phil 1:1, 1 Tim 3:1-13, Titus 1:5-16 and, of course, *Did.* 15.1. This position has been supported and expanded in latter days by proponents such as R. M. Grant,[99] Erik Wolf,[100] W. H. C. Frend[101] and Martin Dibelius with Hans Conzelmann,[102] who have drawn parallels from such post-apostolic witnesses as 1 *Clem.* 54.2[103] and *Herm. Vis.* 2.4.3, where bishops and presbyters assume a somewhat identical role.

Despite the virtues of these three arguments, with each solution one is left with two troubling questions that are not resolved concerning the text of the Didache: 1) Is it indeed to the *community proper* that the charge is made "to appoint" (χειροτονέω) bishops and deacons (*Did.* 15.1);[104] and, 2) Is it indeed to the *community proper* that instructions are given on how to baptize (*Did.* 7.1), how to speak the words of the eucharist (*Did.* 9.1-10.5) and how to evaluate prophets (*Did.* 13.1-7)?

Both apostolic and post-apostolic witnesses characterize the office of presbyter in the early church as a position that was responsible for numerous

---

95 For correctives to the Hatch-Harnack perspectives, see Robinson, "Ministry," and Linton, *Problem*, passim.

96 See for example, Zahn, *Forschungen*, 302-10; Schaff, *Manual*, 73-75; Spence, *Teaching*, 151.

97 See the brief discussion of Schöllgen, "Monoepiskopat," 146-51.

98 Lightfoot, *Apostolic Fathers*, 215; Knopf, *Lehre*, 36-38.

99 Grant, *Apostolic Fathers*, 160-73.

100 Wolf, *Ordnung*, 168-69.

101 Frend, *Christianity*, 139.

102 Dibelius and Conzelmann, *Pastoral Epistles*, 54-57.

103 Compare 1 *Clem.* 1.3, where presbyters are acknowledged as "the community rulers" (ἡγούμενοι); see Herrmann, *Ecclesia*, 27-28.

104 Note that at Acts 14:23 it is Barnabas and Paul who "appoint" elders; at Titus 1:5 the responsibility is given to Titus; at 1 *Clem.* 42.4-5 it is the apostles who "appointed" bishops and deacons, in accordance with the directions of Isa 40:17. See Wengst, *Schriften*, 41 n. 141. Admittedly, early congregations had the right to "confirm" appointees to office; see Herrmann, *Ecclesia*, 27.

facets of community life, both administrative and liturgical, within the body of believers. Presbyters protected the congregation against the dangers of error that threatened from without and from within (Acts 20:29-30; 2 John 10-11; *Herm. Vis.* 2.6.2-3), served as cultic officers of the church's eucharist (1 *Clem.* 40; *Mart. Pol.* 6.1), had charge of the community funds (1 Pet 5:2), directed the administration of charity (*Mart. Pol.* 6.1) and established the normative teaching office for the community (Acts 15; 16:4).[105] One readily finds such functions addressed by the Didache: warnings against errors (chaps. 1-6); administration of community funds (chap. 11); administration of the eucharist (chaps. 9-10, 14); administration of charity (chap. 11); and, establishment of a normative teaching office (chap. 11). In point of fact, the entire writing serves as a witness to the correct practice of broadly-stated administrative and liturgical functions that were associated with the *function*, if not the *office*, of presbyter. One thus sees that while presbyters at no point are mentioned within the text, their duties are expressly outlined.[106]

In its own right the Didache must have been regarded as an ancient classic by third-fourth century "church orders."[107] The subsequent incorporation and manipulation of the text by the Church Fathers indicates that it carried a wide influence both among Syrian and Egyptian communities which no doubt went far beyond the original intention of the Didachist. This popularity of the text among patristic authors, who themselves were struggling with the development of ecclesial order and divergent practices, led no less a scholar than Streeter to observe that[108]

> the main object of the second half of the Didache is to give advice to communities which are in difficulties owing to the lack of an established ministry and to help them in that direction.

Unfortunately, the scholarly community since Streeter appears to have done little toward either correcting or advancing this perspective, though two correctives must be offered.

Firstly, we must forfeit our lingering archaic and unrealistic views of the Didache as a set of generalized instructions that were constructed in a vacuum for use by the church at large. The final redaction of the document no doubt

---

[105] Bornkamm, "πρέσβυς, κ.τ.λ."; Von Campenhausen, *Authority*, 76-84. For a comparable view of bishops, see Chadwick, "Bishop."

[106] The Apostolic Constitutions often appears to explicate in bolder terms what must have been the original intention of the Didachist. Thus one finds at *AC* 7.22 an alteration of *Did.* 7.1: "But concerning baptism, *O bishop or presbyter*, you shall baptize as the Lord commanded us" (emphasis mine).

[107] Streeter, *Church*, 292-93. Numerous authors have argued for the early date of the original text; see Sabatier, *Didachè*, 150-59; Taylor, *Teaching*, 118; Harris, *Teaching*, passim; Harnack, *Lehre*, 158-70; Lightfoot, *Apostolic Fathers*, 215; Audet, *Didachè*, 187-210.

[108] Streeter, *Church*, 293.

was a response to some immediate need that arose within some specific community. Secondly, we may do better to consider the Didache to be a witness to a ministry in transition, rather than a witness to the "lack of an established ministry."

As a response to these correctives, it may be appropriate to suggest that the reason why the *office of* presbyter was not mentioned by the Didachist was determined by the *function* of the text. Later church orders, such as the Apostolic Constitutions, the Church Ordinances, the Canons of Hippolytus and the Didascalia, incorporated the core material of the Didache as a framework around which to construct manuals for the instruction of clergy. If the Didache is indeed a "witness to a ministry in transition" – the recurring dilemma of the primitive church – one must question whether the purpose of the final redaction of the text also might not have been the instruction of clergy, specifically here, persons who aspired to the office of presbyter. Since scholars have traditionally considered the Didache to be a "manual of instruction"[109] (whether for catechumens, for persons in authority or for an undefined community),[110] there is no new observation in our assignment of the text to a didactic genre, but only in the designation of the intended audience as presbyters.

Such a designation also would explain a number of further difficulties that traditionally are associated with the text. The charge in *Did.* 15.1 "to appoint" bishops and deacons would have been directed toward officials in authority, and thus would have been consistent with contemporary practices.[111] The exposition both of liturgical and of community duties throughout the text also would have been directed toward those same officials, and thus to an appropriate audience. Further, the literary unity of the text could be understood in terms of its function, since both the opening didactic instructions in chaps. 1-6, which were to be directed toward catechumens, and the subsequent liturgical regulations in chaps. 7-15 would have fallen within the parameters of presbyterial authority. Finally, the marked change of address from the second person singular to the second person plural, which also is divided roughly along such chapter divisions,[112] might be understood as the difference between materials that were addressed to individual candidates for baptism and materials that were addressed to the presbyters as a group. It thus appears both reasonable and responsible to speculate that the final function of the Didache may have fallen somewhat within the same parameters as those

---

[109] On the usability of the document, see Muilenburg, *Relations*, 78-80.

[110] Johnson, "Motive," 108.

[111] One need not consider here any formal ritual of ordination for bishops, such as that found in Hipp. *trad. ap.* 2.1-4.2 of the third century.

[112] Audet, *Didachè*, 105-10.

that were espoused by the later church orders which used the Didache as an outline for clerical instruction.

As to an exact provenance and socio-political occasion by which the need for such a manual would have originated, it is difficult to be certain. One indeed may continue to consider as valid options the predominant views among scholars of the Didache that likely provenances for the text may have been either Alexandria or Antioch. It is assumed here that Antioch, which was an early gathering place for ethnically and theologically divergent Christians,[113] is perhaps the better of these choices. The historically-diverse religious background of the city,[114] the absence of any distinctive hierarchical structure for the Christian community of the city during the first century[115] and the potential for social conflict in this striving ancient metropolis all lend support to the choice of Antioch as the provenance in which the materials of the Didache were collected.

A likely *occasion* may have stemmed from the seeds of Jewish-Gentile struggles in Antioch, which certainly were present prior to the destruction of Jerusalem in C.E. 70, since the strong Jewish community that arose with the founding of the city[116] would have disdained the increasing religious tolerance of the region, whose dependence upon Rome made it a fertile field for the early seeds of the Hellenistic mission.[117]

The struggles in Antioch, which ensued from the necessity within the congregations there to intermingle divergent Jewish and Gentile cultures around a common Judeo-Christian faith, indeed must have forced a radical transformation of ecclesial offices within the city's growing Christian community. As the structure of those primitive churches in Antioch that were steeped in Jewish polity and organization finally yielded to the swell of a Greco-Roman mindset, the need also would have arisen to reorient and retrain the leaders of such Jewish-oriented communities. Formerly Jewish-Christian *elders,* whose understanding of authority and leadership was based upon the synagogue, would have needed to be instructed concerning their new roles as *presbyters* in a three-tiered church hierarchy that was based upon Hellenistic models.[118]

Such observations, of course, can be little more than suggestions, but they are suggestions that hopefully focus upon the specific needs associated with

---

[113] Herrmann, *Ecclesia*, 33. In support of an Alexandrian presbyter tradition, see pp. 34-37.

[114] Wallace-Hadrill, *Antioch*, 14-26.

[115] At least, this is the impression that one receives from the lack of historical testimony to any dominant ruling structure such as that which arose in the Jerusalem church (see Downey, *History*, 272-87).

[116] See Meeks and Wilken, *Jews*, passim; Stern, "Diaspora," 137-42; and, Tcherikover, *Civilization*, 289, 328-29.

[117] Theissen, *Setting*, 36.

[118] Dix, "Ministry," 244, 267.

ecclesial organization in the early church. In light of the sayings materials that are preserved in *Did.* 1-5, the Didache must somehow be explained by modern scholarship as a document that spans the transition between Jewish and Gentile Christianity, and therefore, must reflect an ecclesial hierarchy that is representative of such a transition. While there is no question that the Didache is neither directly constructed upon the text of the Matthean Gospel, nor that the epistles of Ignatius are immediately dependent upon the materials or the theological emphases of the Didache, the Didache in fact may reflect an indirect witness to the transition in ecclesial hierarchy that occurred as the community of Antioch proceeded from the first to the second centuries. In many ways, the previously unknown transition from Matthew to Ignatius may well have reflected such a shift in emphases, from Jewish patterns of structure to Gentile conceptions of hierarchy.

Further Elements in the Reconstruction of a Community

As has been observed above, the sayings that were collected and preserved in the Didache reveal a number of convergent elements. The orientation of the sayings collection is unquestionably Jewish. And while at least one redactor subsequent to the Didachist has attempted to *Christianize* the collection through the introduction of new theological emphases (1.3b-2.1), there is no question that the original collection was of a Christian-Jewish character. Upon this observation, several points follow.

Firstly, the sayings have been organized into an expansion upon the initial elements of the decalogue. This form of the decalogue again has been enlarged through contemporary concerns, yet it remains as the focus of chaps. 1-5.

Secondly, the influence of a strong wisdom tradition is evident in the Didache, especially in those materials that appear in the text immediately after the decalogue (i.e., chap. 3). The sayings and themes in these materials are scattered and often are disjointed; however, they reveal the influence of wisdom motifs and traditions.[119]

Finally, the Jewish nature of the sayings collection is of concern to the tradents of the Didache only in so far as that collection is a part of the original core of materials. The subsequent redactions of the text, while themselves concerned to preserve additional materials that originally may have been associated with the sayings, are not steeped in the original Jewish mindset from which the sayings themselves have sprung.

We have seen that much of the material in the text, especially that material which appears as an interwoven motif within the sayings, reflects Matthean

---

[119] So it was that Harnack continued to argue for a predominant influence of Sirach upon the text.

themes and concerns. On the other hand, there does not seem to be a concerted effort to reflect either the theology or the structure of the Matthean Gospel.[120] In what way can the Didache have derived from a community tradition that also served as the foundation of the Matthean Gospel? The answer appears in the brief examination of several literary, socio-historical and liturgical features that are paralleled between the two texts.

What is Known from the M Source

At the conclusion of his recent investigation of the special Matthean source (or "M"), Stephenson Brooks attempts to reconstruct the history of the Matthean community as it is known from the witness of M. The results of Brooks' examinations shed significant light upon the types of movements and traditions that may have existed behind the formation of the Matthean Gospel and that would have permitted the additional formation of the Didache within that same community, as we have argued above. The relevant observations from his arguments and conclusions are presented in summary form here.

On the one hand, Brooks determines from the free manner in which the Matthean redactor has incorporated both the Sayings Gospel Q and the Marcan source that the M source probably was used with great freedom as well. On the other hand, Brooks argues that the literary structure which currently unites the various texts in the Gospel must be attributed to the redactor, since there is "scant evidence" for a pre-Matthean narrative tradition.[121] This, he suggests, does not preclude conclusively that the M source may have existed in part as a written document; however, there appears to be "no evidence that compels the postulate of written sources to account for the M sayings traditions."[122]

Based upon the assumption that the M-source materials were available to the Matthean redactor in an oral form alone, Brooks appeals to the work of Kelber[123] to identify the strata of these oral materials. Kelber establishes a law of "social identification" by which sayings may be grouped according to

---

[120] See the comments of Bornkamm, however, who compares the structure of the Sermon on the Mount with that of the Didache (*Tradition*, 17).

[121] Brooks, "History," 177-80.

[122] Brooks, "History," 180. He does admit, however, that Matt 5:19, 21-22, 27-28, 33-35 and 37, because of their antithetical character, may have come to the redactor "from a single tradition," which he also ascribes to a "Jewish Christian community" (pp. 180, 279). Yet, he does not include in this category the materials of Matt 6:1-6, 16-18, which he ascribes to a "Christian Jewish community" (p. 278). Since we have noted the presence of this antithetical format throughout Matt 6:1-18, and in consideration of the Three Rules theme that appears in the antithetical materials of *Did.* 1.3b-6, it may be that the Sermon on the Mount preserves an early written tradition which possessed a consistent literary structure.

[123] Kelber, *Gospel*, 24.

"social locators." With this in mind, Brooks identifies three distinct traditions in the M materials:[124]

#1 – Matt 5:19, 21-22, 27-28, 33-35, 37; 12:36-37; 18:18, 19-20; 19:12(?); 23:8-10
#2 – Matt 6:1-6, 16-18; 23:2-3, 5
#3 – Matt 5:23-24 (?); 23:15, 16-22, 24, 33

Several other texts are suggested as representatives of mutually-exclusive traditions, though they are not excluded necessarily from the above traditions:

#4 – Matt 10:5b-6, 23b
#5 – Matt 6:7-8; 7:6[125]

Brooks argues that the above groupings of sayings represent several developmental stages in the history of the Matthean community. Collections #2 and #4 are "sayings representative of a tradition coming from a Christian Jewish group"; collections #3 and #5 are "sayings from an interim period"; collection #1 is "sayings representative of a tradition coming from a Jewish Christian community."[126] Through his analysis of "social indicators" for each grouping, Brooks thus concludes that the Matthean community was composed of several parties of divergent Christians who maintained oral traditions that were preserved and reinterpreted – a process that was interrupted to some extent by the composition of the Matthean Gospel. It is the "historicizing" element of the Gospel that serves to bind these various oral traditions together into a literary unity.[127]

Based upon Matt 10 and 23, Brooks next suggests a specific view of Christian history that was shared by the Matthean redactor with the community from which the M tradition was derived. In chap. 23[128] one witnesses the gradual removal of authority from the leaders of Judaism, the scribes and the Pharisees. These leaders summarily are judged for their interpretations of tradition, their behavior with respect to that tradition, and finally, their direct persecution of "Christian prophets, wise men, and scribes." Brooks sees here "four distinct historical stages in the relationship between the contemporary readers of specific sayings and the Jewish authorities":[129]

1) the reader's religious life is circumscribed by the authority of the Jewish synagogue leaders
2) in antithesis to this circumscribed position, the reader is subject only to the authority of Jesus as teacher and Christ, and God as Father

[124] Brooks, "History," 174-75.
[125] Matt 5:36 is a verse for which there is no accounting in this schema.
[126] Brooks, "History," 278-80.
[127] Brooks, "History," 181-82.
[128] Brooks, "History," 184-87.
[129] Brooks, "History," 186-87.

3) the reader is given an explanation of the new position, firstly with reference to the invalid interpretation and religious behavior of the synagogue rulers, and secondly with reference to their overt persecution of members of the community of Jesus
4) finally, the reader's ties with Judaism/Israel are severed

Brooks sees further support for this reconstruction of history in the text of chap. 10.[130] While the redactor knows of a time when Jesus and his disciples "engaged exclusively in a mission to Israel," chap. 10 indicates a subsequent mission to the Gentiles – a mission that occurs only after substantial persecution from Jewish authorities.[131]

In his final analysis, Brooks argues for two primary phases in the development of the Matthean community. On the one hand, he envisions a "Christian Jewish group relatively at peace within the synagogue" prior to C.E. 70. On the other hand, he sees a secondary development into a "Jewish Christian community constituted apart from, and in ideological opposition to, the Jewish synagogue."[132] The former group "affirms the teaching authority of its synagogue leadership, while being critical of the pious behavior of both the leadership and other synagogue members." The latter group is organized in antithesis "to conceptions about Torah and community organization that characterized significant portions of Judaism in the first century." While we cannot be certain as to the precise nature of the theology that was held by the first group, the latter group maintains a well-developed Christology and a "theology based upon Jesus as the eschatological spokesperson for God." The Matthean redactor, as heir to these two traditions within the community, assimilates the materials of the Marcan Gospel and Sayings Gospel Q into the traditional community sayings that were preserved by the Matthean community.

Common Elements and Perspectives

Apart from the agreements between sayings that were observed the discussion above, numerous other minor agreements arise between the texts of the Didache and the Matthean Gospel, and should not be omitted in passing. While no one of these agreements can establish an element of certitude with respect to the close association between the Didache and the Matthean Gospel with respect to the history of the writings, the cumulative nature of the

[130] Brooks, "History," 187-89.

[131] Luz (*Matthäus*, 67) observes that the concept of a Gentile mission in the Matthean Gospel probably resulted from the influence of the Jews who fled from Palestine, i.e., those persons who represented either the Q movement or the Marcan community.

[132] Brooks, "History," 191-95.

elements may serve as an argument in support of a common community background for the two texts.

From Jew to Gentile

One immediately notes both within the Didache and within the Matthean Gospel that there is a tension between the concerns and perspectives of a Jewish Christianity and a Hellenistic-Gentile Christianity.[133] Scholars traditionally (and correctly) have eased this tension through the attribution to each text of redactional layers and divergent sources.

The earliest layer of the Didache (1.1-3a; 2.2-6.1a) is constructed upon the Two Ways source and around the decalogue, with the incorporation of additional elements from early Jewish wisdom tradition. There is little question that the community from which this section of the text derives was Jewish in nature and tradition.[134] By the time that the subsequent layer of the text (7-15[16]) was added, however, one already detects the presence of a fervent anti-Jewish element. Thus, in 7.2 the ritual laws of baptism concerning "running water" are emended. Also, in 8.1 the reader is exhorted not to fast "with the hypocrites" on Mondays and Thursdays, but instead to fast on Wednesdays and Fridays. Apart from these two pericopae, the Didache does not seem concerned to attack Judaism or Jewish Christianity. But enough is said in chaps. 7-8 to indicate that a major shift in perspective has occurred. Furthermore, the redactor seems content to pursue other issues in subsequent chapters based upon the understanding that a new theological design and perspective now has become foundational for Christianity in the community that has produced the text.

The problems of Jewish/Gentile questions in the Matthean Gospel are legion and are well-known. As with the earliest materials of the Didache, the Matthean redactor writes with a view toward the demonstration of fulfilled OT prophecy. Thus the Sermon on the Mount, while a source for attacks upon the unacceptable practice of religious piety (6:1-21), reflects an immediate concern to preserve and surpass the Torah, without rejecting the authority of that Torah (5:17-48). Again, in 10:5-23 the disciples are exhorted to avoid the Gentiles in their wandering missions. But throughout the Gospel

---

[133] The focus of both of these community factions into the Gentile mission theme of the Matthean Gospel led to the early circulation of the text within the wider church sphere (Luz, *Matthäus*, 70).

[134] As an instructional code from early Judaism, one can agree with Meeks (*World*, 149) that "we can understand how someone would have thought it appropriate for beginners in the faith and thus added it to instructions for baptism, the Eucharist, and other aspects of church life . . ." This implies, of course, that *Did.* 1-5 was not composed originally for the purpose of catechetical instruction, but that this use of these chapters was the result of a secondary adaptation of the text.

there is an element of testing that is issued to Jesus by the "scribes and Pharisees" and the "Pharisees and Sadducees," a testing which summarily implicates the leaders of Judaism with a legalistic rigor that is rejected by the gospel message. In chap. 23 these very leaders are condemned, while in 28:16-20 the disciples are commissioned to evangelize the "nations," and thus are provided with a new field of mission.

Various scholars have suggested that the special circumstances under which the Matthean text was written indicate that the Gospel arose during a "period of intense hostility between Matthew's Christian community and the synagogue 'across the street.'"[135] From such a set of circumstances the harsh anti-Jewish polemic of the work may be explained – and it is a fierce polemic, no matter how one may argue that an anti-Gentile bias also appears in the Gospel. The Sermon on the Mount, for example, contains several "tongue-in-cheek" references to persecution of the righteous (Matt 5:11-12 [Q]) and the need for the righteous to surpass the "scribes and Pharisees" in that righteousness (Matt 5:20 [Q]). From the redactor's source on almsgiving, prayer and fasting, the theme of "hypocrites" is introduced (Matt 6:1-21 [M]). Elsewhere, Gentiles are acknowledged to be the bearers of the true faith in opposition to the Jews, who bear the tradition of Israel's patriarchs (Matt 8:11-12 [developed from Q]); the Kingdom of God is promised to a nation other than Israel (Matt 21:43 [developed from Mark]); the "scribes and Pharisees" are violently denounced with seven woes (Matt 23 [M and Q]).

While the organized structure of the Matthean text has led many scholars to speculate that the redactor has instituted this polemic as some form of "pedagogical function," this explanation does not appear to be entirely satisfactory. Admittedly, in the Matthean schema the "scribes and Pharisees" may serve as the *antithesis* to the disciples of Jesus.[136] But the polemic of the Matthean redactor is understood better for what it *appears* to be. The redactor faces a real and vibrant "trauma of separation from Judaism," the presence of which is suggested by the following facets of the Matthean text:[137] 1) the mission of Jesus and his followers is directed to Israel as well as to the nations; 2) a strand of anti-Gentile bias remains within the Gospel (e.g., 5:47; 6:7, 32; 18:17; 24:9); 3) there is an increased use of apocalyptic themes that are based upon "external oppression and internal dissension" (chaps. 24-25).

Both the Didache and Matthean Gospel thus reveal signs of a shift of thought, from a concern for Judaism and Jewish tradition to a concern for Gentile Christianity and the establishment of a Hellenistic church community.

---

[135] Stanton, "Gospel," 266. For much of the following argument I am dependent upon the work of Stanton.

[136] Van Tilborg, *Leaders*, 26, 98.

[137] See Stanton, "Gospel," 274-84.

This shift is perhaps in keeping with the movement of thought throughout the first-century church, but here it at least serves as a binding element between the two documents.

Words and Phrases

Several significant associations between the Didache and the Matthean Gospel appear through the various language and terminology that is shared by the two texts. While such words and phrases by no means should be considered to be evidence that one text has borrowed from the other, their very existence indicates that the redactors of each text may have drawn upon materials from a common tradition.

As is argued above, it is assumed here that *Did.* 1.3b-2.1 reflects a firsthand knowledge of the written Matthean Gospel text, and therefore, that some parallels in terminology with that Gospel are to be expected. On the other hand, we have argued that the remainder of *Did.* 1-5 derives from that pre-Gospel community within which the Matthean redactor wrote, and thus, there is little surprise that no "specifically Matthean terminology" appears in these chapters.

In *Did.* 7.1, 3 the hearer/reader is exhorted to baptize "in the name of the Father and of the Son and of the Holy Spirit," which again is an obvious reflection of the formula that appears in the mission charge of Matt 28:19. In *Did.* 8.2 and 10.5 the ritual phrase "for thine is the power and the glory forever" appears in agreement with numerous early manuscripts of the Matthean Gospel that attach some form of this phrase as a conclusion to the Lord's Prayer. In *Did.* 8.6 one finds "Hosannah to the *God* of David," an interesting variation from the "Hosannah to the *Son* of David" of Matt 21:9, 15, which perhaps betrays either an ignorance of the Matthean tradition or a resistance against early Matthean efforts to establish the historical Jesus within the messianic tradition of Israel.

These few key phrases betray an awareness of the Matthean liturgical tradition within the secondary materials of the Didache, which thereby at least place the texts in a stream of consciousness apart from the remaining Synoptic Gospels.

The Witness of Ritual and Tradition

The Didache addresses four topics in chaps. 7-10 that traditionally are associated with the concerns of community organization. Each topic is directed toward a question of "correct practice," and presumably, is dictated by a community tradition which has been received by the redactor of these chapters. The role of these four topics in relation to the tradition that is found in the Matthean Gospel is significant enough for consideration here.

On Ritual Immersion

After the conclusion of the Two Ways instruction (chaps. 1-5), and hence after the conclusion of the earliest layer of materials, the initial concern of the Didache is directed toward the question of baptismal ritual. The text begins with the conditional charge ταῦτα πάντα προειπόντες ("after proclaiming all of these things [publicly]"), which presumably refers to the charge to the catechumens that appears in chaps. 1-5(6). Immediately thereafter appears the phrase

> βαπτίσατε εἰς τὸ ὄνομα τοῦ πατρὸς καὶ τοῦ υἱοῦ καὶ τοῦ ἁγίου πνεύματος (7:1; cf. 7:3c)
>
> (baptize in the name of the Father and of the Son and of the Holy Spirit)

This type of Trinitarian language suggests the introduction here of a tradition that was not originally associated with chaps. 1-5. In the previous materials, the only Christological title in use was that of Lord (κύριος), which provided a nebulous term by which the hearer/reader could understand all such usages of the term as an indication either of the figure of Jesus the Christ (the more recent Christian understanding of the text) or of יהוה the God of Israel (the older, more Jewish understanding of the text).[138] With the exception of 1.3-2.1, the possibility of this "dual perception" of the sayings is held consistently throughout chaps. 1-5.

The Trinitarian formula that is offered here (*Did.* 7.1) readily suggests a dependence upon the phraseology of the Matthean Gospel (cf. Matt 28:19):

> βαπτίζοντες αὐτοὺς εἰς τὸ ὄνομα τοῦ πατρὸς καὶ τοῦ υἱοῦ καὶ τοῦ ἁγίου πνεύματος
>
> (baptizing them in the name of the Father and of the Son and of the Holy Spirit)

It is uncertain as to whether the second redactor of the Didache simply has drawn upon the same tradition as that from which the Matthean redactor also has borrowed,[139] or whether s/he in fact relies upon this particular form of the text as it appears in the Matthean Gospel. On the one hand, the formulaic structure and the liturgical nature of the wording argue for the timelessness of the phrase within the early Christian tradition.[140] On the other hand, the unique use of this phrase in the Matthean Gospel (in distinction from the remaining NT Gospels) and the specific association of the charge with baptism in both the Matthean text and the Didache argue for some form of direct

---

[138] From this Meeks infers that the presumed authority figure behind the text can be seen either as the figure of God or as the figure of Jesus, the sage who reveals the commandments of God (*World*, 150-51).

[139] So for example, Köhler, *Rezeption*, 40-41.

[140] Kelber, *Gospel*, 64-70.

dependence by the redactor of the Didache. These latter criteria serve as the focus of discussion for S. E. Johnson (1946), who claims, with numerous convincing arguments, that the purpose of the Didache was to serve as the practical application of this "Great Commission" from Matt 28:16-20.[141] Johnson's thesis, if correct, has no direct bearing upon the age of the materials that are preserved in chaps. 1-5, but would substantiate that the redactor of chaps. 7-15 was concerned to respect the authority and the challenge of the Matthean text.

While the remainder of the discussion in *Did.* 7.2-3 is an interesting witness to the early Jewish practice of baptism by running water, its application to our present review is inconsequential.

On Fasting

In 7.4-8.1 the question of fasting becomes the central focus for the redactor. As was mentioned above in our discussion of 1.3b-2.1, there is a reasonable possibility that the second redactor was familiar with the text on almsgiving, fasting and prayer that was used by the Matthean redactor in Matt 6:1-18. Unlike the discussion of the Matthean text, however, the concern for fasting here is not that of fasting "*in the manner* of the hypocrites," but is that of fasting "*with* the hypocrites." To be sure, this is a distinctive step towards defining the community of the Didache with respect to Judaism and the synagogue. One also finds here the exhortations against the custom of fasting δευτέρᾳ σαββάτων καὶ πέμπτῃ ("Monday and Thursday") but for the practice of fasting on τετράδα καὶ παρασκευήν ("Wednesday and Friday"). Again, as with the question of baptismal ritual, it is difficult to know whether this charge stems from a source that also was used by the Matthean redactor, or whether these materials were constructed around the text in Matt 6:16-18. In either case, the text of the Didache here shows a definite reflection of materials that are peculiar to the Matthean Gospel.

On Prayer

The issue of fasting is presented in 7.4-8.1 as a prelude to the question of prayer. The relationship of the two motifs again reflects that concern for prayer which appears in Matt 6:1-18 (though the presentation in the Didache is in reverse order; but see *Gos. Thom.* 14). Little actually is said concerning prayer in *Did.* 8.2, except to outline as an authoritative practice the recitation of the "Lord's Prayer" itself. These words, which are paralleled virtually verbatim in Matt 6:9-13, are charged to the catechumen as a prayer that should

[141] Johnson, "Motive," 107-22.

be said three times daily (8.8), and are openly acknowledged to be the words of the Lord (κύριος), who here is defined specifically as Jesus.[142]

As with the discussions and conclusions concerning baptism and fasting above, one hardly can determine the source behind the Didache's version of the "Lord's Prayer."[143] The stylized form of the prayer offers no clear evidence concerning a date for its usage (so the prayer in this form is well-recognized even today), though the addition of ὅτι σοῦ ἐστιν ἡ δύναμις καὶ ἡ δόξα εἰς τοὺς αἰῶνας ("for yours is the power and the glory forever") would seem to suggest that the Didache recognizes the longer, and therefore presumably later, form of the prayer. Of additional concern here is the possibility of direct influence by the Sayings Gospel Q. As was seen above, the witness of the Lucan Gospel in 1.3b-2.1 and chap. 16 continually offers the Q source as a possible text that was used by a later redactor of the Didache. With respect to the prayer in *Did.* 8.2, however, the literary structure of the piece reflects that of the Matthean Gospel to such an extent that one probably need go no further than the composition of the Matthean text for the source of the Didache's reading.

On Table Fellowship

Of primary concern to the second redactor with respect to the preservation of and comment upon community ritual and tradition is the question of table fellowship. The issue arises in chaps. 9-10 in a complex association of key words and phrases that are to be spoken with reference to table fellowship occasions. In addition to the witness of H at this point, we also can refer to the testimony of the Coptic manuscript, which shows a divergence from the H reading at several junctures.[144]

As with the versions of the eucharist that appear in the NT Gospels and

---

[142] Thus, one reads in *Did.* 8.2: "And do not pray as the hypocrites, but as the Lord commanded in his Gospel . . ." (μηδὲ προσεύχεσθε ὡς οἱ ὑποκριταί, ἀλλ' ὡς ἐκέλευσεν ὁ κύριος ἐν τῷ εὐαγγελίῳ αὐτοῦ). While some scholars argue that the reference to gospel here and elsewhere in the Didache (cf. 11.3; 15.3-4) refers simply to the general "Good News" message, I would argue that the late date of those passages in which the term appears certainly would not be inconsistent with the conclusions that the second redactor of the Didache reflects some knowledge of the Matthean text here.

[143] For an interesting discussion of the Jewish elements that lie behind the construction of the prayer, however, see Finkel, "Prayer," 131-70.

[144] See specifically on these materials the discussions of Gibbins, "Problem," 373-86; Middleton, "Prayers," 259-67; Dibelius, "Mahl-Gebete," 32-41; Lietzmann, *Mass*, 188-94; Riggs, "Table," 83-102; and, Clayton N. Jefford and Stephen J. Patterson, "A Note on *Didache* 12.2a (Coptic)" (*SecCent*) forthcoming. The monograph of Vööbus on this subject (*Traditions*), while sometimes far-afield in its approach, is not without merit. Helpful reviews of the Coptic text are available in Horner, "Fragment," 225-31; Schmidt, "Didache-Fragment, " 81-99; and, Audet, *Didachè*, 28-34.

in the witness of Paul (Matt 26:26-29; Mark 14:22-25; Luke 22:15-20; John 6:51-58; 1 Cor 11:23-25), the Didache reveals both the elements of the bread and the cup, though these elements are presented in the reverse order, i.e., cup first and bread second. Unlike the NT versions, however, the Didache does not reveal the ritualistic structure of the eucharist – neither the association of the event with Jesus nor the association of the specific elements of the meal with the body and blood of Jesus. This divergence from the Gospel accounts may best be explained by one of two different scenarios.

Firstly, there is a possibility that the account of the eucharist which appears in the Didache in fact is not a eucharistic moment like that of the Gospels at all. Instead, the Didache's rendering may reflect more accurately a witness to the "*agape* feast" of early Christianity.

Two objections arise against this thesis. On the one hand, the so-called and well-known "*agape* feast" is not so well documented within the historical record. This argument from silence, however, can hardly be considered as sufficient evidence to deny the existence of such an event in early Christian tradition. To be sure, the elements of the Didache's account are typically Jewish in content: the reference to the "Holy Vine of David" (9.2); the address to God the Father (8.3; 10.2); the reference to the "Holy Name" (10.2); the use of the phrase "God of David" (10.6); etc. In addition, the implications for a messianic understanding of the figure of Jesus are present, yet are greatly subdued (unlike that of the NT Gospel accounts): "Jesus your child" (9.2, 3; 10.2, 3); "Jesus Christ" (9.4); and, "Lord" (9.5). Without question, however, there is no apparent comment upon the cross/resurrection theology that is dominant in the NT Gospel accounts.

The second objection to the "*agape* feast" concept derives from our previous observations about the ritual materials in *Did.* 7-8, i.e., that the entire corpus of topics in the latter chapters of the text have unquestioned parallels in the Matthean Gospel. Therefore, this level of the Didache must be highly dependent upon the Matthean tradition. If this is so, as would seem obvious, then one must explain the divergence between the account of the Matthean Gospel and the account of the Didache. An explanation is forthcoming based upon the understanding that chaps. 1-5 of the Didache have preserved materials that stem from the Matthean community as that community existed prior to the composition of the Matthean Gospel text. It is quite likely that the second redactor of the Didache has preserved in the complicated construction of chaps. 9-10 the reminiscence of a table fellowship that was known and used within the earliest configurations of the Matthean community. This is to say that the Matthean redactor has not preserved the original form of table fellowship that was common to his/her community (a process which we have seen above with respect to the specific sayings of the historical Jesus), but instead, that the Matthean redactor once more is dependent upon a tradition which was imported from outside of the community. This tradition, of course, is borrowed directly from the Marcan text. There is no question that the Matthean version of the eucharist is simply an elaboration of the Marcan account.

The second scenario that also may serve as an explanation of the unique nature of the Didache's table fellowship does not seek to explain the text as a representation of a divergent practice from that which is found in the text of the Matthean Gospel. Clearly the Didache preserves a series of ancient Jewish prayers, which themselves have been *Christianized* into a context that is suitable for table fellowship in the early church. In modern considerations of the NT eucharist accounts we have grown accustomed to the understanding that the "quoted words of Jesus" are the actual form of expression which accompanied the ancient practice of liturgical ritual. This recognition has been inherited through the interpretation of a long church tradition.

In fact, the NT accounts of the eucharist – though certainly highly formulaic – do not necessarily offer the words that are to be spoken in accompaniment of the ritual itself. Instead, they only describe the *process* of the ritual. One must ask, therefore, whether the Didache may not maintain the specific words/prayers which were meant to accompany that ritual as it was practiced within the Matthean community. Such a thesis, of course, is only a conjecture. But if the table fellowship motif of the Didache is to stand in consistent association with the Matthean tradition (as do the motifs of baptism, fasting and prayer which appeared before), this may seem a reasonable explanation for serious consideration.

Some additional support for this conjecture is provided by the saying in *Did.* 9.5b that parallels the saying of Matt 7:6:

> *Did.* 9.5b – Μὴ δῶτε τὸ ἅγιον τοῖς κυσί.
> ("Do not give anything holy to the dogs")
>
> Matt 7:6 – Μὴ δῶτε τὸ ἅγιον τοῖς κυσὶν
> ("Do not give anything holy to the dogs")

There is no question that this saying comes from the Matthean tradition, since the basis for Matt 7:6 is the special Matthean M source. It is interesting to note that the other saying in Matt 7:6 ("do not throw your pearls before swine" [μηδὲ βάλητε τοὺς μαργαρίτας ὑμῶν ἔμπροσθεν τῶν χοίρων) is not found in *Did.* 9.5b, nor is the context for the Didache's version (those who may eat of the eucharist) reflected in the Matthean account. Again, while it is not possible to prove that the second redactor of the Didache has borrowed directly from the Matthean Gospel, this saying does indicate some dependence upon the Matthean tradition.

Christology in Perspective

The Christological perspective of a writing/writer generally serves as a ready indicator of the theological development of the religious community from which the text derives.

The Matthean Gospel possesses one of the more well-developed Christologies of the NT corpus. It reveals a compilation of names and appellations for Jesus that betrays at once both common titles of respect for persons of renown in the early Mediterranean world as well as specific labels that were restricted to the holiest representatives of God. Thus, in the Matthean text one discovers names for the figure of Jesus that were drawn from among the M, Q and/or Marcan materials. Among these designations are "Christ" (Χρίστος; 1:1 [from the redactor]), "Son of God" (ὑιὸς τοῦ θεοῦ; 4.3 [from Q]), "Lord" (κύριος; 7:22 [from Q]), "Teacher" (διδάσκαλος; 8:19 [from the redactor]), "Son of David" (ὑιὸς Δαυίδ; 9:27 [from Mark]), "Son of Man" (ὑιὸς τοῦ ἀνθρώπου; 11:19 [from Q]), etc. In each case the distinctive title is attributed to the figure of Jesus without any confusion.

With respect to the Didache, however, an entirely different situation occurs. The list of titles that appears within the document is far more restricted than that list which appears within the Matthean Gospel. The total listing of such titles, which, as is provided here, includes any name within the text that could be applied to the figure of Jesus or to the image of God, includes "Lord" (κύριος), "God" (θέος), "Paymaster" (ἀνταποδότης; 4.7), "Father-Son-Holy Spirit" (πάτρος-υἱός-ἁγίος πνεύματος), "Holy Vine of David" (ἅγιας ἅμπελος Δαυεὶδ; 9.1), "Child" (τέκνον [of God]), "Christ" (Χρίστος – from χριστέμπορος ["one who used Christ for gain"]; 12.5), "Lord Almighty" (δεσπότης παντοκράτωρ; 10.3); "God of David" (θεὸς Δαυείδ; 10.6) and "Son of God" (υἱὸς θεοῦ; 16.4). While one notes immediately that the bulk of these titles are reserved only for the figure of God "the Father," two other parameters to these titles must be observed.

Firstly, the use of the term "Lord" (κύριος) is not distinctly defined throughout the text with respect to the specific *persona* that is indicated. One thus finds that usages of the title generally may be as applicable to the figure of God the Father as to that of Jesus. Since much of the material that is incorporated into the text of the Didache is derived either from OT sources or from parallel Jewish traditions, in most cases it probably would be more accurate to assume that the Didachist indeed refers to the figure of God the Father rather than to the figure of Jesus.

Secondly, those titles that are restricted specifically to the figure of Jesus as the messiah do *not* appear in the earliest portions of the text. Thus there are no such usages in chaps. 1-5. Those traditions that may stem from earlier sources (e.g., chaps. 9-10, 16) obviously include such titles as they are provided from the hand of a later, "Christianizing" redactor.

It must be assumed, therefore, that the witness of a Christological stance for the earliest layer of the Didache is an attestation for a very low Christology. It is only under the attention of later redactors, who themselves were concerned to adapt the theology of the Didache into a more meaningful or theologically orthodox view, that the text was endowed with the benefits and the privileges of a higher Christology (in the opinion of the redactors). As with the remainder of those materials in the Didache that have been adjusted to coincide with the theological view of the Matthean text, so too, these Christological terms must be seen in the light of that canonical Gospel.

Summary of Conclusions

The preceding series of investigations has served to reinforce the findings of our initial textual study, i.e., that the text of the Didache contains a collection of early sayings whose roots may be traced to the influence of several different sources within the Judeo-Christian tradition. These sources appear to include 1) a tradition of sayings materials that were similar in nature to those materials which were collected in the Sayings Gospel Q and in the Marcan Gospel, 2) the OT, 3) the Synoptic Gospels in some final literary form (or some harmony of those Gospels) and 4) a corpus of apocalyptic sayings, whose origin is unknown.

The order in which these sayings sources were used to construct the text of the Didache occurred in two primary stages:

1) The majority of "sayings materials" that are incorporated into the Didache appear in *Did.* 1.1-6.1a, which is a collection of sayings that primarily reflects a dependence upon the text of the OT and upon early Jewish wisdom sources that were preserved and interpreted within the early Christian community. These sayings, with the exception of 1.3b-2.1, are among the oldest materials in the Didache. They do not include any elements that would associate them specifically with the Christian tradition. The source(s) from which this collection was derived and the original organization of these sayings materials are unknown.

The Didachist provided a format for these sayings through the use of the framework that existed in the Two Ways source, which was an early literary text that also was incorporated into *Barn.* 18-20. Because much of this source is paralleled verbatim between the Didache and Barnabas, scholars generally agree that the Two Ways source was a written document, not an oral tradition. The Didachist incorporated the original collection of sayings materials into the structure of the Two Ways source in accordance with the order of the various motifs that were suggested by the source itself (as least as one can determine from the witness to the Two Ways source that is preserved in Barnabas).

In addition, the framework of the Two Ways source was segmented in order to permit the Didachist to include an additional structural guideline for the sayings, i.e., the framework of the decalogue. The decision of the Didachist to utilize the format of the decalogue probably was not arbitrary, particularly in consideration of the limited use of that text that appears in later writers. Instead, one must assume that the presence of the decalogue, which is used as a literary authority through which the sayings themselves gain validity and authoritative recognition, reflects the Jewish orientation of the Didachist, as well as the community for whom *Did.* 1.1-3a, 2.2-6.1a initially were constructed.

2) The text of *Did.* 7-15 was added to the sayings of *Did.* 1.1-3a, 2.2-6.1a at a later date. These materials, which are primarily of a liturgical or an ecclesial nature, included formulaic sayings that easily could have been transmitted in early Christian communities with little or no alteration. Because the general nature of the texts in chaps. 7-15 is consistent with parallels that occur throughout the Synoptic Gospels (and are consistent especially with the parallels that are preserved in the Matthean Gospel), it must be assumed that the majority of these materials were influenced by the written form of those Gospels or, at least, that these materials were introduced into the Didache after the composition of the Gospels. In distinction from the collected sayings in chaps. 1-5, a specifically Christian emphasis is found throughout the materials of chaps. 7-15. The sayings of *Did.* 1.3b-2.1 and 6.2-3 also may have been attached to the structure of the Didache at the time that chaps. 7-15 were added, or they may have been inserted a short time thereafter. *Did.* 1.3b-2.1 was included to adjust the theology of 1.1-3a, 2.2-6.1a toward a more specifically Christian perspective. *Did.* 6.2-3 was included in order to provide a smooth transition between the materials of 1.1-3a, 2.2-6.1a and 7.1-15.4.

The collection of materials that is found in *Did.* 16, which is concerned to characterize the event of the return of Christ, is of such a nature that it cannot be dated with accuracy. The form and presentation of this collection are those of apocalyptic exhortation – an early oral and literary genre whose elements were adapted and altered continually according to the needs of the first-second century church. Specific sayings in this collection often parallel materials that are contained either in the Matthean or Lucan Gospels apart from the remaining Synoptic witness. It is not known whether some of the sayings in these materials originally were associated with the sayings of 1.1-6.1a, though there is no specific evidence to support this assertion.

A historical rationale behind the collection of these sayings materials is difficult to reconstruct. An analysis of the nature of the sayings and of the form of the attendant materials suggests at least three stages in a tradition of growth within an early Christian community:

1) The original corpus of sayings materials was collected by an early com-

munity of Christian Jews who continued to be influenced by the religious life and thought of the first-century synagogue. Thus, the sayings are consistent with materials that appear in the OT and in early Jewish thought. These sayings are dominated by and constructed around the structure of the decalogue, which serves both as a literary framework and as an axis for ethical instruction. Also evident in the sayings materials are traces of early Jewish wisdom tradition and a concern for a land theology. The original collection of sayings did not reflect the theological concerns of the later church (i.e., a developed Christology, a discussion of ecclesial polity, etc.), but instead, they probably were envisioned as prophetic interpretations by Jesus that were offered upon the Jewish tradition.

2) This community of Christian Jews eventually was expanded by the addition of Christian Gentiles, for whom the significance of the OT in the light of the Jewish tradition of interpretation may not have been as great. As the community was enlarged through the influx of this latter group, the general theological orientation of the community shifted toward a concern for the kerygmatic gospel of the Hellenistic world. At this time, the original group of Christian Jews probably became seen as the more conservative faction within the community whose perspective of religion, which was dominated by Jewish ideas and theology, quickly diminished into the minority view.

3) During the shift from a Jewish orientation to a Hellenistic orientation, the community acquired the materials of the Marcan Gospel and of the Sayings Gospel Q, which were added to texts that were used within the community. Many of the sayings materials that originally had been collected by the early community of Christian Jews were paralleled in these two texts. Subsequently, persons within the community constructed a new text in the form of a Gospel (i.e., the Matthean Gospel) that incorporated the old materials which had been preserved by the community and the new materials which were added from the two outside sources. In most of those instances where it was necessary to choose between the incorporation of sayings that were contained in the Sayings Gospel Q or the Marcan Gospel, on the one hand, and the incorporation of sayings that were preserved from the immediate community, on the other hand, the authors of the Matthean Gospel opted for the former materials.

4) With the new Gospel as an authoritative standard for the community, the original collection of sayings materials (i.e., 1.1-3b and 2.2-6.1a) was transformed into a text that could be used for the instruction of catechumens. At some time thereafter, the problems of hierarchy and of ecclesial structure that were associated with the shift from a Jewish orientation to a Hellenistic orientation were resolved through the decision to incorporate the office of "elder," which had been maintained from the days of worship in the synagogue, into the office of "presbyter," which was suggested from a three-

tiered hierarchy of authority that commonly was used in Hellenistic congregations. The materials of *Did.* 7-15 then were added to the original collection of sayings (perhaps in two separate phases [chaps. 7-10 and chaps. 11-15]) in order to construct a manual of instruction for those Christian Jews who needed to become familiar with the role and duties of the office of presbyter. Additional alterations (1.3b-6.1a and 6.2-3) were made to this manual on occasion in order to adjust the theology of the text to that of the Gospel, which had become the authoritative standard of the community.

5) With the eventual demise of the original community of Christian Jews through attrition and with the new prominence of the new Gospel that had been fashioned within the community, the manual of instruction (or the Didache) ultimately was relegated to a position of neglect.

To be sure, this scenario, which seems to suit the criteria by which the text of the Didache and the text of the Matthean Gospel may once have related to one another, is not attested directly within the historical tradition. On the other hand, such an understanding of the traditio-historical development of these two texts appears to explain the majority of questions concerning the composition and the redaction of the Didache text.

With respect to "the new problem of the Didache" which was raised in Chapter One, the questions of date and of provenance for the text of the Didache are limited for the biblical scholar only insofar as one can date and place the composition of the Matthean Gospel. The city of Antioch, with its many divergent communities of Christians and with its active influx both of Jewish and Hellenistic thought, seems a reasonable provenance for the text. The formation of the original sayings materials that appear in *Did.* 1-5(16?) and the association of those materials with the Two Ways source with some justification may be placed prior to the construction of the Matthean Gospel (i.e., certainly before C.E. 80; probably before C.E. 70; possibly ca. C.E. 50). Most of the remaining materials (i.e., *Did.* 7-15) should be dated to the composition of the Matthean Gospel or shortly thereafter (ca. C.E. 80-100). Several other passages, including 1.3a-2.1, 6.2-3 and most of chap. 16, cannot be dated with accuracy, since they reflect concerns of the early church that continued into the second century and beyond.

APPENDIX A: Q 13:23-24 (MATT 7:13-14/LUKE 13:23-24)[1]

Q 13:[23]-24

[1]/ after 13:21; before 13:[25]-26	
[ ][2]	
[ ][6] εἰσελθ[ατε][6]	Enter
διὰ τῆς στενῆς [[[θ][7]]]ύ[[[ρα][7]]]ς	through the narrow [[door]]
ὅτι ( )[8]	for
πολλοί [[[ ][9]]]	many
(ζητήσου)[10]σιν ( )[10] εἰσε(λθεῖν)[10]	will seek to enter
[[( )[11]]]	
[ ][12]	
( )[13]	
[3]/(καὶ)[3]	and
ὀλίγοι [[(εἰσιν)[4]]]	few [[are]]
οἱ (εὑρίσκοντες αὐτήν)[5].	those who will find it.
\[3]	
\[1]→ Q 13:[25]	

Matt 7:13-14	**Luke 13:23-24**
0·1/	0·1/
[ ][2]	[Εἶπεν δέ τις αὐτῷ· κύριε, εἰ][2]
	[3]/( )[3]
	ὀλίγοι ( )[4]
	οἱ [σῳζομενοι][5]
∧[3]	\[3];
[ ][2]	[ὁ δὲ εἶπεν πρὸς αὐτούς·][2]
[ ][6] Εἰσέλθ(ατε)[6]	[ἀγωνίζεσθε][6] εἰσελθ[εῖν][6]
διὰ τῆς στενῆς (π)[7]ύ(λη)[7]ς·	διὰ τῆς στενῆς [θ][7]ύ[ρα][7]ς,
ὅτι (πλατεῖα ἡ πύλη καὶ	ὅτι

---

[1] The following materials have been patterned along the guidelines for the examination of those NT pericopae which have been determined to be Q passages according to the criteria of the Institute for Antiquity and Christianity's project "Q: A Lost Collection of Jesus' Sayings" (directed by James M. Robinson). Variants in the text are marked by raised numerals (= [1]); materials only in the Matthean Gospel are indicated within parentheses; materials only in the Lucan Gospel are indicated within brackets; variations in position between texts are indicated within slashes (= ∧). Because of the limitations of the present study, only Q 13:23-24 is considered in the present analysis. The broader question of the complete Q 13:23-27 section, as it has been defined by the project, has not been taken into consideration. In addition, Q 13:23-24 is analyzed as a single unit, since the division of the text into separate verses serves no immediate purpose for the examination of the saying. Unlike the remainder of the study, in which translations are given for such sources, secondary sources have been left in their original languages here in order to insure accuracy in the presentation of scholarly considerations for each variant. Finally, with respect to the text of the pericope, an examination of possible textual variations within ancient manuscripts indicates that there are no known major deviations in the tradition which would be pertinent for the present analysis.

εὐρύχωρος ἡ ὁδὸς ἡ	
ἀπάγουσα εἰς τὴν	
ἀπώλειαν καὶ)[8]	( )[8]
πολλοί [ ][9]	πολλοί, [λέγω ὑμῖν][9],
(εἰ)[10]σιν (οἱ)[10]	[ζητήσου][10]σιν ( )[10]
εἰσε(ρχόμενοι)[10]	εἰσε[λθειν][10]
(δι' αὐτῆς)[11]·	( )[11]
[ ][12]	[καὶ οὐκ ἰσχύσουσιν][12].
(τί στενὴ ἡ πύλη καὶ	
τεθλιμμένη ἡ ὁδὸς	
ἡ ἀπάγουσα	
εἰς τὴν ζωὴν)[13]	( )[13]
[3]/(καὶ)[3]	
ὀλίγοι (εἰσὶν)[4]	
οἱ (εὑρίσκοντες αὐτήν)[5].	
\\[3]	/\\[3]
\\[0·1]	\\[0·1]

Q 13:23-24[0]: Is the pericope in Q?
Luke and Matthew = Q

Pro:

Con:

Evaluation:
CJ 22 ii 88:

This issue has not been argued in the current reconstruction. The material is assumed to be in Q.

Q 13:23-24[1]: Position of 13:23-24 in Q.
Luke = *Q:* After Q 13:21; before Q 13:[25]-26.

Pro: **Streeter** 1924, 283: "But Luke's version comes in the middle of a section of which the beginning (Mustard Seed and Leaven), xiii. 18-21, the middle, xiii. 28-29, and the end, xiii. 34-35 ("Jerusalem, Jerusalem"), are certainly Q, and of which, as we shall see later, much of the rest is probably Q; the probability, then, is that Luke here also follows Q." **Hirsch** 1941, 130: "So halte ich Luk 13 24-30 für einen in sich geschlossenen Q-Abschnitt." **Kilpatrick** 1946, 23: "We may, accordingly, assume that the evangelist [Matthew] has used both the Q saying much as it appears in Luke and also a saying about the Two Ways from another source." **Dupont** 1958, 94-95: "Les vv. 23-24 constituent une unité . . . elle doit avoir été fournie à Luc par une tradition ancienne, et tout porte a penser qu'elle lui a été transmise précisément comme introduction au logion du v. 24." **Luz** 1985, 395[7]: "Weil Lk 13,23-29 in Mt 7,13f.22f; 8,11f fortlaufend benutzt wurde." Reconstructions: **Harnack** 1907, ET 142. **Edwards** 1976, xii. **Polag** 1979, 68-69. **Crossan** 1983, 338 and 345.

Con: **Schmid** 1930, 243: "Die Lk-Parallelen stehen wiederum beisammen (Lk 13 23-27) in einem Abschnitt, dessen Einheitlichkeit durch mehrere Sprünge im Gedankengang ausgeschlossen wird." **Fitzmyer** 1985, 1022: "There is no certainty that vv. 24-29 formed a unit in 'Q.'"

Matt = *Q:* After Q 6:31 (Matt 7:12); before Q 6:43 (Matt 7:18).

Pro: **Hirsch** 1941, 88: "Der Q-Abschnitt, aus dem sie stammt, ist bei Matth ganz aufgelöst worden (Luk 13 23-30). Für die ersten Verse dieses Abschnitts (Luk 13 23-24) hatte Matth in seiner MaS-Rede [M] von wahrer Gesetzeserfüllung eine Dublette . . ."

129: "... wir haben für die zu 24 [= Matth 7 13-14] eine Luk unbekannte Vorlage des Matth, MaS [M], angesetzt, und fur die zu 25 [= Matth 25 10-121] ist eine solche Vorlage selbstverständlich. Wenn Matth diese Verse in Q-Fassung fand, so hat er sie wegen der reicheren Entsprechung seiner andern Vorlage weggelassen." **Beare** 173: "the wording is so different as to suggest that the Evangelists have drawn upon two different sources." **Morgenthaler** 1971, 192.

Con: **Kilpatrick** 1946, 23: "The verbal differences make possible the view that the evangelist [Mt] has employed two sources, but the presence of a substantial difference gives this view greater probability. The rhythmic structure of the saying in Matthew differs from the Lucan form of the saying and this fact may support the suggestion that two sources have been conflated. We may, accordingly, assume that the evangelist has used the Q saying much as **Knox** 31: 'The new Torah proper is then enforced by a series of warnings (Matt. vii.13ff.); it is probable that Matthew had in mind the warnings and promises with which Leviticus and Deuteronomy conclude their versions of the Torah (Lev. xxvi.3-end, Deut. xxviii-xxx). For this purpose he detaches from their original position the sayings on the narrow gate, which in Luke appear in the collection of sayings xiii.22ff., which appears to be a Lucan compilation of unattached material.'" **Lambrecht** 1985, 185. Reconstructions: **Harnack** 1907, ET 142. **Edwards** 1976, xii. **Polag** 1979, 68-69. **Crossan** 1983, 338 and 345.

Evaluation:

CJ 18 ii 88: {B}, After Q 13:21; before Q 13:[25]-26.

The majority view of scholarship argues either that the Lucan redactor has preserved this section in the order of Q or, conversely, that the Matthean redactor has not done so. The sequence of materials in the Lucan and Matthean texts is the same, which indicates a knowledge of a common source that was used by each redactor. In addition, the position of the Matthean version of this Q saying may have been influenced by its association with another saying (the Two Ways) and may have been influenced by the source from which this second saying was derived (see the discussion of variants ^{8} and ^{13} below). The nature of this possible influence by a second saying, however, cannot be known from the available data.

Q 13:23-24^{2}: Luke's introduction with a question and answer.

Luke = Q: [Εἶπεν δέ τις αὐτῷ κύριε, εἰ]^{2} ^{3}/( )^{3} ὀλίγοι ( )^{4} οἱ [σῳζόμενοι]^{5}\$^{3}$; [ὁ δὲ εἶπεν πρὸς αὐτούς]^{2}:

Pro: **Schmidt** 1930, 244: "Dafür behalt aber Lk das Plus der Situationsangabe (13 23), die man doch nicht als aus dem Text des Spruches erschlossene freie Erfindung des Evangelisten bezeichnen darf." **Manson** 1937, 124: "v. 23 may well be part of Q. Cf. Lk. 9:57-62 for similar openings." **Marshall** 1978, 563: "...it is possible that it constituted the original introduction to the saying (Lucan: **Bultmann**, 359f.; **Dibelius**, 162 ...; **Flender**, 81f ...)"; 564: "The introductory formula may be pre-Lucan, but this is not certain. For εἰ introducing a direct question cf. 22:42; 22:49; Acts 1:6; et al .... The word 'few' appears in Mt. 7:14; this suggests that either Luke (or his source) constructed the question out of Jesus' answer, or the answer in its Matthaean form is based on the question posed in Lk."

Con: **B. Weiss** 1876, 214: "Vor Allem aber muss ich jetzt (anders a. a. O. S. 125ff.) annehmen, dass dem Abschnitt Luc. 13, 22-30 ein echtes Redestück der Quelle zu Grunde liegt, das sich sehr passend an die Parabeln v. 18-21, wie diese an v. 1-9 (Vg. S. 32), anschloss, obwohl Luc., der diesen Zusammenhang durch die Einschaltung von v. 22 und die in seiner Weise gebildete Zwischenfrage v. 23 durchschnitten hat, ihn sichtlich nicht mehr erkannte." 1907, 94^{1}: "Was bei Lk. 13,22 dazwischen steht, ist eine bei ihm mehrfach wiederkehrende Erinnerung daran, dass Jesus sich immer noch in dem Umherreisen befand, dessen Ziel Jerusalem war, wie es Lukas in seinem zweiten Teile schildert. Dieselbe will, wie das διδάσκων zeigt, 13, 26, und wie das πορ. ποιούμ. εἰς ἱεροσ. zeigt, 13,33 vorbereiten, woraus folgt, dass ihm alles folgende (13, 24-33) in Q vorlag. Dagegen ist Lk. 13, 23 eine der dadurch notwendig gewordenen Übergangsfragen, wie wir sie aus 12, 41. 17, 37 bereits kennen, und zwar genau wie dort, durch κύριε eingeleitet, in der noch deutlich in dem εἰ ὀλίγοι οἱ σῳζόμενοι eine Reminiszenz an den folgenden Spruch aus Q anklingt." **Müller** 1908, 13-14: "Neubildungen des Lk, entweder unter Benutzung von nicht völlig übernommenen Versen aus Mk, Q oder S, oder aus dem Inhalte des vorhergehenden oder nachfolgenden Zusammenhanges heraus, sind . . . 13:23 Einleitungsfrage zum Folgenden." **Haupt** 1913, 258. **Bussmann** 1929, 22: vs. 24 alone is from Q. 77: ". . . v. 23 ist vielleicht eine aus dem folgenden Wort erschlossene Frage, die L gebildet hat, aber v. 24 ist in Mt erweitert." **Hirsch** 1941, 130: " Der Vers 23 gibt dem ganzen Stück eine etwas andre Beleuchtung, als es an sich hat; er dient sachlich dazu, aus einer Drohnung gegen jüdische Zeitgenossen eine Lehre für Christen zu machen." **Beare** 1962, 67: ". . . he [Luke] has provided it with an artificial setting." **Schulz** 1972a, 310: "Die Umformungen des Lk lassen sich weitgehend aus dem unmittelbaren Kontext erklären: Lk 13,22-30 ist eine aus verschiedenen trad Materialien red komponierte eschatologische Rede des Lk . . . Auch V 23 dürfte von Lk stammen. Das Vokabelmaterial ist wiederum lk: εἶπεν δέ; κύριε; σῴζειν bei Lk oft ohne Objekt als Terminus technicus für das Heil; ὁ δέ häufig im Dialog; εἶπεν πρός + Akk ist eine typisch lk Konstruktion. ὀλίγος ist möglicherweise Nachklang der Mt-Fassung des Logions Mt 7,13f, wo das Stichwort ὀλίγος vorkommt." **Edwards** 1976, 131: "Luke's introduction creates an apophthegm . . . **Marshall** 1978, 563: "The question in v. 23 may have been composed by Luke as an introduction to the following saying . . ." **Jeremias** 1980, 231: "εἶπεν δέ: ist lukanisch → Red – εἰ: die seltene Konstruktion: εἰ als Fragepartikel vor direkter Rede (unklassisch, Septuagintismus) begegnet im NT abgesehen von Mt 12,10; 19,3 und Mk 8,23 ausschliesslich im Doppelwerk Lk 13,23; 22,49/Apg 1,6; 7,1; 19,2; 21,37; 22,25, wird also von Lukas nicht ungern geschrieben . . . πρός *c. acc.*: nach Verbum dicendi → Red . . . κύριε: als Anrede des irdischen Jesus ist vorlukanischer Sprachgebrauch → Trad." **Schmithals** 1980, 155: "Erst Lukas hat dem ganzen Stück einen Eingangsrahmen gegeben (V.22f.; vgl. 8,1; 9,51; 12,13.41). Die Frage V.23 verschiebt leicht den Sinn von V.24: Nicht mehr wird nur zur Entscheidung aufgerufen, Lukas weist auch und vor allem auf die Schwierigkeit dieser Entscheidung hin, der nur wenige wirklich gewachsen sind; 'ihr musst euch anstrengen' stammt erst von Lukas (nach Mark. 10,26?, vgl. 1.Tim.6,11f.; 2.Tim. 4,7f.), der damit möglicherweise auch einem Missverständnis der beiden in V.18-21 vorangehenden 'universellen' Gleichnisse vorbeugen will." **Steinhauser** 1981, 149: "Der redaktionelle Satz Lk 13,22 (vgl. Lk 8,1) setzt den lukanischen Reisebericht fort. In Vers 23 leitet Lukas drei Herrenworte 13,24. 26f.28f ein; der Vers enthält typisch lukanische Wendungen. εἶπεν δέ ist charakteristisch lukanisch. κύριε als Anrede an Jesus finden wir oft bei Lukas. Auch σῴζειν ohne Objekt kommt bei Lukas als Terminus technicus für das Heil vor. εἶπεν πρός mit dem Akkusativ ist ebenfalls lukanische Konstruktion. Deshalb ist die Meinung, Lukas hatte durch die Uebernahme der Frage in Vers 23 die Situation des Logions erhalten, unwahrscheinlich. Lukas hat ὀλίγος aus Mt 7,13f bei der Formulierung der Frage angewendet." **Denaux** 1982, 318: "Lk hat seinerseits dem ursprünglichen Logion eine erzählende Einleitung vorangestellt." **Fitzmyer** 1985, 1021: ". . . fashioned by Luke himself to introduce the traditional material which follows." **Lambrecht** 1985, 196: "The introductory verse Lk 13:23 is probably entirely

Lucan redaction, although the 'few' may have come from Q." **Kloppenborg** 1987, 223 n. 213: "the presence of several Lucanisms . . . makes it more probable that 13:23 is a Lucan construction." Reconstructions: **Harnack** 1907, ET 142. **Polag** 1979, 68-69. **Denaux** 1982, 322, 327. **Kloppenborg** 1988, 246.

Matt = *Q:* [ ]^{2} $\wedge^{3}$ [ ]^{2}

Pro: Reconstructions: **Harnack** 1907, ET 142. **Polag** 1979, 68-69. **Schenk** 1981, 102. **Steinhauser** 1981, 152.

Con: **Dupont** 1958, 100: ". . . Matthieu a connu l'introduction de Luc, 13,23 et l'a omise; il n'est pourtant pas négligeable quand on sait par ailleurs que Matthieu ne pouvait pas reprendre cette introduction dans le Sermon sur la montagne."

Evaluation:

CJ 18 ii 88: {A}, [ ]^{2} $\wedge^{3}$ [ ]^{3}

The Lucan question-answer introduction is a typical construction for the redactor. Further, v 23 contains numerous Lucanisms, which suggests that the redactor has chosen to formulate a specific setting for the introduction of the Q saying which immediately follows.

Q 13:23-24^{3}: Position of the "many" in reference to the "few." Luke has them before the "many"; Matthew mentions them after reference to "many."

Luke = *Q:* [Εἶπεν δέ τις αὐτῷ· Κυριε, ε]^{2} ^{3}/( )^{3} ὀλίγοι ( )^{4} οἱ [σῳζόμενοι]^{5}\\$^{3}$; . . . [καὶ οὐκ ἰσχύσουσιν]^{12}. ( )^{13} $\wedge^{3}$

Pro:

Con: **Haupt** 1913, 258. **Bussmann** 1929, 77: "Das οὐκ ἰσχύσουσιν wird L vielleicht für οὐκ εὑρήσουσιν geschrieben haben." **Fitzmyer** 1985, 1021: ". . . fashioned by Luke himself to introduce the traditional material which follows." Reconstructions: **Harnack** 1907, ET 142. **Polag** 1979, 68-69. **Denaux** 1982, 322, 327.

Matt = *Q:* [ ]^{2} $\wedge^{3}$ [ ]^{2} (. . . ἡ ὁδὸς ἡ ἀπάγουσα εἰς τὴν ζωὴν)^{13} ^{3}/(καὶ)^{3} ὀλίγοι (εἰσὶν)^{4} οἱ (εὑρίσκοντες αὐτήν)^{5}.\\$^{3}$

Pro: **Schmid** 1930, 243-44: "Dass Mt 7 13f die ursprüngliche Fassung des ersten Spruches bewahrt haben dürfte, die Lk verkürzt hat, wird vor allem durch den streng durchgeführten Parallelismus nahegelegt." Reconstructions: **Harnack** 1907, ET 142. **Polag** 1979, 68-69. **Schenk** 1981, 102. **Steinhauser** 1981, 152. **Kloppenborg** 1988, 246.

Con: **Lambrecht** 1985, 196: "Moreover, [Matthew] sets the 'many' (the crowd) in opposition to the 'few' (cf. Lk 13:23)."

Evaluation:

CJ 18 ii 88: {A} [ ]^{2} $\wedge^{3}$ [ ]^{2} . . . ἡ ὁδὸς ἡ ἀπάγουσα εἰς τὴν ζωὴν)^{13} ^{3}/(καὶ)^{3} ὀλίγοι (εἰσὶν)^{4} οἱ (εὑρίσκοντες αὐτήν)^{5}.\\$^{3}$

The position of the "many" and "few" is determined primarily by the decision concerning the originality of the question-answer introduction in the Lucan version (see the discussion of variant ^{2} above). The Matthean version thus is the preferred reading.

Q 13:23-24^{4}: Matthew's use of εἰσίν.

Luke = *Q:* ὀλίγοι ( )^{4} οἱ [σῳζόμενοι]^{5}

Pro: **Jeremias** 1980, 231$^{20-22}$: " – Das Fehlen von εἶναι als Kopula ist zwar dem klassischen Griechisch nicht unbekannt, ihm jedoch längst nicht so geläufig wie den semitischen Sprachen, in denen das Fehlen der Kopula überaus gebräuchlich ist. Das Phänomen begegnet reichlich im lukanischen Doppelwerk, aber in ganz unterschiedlicher Streuung. So finden sich in der Apostelgeschichte nur 27 Belege, in auffälligem Kontrast dazu aber allein in der lukanischen Kindheitsgeschichte 22; da die Apg genau 10 mal so umfangreich ist wie die Kindheitsgeschichte, wären bei gleicher Proportion nicht weniger als 220 Belege in der Apg zu erwarten. Es kann kein Zweifel daran bestehen, dass die Häufung der Belege (unsere Stelle, Lk 1,5, biete zwei) als unlukanischer semitisierender Sprachgebrauch anzusprechen ist. Dieses Ergebnis bestätigt sich, wenn man den von Lukas ubernommenen Markusstoff für sich analysiert. An mindestens 21 Stellen in diesen Markuskapiteln stiess Lukas auf das Fehlen von Formen von εἶναι. Er liess von ihnen sieben passieren, offensichtlich, weil sie ihm stilistisch vertretbar erschienen; aber an 14 Stellen beseitigte er die Ellipse. **N. Turner** hat richtig beobachtet, wenn er feststellte: 'Luke prefers the copula on every possible occasion, apart from set phrases, titles, and a few exclamations and questions' [**Moulton-Turner**, Grammar III 304]. Das heisst: die Weglassung der Kopula ist im allgemeinen Kennzeichen der vorlukanischen Tradition, da Lukas die Kopula nach Möglichkeit nicht streicht, sondern zufügt. Im LkEv finden sich 91 Fälle von fehlender Kopula; als vorlukanisch ist vor allem das Fehlen von Formen von εἶναι bei Demonstrativa, in Ausrufen, in sprichwortartigen Sentenzen sowie in Lob- und Segenssprüchen anzusehen." Reconstructions: **Polag** 1979, 68-69.

Con: **Fitzmyer** 1985, 1021: ". . . fashioned by Luke himself to introduce the traditional material which follows." **Haupt** 1913, 258. Reconstructions: **Harnack** 1907, ET 142. **Denaux** 1982, 322, 327.

Matt = Q: ὀλίγοι (εἰσὶν)^4 οἱ (εὑρίσκοντες αὐτήν)^5.

Pro: **Schmid** 1930, 243-44: "Dass Mt 7 13f die ursprüngliche Fassung des ersten Spruches bewahrt haben dürfte, die Lk verkürzt hat, wird vor allem durch den streng durchgeführten Parallelismus nahegelegt." Reconstructions: **Harnack** 1907, ET 142. **Schenk** 1981, 102. **Steinhauser** 1981, 152. **Kloppenborg** 1988, 246.

Con: Reconstructions: **Polag** 1979, 68-69.

Evaluation:

CJ 18 ii 88: {C}, ὀλίγοι (εἰσὶν)^4 οἱ (εὑρίσκοντες αὐτήν)^5.

While there is insufficient evidence to make an informed decision, the Lucan redactor may have altered the text in the process of constructing the introduction. There is no apparent rationale for such an alteration on the part of the Matthean redactor.

Q 13:23-24^5: Luke's predication for the few, "being saved," or Matthew's "finding it."

Luke = Q: ὀλίγοι ( )^4 οἱ [σῳζόμενοι]^5

Pro:

Con: **Haupt** 1913, 258. **Fitzmyer** 1985, 1021: ". . . fashioned by Luke himself to introduce the traditional material which follows." Reconstructions: **Polag** 1979, 68-69. **Denaux** 1982, 322, 327.

Matt = Q: ὀλίγοι (εἰσὶν)^4 οἱ (εὑρίσκοντες αὐτήν)^5.

Pro: **Schmid** 1930, 243-44: "Dass Mt 7 13f die ursprüngliche Fassung des ersten Spruches bewahrt haben dürfte, die Lk verkürzt hat, wird vor allem durch den streng durchgeführten Parallelismus nahegelegt." Reconstructions: **Polag** 1979, 68-69 (εὑρήσουσιν). **Schenk** 1981, 102. **Steinhauser** 1981, 152. **Kloppenborg** 1988, 246.

Con:

Evaluation: CJ 18 ii 88: {A}, ὀλίγοι (εἰσὶν)^4 οἱ (εὑρίσκοντες αὐτήν)^5.

The predication for "being saved" or "finding it" is determined primarily by the decision concerning the originality of the question-answer introduction in the Lucan version (see the discussion of variant ^{2} above). The assumption is that the Lucan redactor has changed the Matthean reading in order to make more specific the nature of the question that is addressed to Jesus. On the other hand, the future tense of the Lucan verb is preferred in the saying (see the discussion of variant ^{10} below), which suggests that Polag's εὑρήσουσιν may be the most accurate reading of the text. To be sure, the Lucan redactor has abandoned the metaphor of "seeking" and approaches the issue of salvation directly.

Q 13:23-24[6]**:** Luke's verb and complementary infinitive or Matthew's verb.
Luke = Q: [ἀγωνίζεσθε][6] εἰσελθ[εῖν][6]

Pro: **B. Weiss** 1907, 94: "Wenn er mit dem ἀγωνίζεσθε εἰσελθεῖν διὰ τ. στενῆς θύρας begann, so haben wir hier im Zusammenhang von Q noch deutlich die konkrete Beziehung des Spruchs, die in dem εἰσέλθατε διὰ τῆς στενῆς πόλης Mt. 7, 13 verlorgen gegangen ist." **Denaux** 1982, 324: "'ἀγωνίζεσθαι ist in den Evangelien sonst nicht belegt und wird auch von Lukas nur an dieser Stelle verwendet, so dass von der Wortstatistik her die Frage der Redaktion nicht entschieden werden kann,' so sagt mit Recht P. Hoffmann, der das Wort nachher dann doch aus anderen Gründen der Lk-Redaktion zuschreibt [**Paul Hoffmann**, "Πάντες ἐργάται ἀδικίας: Redaktion und Tradition in Lc 13 22-30" *ZNW* 58 (1967): 188-214]. In diesem Fall würde das lukanische ἀγωνίζεσθε gemäss unserer Sehweise ein ursprünglicheres ζητεῖτε oder ζητησάτε ersetzt haben. Die Argumente Hoffmanns können aber ebensogut für die Anwesenheit des Wortes in Q angeführt werden. Zunächst: 'Das Bildwort vom ethischen Agon war in der hellenistischen Diatribe verbreitet und wurde sowohl von der jüdischen als auch von der urchristlichen Paränese aufgenommen.' Warum konnte dann der Q-Redaktor dieses geläufige Bildwort nicht schon aufgenommen haben? Zweitens: Die Zusammenordnung von Ethik (vgl. das Agonmotiv in der Aufforderung) und Eschatologie (vgl. die Future in der Begründung) stimmt mit der theologischen Konzeption des Lukas im allgemeinen überein. Gilt nicht daselbe für den Q-Redaktor? Man darf demnach die Möglichkeit nicht von vornherein ausschliessen, dass Lk den Imperativ ἀγωνίζεσθε schon in Q vorgefunden hat." Reconstructions: **Denaux** 1982, 322, 327.

Con: **Harnack** 1907, 67: ". . . St. Luke gives only an extract, wherein, however, he develops the teaching by means of ἀγωνίεσθε and ζητήσουσιν . . ." **Schulz** 1972a, 310: "Schon das zusammengesetzte ἀγωνίζεσθε εἰσελθεῖν ist sicher sek gegenüber εἰσέλθατε bei Mt. Vom ethischen Agoon spricht auch die hellenistische Diatribe, und Lk gestaltet im Sinne einer 'verbreiteten paränetischen Tradition' um und akzentuiert ethisch." **Jeremias** 1980, 232: "ἀγωνίζομαι wird im NT nur Lk 1,24 mit dem Infinitiv konstruiert." 93: "Die *Ergänzung von Verben durch einen Infinitiv* ist ein dem klassischen Griechisch geläufiger Sprachgebrauch, der jedoch im hellenistischen Griechisch weithin durch die Konstruktion mit ινα und οτι verdrängt wird." **Steinhauser** 1981, 149: "ἀγωνίζεσθε εἰσελθεῖν ist gegenuber εἰσέλθατε in Mt 7,13 als sekundär anzusehen." Reconstructions: **Harnack** 1907, ET 142. **Polag** 1979, 68-69.
Matt = Q: [ ][6] Εἰσέλθ(ατε)[6]

Pro: **Schmid** 243-44: "Dass Mt 7 13f die ursprüngliche Fassung des ersten Spruches bewahrt haben dürfte, die Lk verkürzt hat, wird vor allem den streng durchgeführten Parallelismus nahegelegt." Reconstructions: **Harnack** 1907, ET 142. **Polag** 1979, 68-69. **Schenk** 1981, 102.

Con:
Evaluation:
CJ 18 ii 88: {B}, [ ][6] Εἰσέλθ(ατε)[6]

The use of the verb with the complimentary infinitive appears to be a stylistic preference of the Lucan redactor. There is no specific reason to argue against the construction that is offered in the Matthean version.

Q 13:23-24[7]: Luke's "door" or Matthew's "gate."
Luke = Q: διὰ τῆς στενῆς [θ]⁷ύ[ρα]⁷ς,

Pro: **J. Weiss** 1907, 297: "Von diesem Spruchgebilde hat Lukas nur die erste Mahnung . . . Bei Matthaüs ist mit dem Bilde von der engen Pforte das im Judentum (Jer. 21,8) und Urchristentum häufige . . . von den zwei Wegen verbunden . . ." **Dupont** 1958, 95: "Nous pouvons ajouter qu'il [Luke] a trouvé le logion à la place où il le transmet, car il s'y rattache au v. 24 suivant le procédé archaïque du mot-agrafe (θύρα), qu'on n'attribuera pas facilement à Luc." **Marshall** 1978, 563: "No certain answer to the problem of priority can be given, and the possibility of separate developments in the tradition is perhaps most likely"; 565: "It seems highly improbable that if Luke had known of the metaphor of 'the way' in Mt. he would have omitted it; on the other hand, there is nothing to suggest Matthaean formulation of the metaphor in Mt. The same basic thought of the narrow entrance has been developed in two different ways, probably in Christian catechetical usage."

Con: **Harnack** 1907, ET 68: "St. Luke thinks of the door of a house." **Bussmann** 1929, 77: According to **Harnack**, "L biete nur einen Auszug und habe darum πύλη in θύρα geändert, weil er die Strasse fortgelassen habe." **Schulz** 1972a, 310: "Für die Ersetzung von πύλη durch θύρα sprechen Argumente aus dem unmittelbaren Kontext (s u). θύρα ist darüber hinaus ein von Lk häufig gebrauchtes Wort." **Schmithals** 1980, 154: "V. 24 differiert spürbar von der Parallele Mat. 7,13f., die neben die Metapher von der engen Türe (sekundär) das Bild vom schmalen (und von breiten) Weg setzt. Die Metapher von der Türe begegnet auch 4.Ezra 7,3ff." **Steinhauser** 1981, 149-50: "Der Evangelist [Luke] formuliert ethisch und fordert seine Leser auf, alle Kraft einzusetzen, um durch die Türe (sc. in den Festsaal) einzutreten und am eschatologischen Mahl teilzunehmen. In diesem Zusammenhang ist deshalb θύρα gegenüber πύλη bei Mattäus als sekundär anzusehen. Die Ersetzung des Wortes πύλη (das Stadttor) durch θύρα (die Haustür) verknüpft Vers 24 mit dem folgenden Vers 25. Damit ist auch das Fortlassen von ὁδός bei Lukas erklärt." **Fitzmyer** 1985, 1021: "The Lucan form speaks only of a 'narrow door,' and it is linked to vv. 25-27a by catchword bonding; both have to do with a 'door.' Luke may have modified his source to create this bond." Reconstructions: **Harnack** 1907, ET 142. **Polag** 1979, 68-69. **Denaux** 1982, 322, 327.

Matt = Q: διὰ τῆς στενῆς (π)⁷ύ(λη)⁷ς·

Pro: **Harnack** 1907, ET 68: "Q and St. Matthew think of the gate of a city." **Schmid** 1930, 243-44: "Dass Mt 7 13f die ursprüngliche Fassung des ersten Spruches bewahrt haben dürfte, die Lk verkürzt hat, wird vor allem durch den streng durchgeführten Parallelismus nahegelegt." **Marshall** 1978, 563: "No certain answer to the problem of priority can be given, and the possibility of separate developments in the tradition is perhaps most likely." 565: "It seems highly improbable that if Luke had known of the metaphor of 'the way' in Mt. he would have omitted it; on the other hand, there is nothing to suggest Matthaean formulation of the metaphor in Mt. The same basic thought of the narrow entrance has been developed in two different ways, probably in Christian catechetical usage." **Schmithals** 1980, 154: "V. 24 differiert spürbar von der Parallele Mat. 7,13f., die neben die Metapher von der engen Türe (sekundär) das Bild vom schmalen (und von breiten) Weg setzt. Die Metapher von der Türe begegnet auch 4.Ezra 7,3ff." **Steinhauser** 1981, 151: "Die ursprüngliche Fassung des Logions hat mit der Anrede begonnen: εἰσέλθατε διὰ τῆς στενῆς πύλης." Reconstructions: **Harnack** 1907, ET 142. **Polag** 1979, 68-69. **Schenk** 1981, 102.

Con: **Streeter** 1924, 283-84: "But the words ἡ πύλη ("*is* the gate") are omitted in Matthew on their second (א Old Lat.) and third (544 Old Lat.) occurrence. If this reading is original, Q had the Lucan saying about "the narrow *gate*," M had one quite different – the antithesis between the "broad and the narrow *ways*." (The contrast of the Two Ways occurs in the Didache and elsewhere.) Matthew has conflated Q and M." **Bussmann** 1929, 77: "Aber wenn Mt erweitert hat, wie nach seinem sonstigen Verfahren wahrscheinlicher ist, dann hat er um der Strasse willen die Tür in ein Tor verwandelt." Beare 1962, 174: ". . . in Matthew, we begin with the slight change from a 'narrow door' to a 'narrow gate.'" **Denaux** 1982, 322: "Die Zufügung des Wegmotivs veranlasste Mt das Q-Wort θύρα (vgl. die Stichwortverbindung in Lk 13,24.25) durch die Vokabel πύλη zu ersetzen." **Lambrecht** 1985, 196: "Matthew has added the way-motif, so he changed the 'door' into the 'gate.'"

Evaluation:

CJ 18 ii 88: {C}, διὰ τῆς στενῆς (θ)[7]ύ(ρα)[7]ς·

While there are sufficient arguments on both sides of the issue to suggest that one redactor or another has changed the original wording of the Q saying, the Matthean version probably has been influenced by its assocation with another saying (the Two Ways; see the discussion of variant [2] above and variants [8] and [13] below). Further, the original position of the saying with respect to the order of the Lucan text (see the discussion of variant [1] above) suggests that the term "door" would have been used consistently.

Q 13:23-24[8]: Matthew's description of the path to destruction.

Luke = Q: ὅτι ( )[8]

Pro: **J. Weiss** 1907, 297: "Von diesem Spruchgebilde hat Lukas nur die erste Mahnung . . . Bei Matthaüs ist mit dem Bilde von der engen Pforte das im Judentum (Jer. 21,8) und Urchristentum häufige . . . von den zwei Wegen verbunden . . ." **Marshall** 1978, 563: "No certain answer to the problem of priority can be given, and the possibility of separate developments in the tradition is perhaps most likely"; 565: "It seems highly improbable that if Luke had known of the metaphor of 'the way' in Mt. he would have omitted it; on the other hand, there is nothing to suggest Matthaean formulation of the metaphor in Mt. The same basic thought of the narrow entrance has been developed in two different ways, probably in Christian catechetical usage." Reconstructions: **Polag** 1979, 68-69.

Con: **Harnack** 1907, ET 68: "St. Luke has written θύρα for πύλη, because he has omitted 'the way' . . ." Reconstructions: **Harnack** 1907, ET 142. **Denaux** 1982, 322, 327.

Matt = Q: ὅτι (πλατεῖα ἡ πύλη καὶ εὐρύχωρος ἡ ὁδὸς ἡ ἀπάγουσα εἰς τὴν ἀπώλειαν καὶ)[8]

Pro: **Schmid** 1930, 243-44: "Dass Mt 7 13f die ursprüngliche Fassung des ersten Spruches bewahrt haben dürfte, die Lk verkürzt hat, wird vor allem durch den streng durchgeführten Parallelismus nahegelegt." **Schulz** 1972a, 311: "Die ursprüngliche Fassung hat Mt aufbewahrt, wahrend Lukas wie öfter den semitischen Parallelismus umgearbeitet hat. Der Aufbau dieses Weisheitswortes ist stilistisch geschlossen und besonders kunstvoll: Auf den prophetischen Imperativ – auch hier dürfte ein ursprüngliches 'Ich sage euch' dem Prozess der Verschriftung zum Opfer gefallen sein – folgt das Aussagewort als Erfahrungssatz. Die beiden Doppelzeiler, jeweils mit ὅτι eingeleitet, erläutern mit Hilfe der traditionellen Motive vom breiten Weg = Verderben und vom schwierig-engen Weg = endzeitliches Leben diesen prophetischen Imperativ. Wie wir schon mehrmals gesehen haben, besteht kein Grund, die besonders symmetrisch-kunstvolle Form als sekundär anzusehen; denn prophetische Improvisation und rhythmisch-kunstvolle Form bildeten in diesem Enthusiasmus eine untrennbare Einheit!" **Zeller** 1977, 139: "So wird das bei Lk nicht vorhandene Motiv der zwei Wege durch Mt oder schon seine Gemeinde nachgetragen sein . . . . Aber ist der Kontrast zwischen dem engen und dem breiten Tor überhaupt ursprünglich, wo doch Lk nur von der schmalen Tür spricht? Dieser Unterschied weist auch den 'Vielen' eine je andere Rolle zu: Während sie sich bei Lk vergeblich vor dem einzigen Einlass drängen, sind sie bei Mt schon auf der geräumigen Strasse des Verderbens. Das Resultat ist dennoch dasselbe: Nur wenige gelange ins rettende Innere. Gegen die Ursprünglichkeit des Kontrastes spricht das zweimalige schwerfällige ὅτι bei Mt. Wenn man sich nur mit einer Hälfte des Parallelismus begnügt, scheint andererseits die Motivation zu schwach; auch das wohl für Q bezeugte Wortpaar πολλοί – ὀλίγοι kann nicht untergebracht werden." **Marshall** 1978, 565: "It seems highly improbable that if Luke had known of the metaphor of 'the way' in Mt. he would have omitted it; on the other hand, there is nothing to suggest Matthaean formulation of the metaphor in Mt. The same basic thought of the narrow entrance has been developed in two different ways, probably in Christian catechetical usage." **Marguerat** 1981, 175: ". . . la version mt est probablement le fruit d'une jonction secondaire du motif de la porte étroite avec le thème des deux chemins au sein de QMt; une telle combinaison est attestée dans le bas-judaïsme (4 Esd 7,6-8)." Reconstructions: **Harnack** 1907, ET 142. **Schenk** 1981, 102. **Steinhauser** 1981, 152.

Con: **Loisy** 1907, 635: "Matthieu aurait combiné l'image de la porte étroite avec celle des deux chemins, familière à l'ancienne tradition chrétienne, mais qui paraît venir de la tradition juive." **Streeter** 1924, 283-84: "But the words ἡ πύλη ("*is* the gate") are omitted in Matthew on their second (א Old Lat.) and third (544 Old Lat.) occurrence. If this reading is original, Q had the Lucan saying about "the narrow *gate*," M had one quite different – the antithesis between the "broad and the narrow *ways*." (The contrast of the Two Ways occurs in the Didache and elsewhere.) Matthew has conflated Q and M." **Dupont** 1958, 99: "On peut se demander si le texte de Matthieu ne résulte pas de la combinaison du thème habituel des deux voies avec la sentence sur la porte étroite." 99[3]: ". . . ainsi **Soiron**, *Logia*, pp. 33s; **Klostermann**, *Mat.*, 68) . . ." **Denaux** 1982, 318: "Mt hat das Q-Logion mit dem Bild von den zwei Wegen bereichert; er ist wahrscheinlich auch verantwortlich für die straffe Symmetrie des Logions." **Lambrecht** 1985, 196: "Matthew has expanded Q a great deal and constructed two long antithetical-symmetrical sentences after 'Enter by the narrow gate.'" **Luz**, 1985, 396: "Der semitisierende Parallelismus membrorum ist ein mt Stilelement." Reconstructions: **Polag** 1979, 68-69.

Evaluation:

CJ 18 ii 88: {B}, ὅτι ( )[8]

Those arguments which place the Matthean description of the path to destruction within the original construction of the Q saying typically argue that this association was peculiar to that form of the Q saying which was received by the Matthean redactor, and was not found in that form which was received by the Lucan redactor. On the one hand, this indeed seems to be a more plausible explanation than the view that the Lucan redactor has omitted such a large segment of the saying with its attendant parallelism (see variant [13] as well). On the other hand, the descriptions of the path to destruction and the path to life are presented in such a manner as to have been inserted into the original Q saying without significant alteration of the basic Q structure. This structural pattern argues for the insertion of a separate Two Ways text by the Matthean redactor himself, or at least, this structure makes such a possibility more probable.

Q 13:23-24[9]: Luke's use of λέγω ὑμῖν.
Luke = *Q:* πολλοί, [λέγω ὑμῖν][9],
Pro: **Jeremias** 1980, 232[106]: "Sie ist also vorlukanisch, was durch die zahlreichen Parallelen zwischen Matthäus und Lukas im Logiengut . . . bestätigt wird."
Con: **Schulz** 1972a, 310: "λέγω ὑμῖν wirkt eingeschoben, könnte aber doch den Spruch des urchristlichen Propheten ursprünglich eingeleitet haben; es wäre dann bei der Schriftwerdung des Spruches weggefallen." **Zeller** 1977, 139: "als redaktionell verdachtig." **Steinhauser** 1981, 150: in agreement with **Schulz**, "λέγω ὑμῖν wie eingeschoben wirkt . . ." Reconstructions: **Harnack** 1907, ET 142. **Polag** 1979, 68-69. **Denaux** 1982, 322, 327.
Matt = *Q:* πολλοί [ ][9]
Pro: **Schmid** 1930, 243-44: "Dass Mt 7 13f die ursprüngliche Fassung des ersten Spruches bewahrt haben dürfte, die Lk verkürzt hat, wird vor allem durch den streng durchgeführten Parallelismus nahegelegt." Reconstructions: **Harnack** 1907, ET 142. **Polag** 1979, 68-69. **Schenk** 1981, 102. **Steinhauser** 1981, 152.
Con:
Evaluation:
CJ 18 ii 88: {C}, πολλοί, [[lέγω ὑμῖν]][9],
No convincing data is offered either for the inclusion or for the rejection of the phrase. According to the "minimalist" definition of Q, there is no reason to include it in the reconstructed text.

Q 13:23-24[10]: Luke's predication for the many with verb and complementary infinitive or Matthew's verb εἰσίν with articular participle.
Luke = *Q:* [ζητήσου][10]σιν ( )[10] εἰσε[λθεῖν][10]
Pro: **J. Weiss** 1907, 297: "Von diesem Spruchgebilde hat Lukas nur die erste Mahnung . . . Bei Matthäus ist mit dem Bilde von der engen Pforte das im Judentum (Jer. 21,8) und Urchristentum häufige. . .von den zwei Wegen verbunden. . ." Reconstructions: **Polag** 68-69.
Con: **Schulz** 1972a, 310: "ζητεῖν ist bei Lk gut bezeugt . . ." **Zeller** 1977, 139: "als redaktionell verdächtig." **Steinhauser** 1981, 150: "Das Wort ζητεῖν kommt bei Lukas öfter vor und ist als sekundär anzusehen." Reconstructions: **Harnack** 1907, ET 142. **Denaux** 1982, 322, 327.
Matt = *Q:* (εἰ)[10]σιν (οἱ)[10] εἰσε(ρχόμενοι)[10]
Pro: **Schmid** 1930, 243-44: "Dass Mt 7 13f die ursprüngliche Fassung des ersten Spruches bewahrt haben dürfte, die Lk verkürzt hat, wird vor allem durch den streng durchgeführten Parallelismus nahegelegt." **Denaux** 1982, 322: "Der Satzteil οἱ εἰσερχόμενοι δι' αὐτῆς, 'die *durch* sie *hinein*gehen' (7,13b), passt eigentlich nicht zu dem Bild von dem Weg, sondern nur zu dem der Pforte. Gerade dieser Ausdruck hat Lk in 13,24: 'viele werden suchen *hinein*zugehen,' d.h. durch die enge Tür. In 7,13b übernimmt Mt den Wortlaut der Quelle, aber er fügt eine Unebenheit ein durch das hinzugefügte Wegmotiv." Reconstructions: **Harnack** 1907, ET 142. **Schenk** 1981, 102. **Steinhauser** 1981, 152.
Con: Reconstructions: **Polag** 68-69.
Evaluation:
CJ 18 ii 88: {B}, [ζητήσου][10]σιν ( )[10] εἰσε[λθεῖν][10]
Presumably, on the one hand, the argument of variant [6] holds true here as well, i.e., that the use of the verb with the complimentary infinitive is a stylistic preference of the Lucan redactor. On the other hand, the argument of variants [8] and [13], i.e., that the Matthean redactor has included an additional Two Ways saying, suggests that the

Matthean verb with the articular participle has been constructed to accommodate the inclusion of the Two Ways materials. While a decision is difficult here, there is no persuasive reason to deny the presence of the Lucan verb with the complimentary infinitive in this instance.

Q 13:23-24[11]: Matthew's prepositional phrase.
Luke = Q: ( )[11]
Pro: **J. Weiss** 1907, 297: "Von diesem Spruchgebilde hat Lukas nur die erste Mahnung . . . Bei Matthäus ist mit dem Bilde von der engen Pforte das im Judentum (Jer. 21,8) und Urchristentum häufige. . .von den zwei Wegen verbunden. . ." Reconstructions: **Polag** 1979, 68-69.
Con: Reconstructions: **Harnack** 1907, ET 142. **Denaux** 1982, 322, 327.
Matt = Q: (δι' αὐτῆς)[11]
Pro: **Schmid** 1930, 243-44: "Dass Mt 7 13f die ursprüngliche Fassung des ersten Spruches bewahrt haben dürfte, die Lk verkürzt hat, wird vor allem durch den streng durchgeführten Parallelismus nahegelegt." **Denaux** 1982, 322: "Der Satzteil οἱ εἰσερχόμενοι δι' αὐτῆς, 'die *durch* sie *hinein*gehen' (7,13b), passt eigentlich nicht zu dem Bild von dem Weg, sondern nur zu dem der Pforte. Gerade dieser Ausdruck hat Lk in 13,24: 'viele werden suchen *hinein*zugehen,' d.h. durch die enge Tür. In 7,13b übernimmt Mt den Wortlaut der Quelle, aber er fügt eine Unebenheit ein durch das hinzugefügte Wegmotiv." Reconstruction: **Harnack** 1907, ET 142. **Schenk** 1981, 102. **Steinhauser** 1981, 152.
Con: Reconstructions: **Polag** 1979, 68-69.
Evaluation:
CJ 18 ii 88: {C}, ( )[11]
No convincing data is offered either for the inclusion or for the rejection of the phrase. According to the "minimalist" definition of Q, there is no reason to include it in the reconstructed text.

Q 13:23-24[12]: Luke's second clause describing the many.
Luke = Q: [καὶ οὐκ ἰσχύσουσιν][12].
Pro: **J. Weiss** 1907, 297: "Von diesem Spruchgebilde hat Lukas nur die erste Mahnung . . . Bei Matthaus ist mit dem Bilde von der engen Pforte das im Judentum (Jer. 21,8) und Urchristentum häufige. . .von den zwei Wegen verbunden. . ."
Con: **Bussmann** 1929, 77: "Das οὐκ ἰσχύσουσιν wird L vielleicht für οὐκ εὑρήσουσιν geschrieben haben." **Jeremias** 232[150]: "ἰσχύω kommt im LkEv achtmal vor, an allen acht Stellen (6,48; 8,43; 13,24; 14,6.29f.; 16,3; 20,26) negiert und mit folgendem Infinitiv . . .; an zwei Stellen hat Lukas diese Konstruktion in den Markustext eingetragen (Lk 8,43 diff. Mk 5,26; Lk 20,26 Zusatz zu Mk 12,17); er schreibt sie viermal in der Apg (6,10; 15,10; 25,7; vgl. 27,16). Sonst findet sie sich im NT nur Mt 8,28; 26,40 (par. Mk 14,37); Mk 5,4; (9,18); Joh 21,6." **Schulz** 1972a, 310: ". . . ἰσχύειν ist ein typisch lk Verb." **Zeller** 1977, 139: "als redaktionell verdächtig." **Steinhauser** 1981, 150: "Ebenfalls ist οὐκ ἰσχύσουσιν als lukanische Redaktion anzusehen (vgl. Lk 8,43)." Reconstructions: **Harnack** 1907, ET 142. **Polag** 1979, 68-69. **Denaux** 1982, 322, 327.
Matt = Q: [ ][12]
Pro: **Schmid** 243-44: "Dass Mt 7 13f die ursprüngliche Fassung des ersten Spruches bewahrt haben dürfte, die Lk verkürzt hat, wird vor allem durch den streng durchgeführten Parallelismus nahegelegt." Reconstructions: **Harnack** 1907, ET 142. **Polag** 1979, 68-69. **Schenk** 1981, 102. **Steinhauser** 1981, 152.

Con:
Evaluation:
CJ 18 ii 88: {A}, [ ][12]
The general agreement is that the Lucan redactor has added these words, which are typical of Lucan style.

Q 13:23-24[13]: Matthew's description of the gate and the path to life.
Luke = Q: ( )[13]
Pro: **J. Weiss** 1907, 297: "Von diesem Spruchgebilde hat Lukas nur die erste Mahnung . . . Bei Matthäus ist mit dem Bilde von der engen Pforte das im Judentum (Jer. 21,8) und Urchristentum haufige. . .von den zwei Wegen verbunden. . ." **Haupt** 1913, 82: "Q^3 [the final form of Q] hat ζωή nicht." **Marshall** 1978, 563: "No certain answer to the problem of priority can be given, and the possibility of separate developments in the tradition is perhaps most likely"; 565: "It seems highly improbable that if Luke had known of the metaphor of 'the way' in Mt. he would have omitted it; on the other hand, there is nothing to suggest Matthaean formulation of the metaphor in Mt. The same basic thought of the narrow entrance has been developed in two different ways, probably in Christian catechetical usage."
Con: **Schulz** 1972a, 311: "Die ursprüngliche Fassung hat Mt aufbewahrt, während Lukas wie öfter den semitischen Parallelismus umgearbeitet hat. Der Aufbau dieses Weisheitswortes ist stilistisch geschlossen und besonders kunstvoll: Auf den prophetischen Imperativ – auch hier dürfte ein ursprüngliches 'Ich sage euch' dem Prozess der Verschriftung zum Opfer gefallen sein – folgt das Aussagewort als Erfahrungssatz. Die beiden Doppelzeiler, jeweils mit ὅτι eingeleitet, erläutern mit Hilfe der traditionellen Motive vom breiten Weg = Verderben und vom schwierig-engen Weg = endzeitliches Leben diesen prophetischen Imperativ. Wie wir schon mehrmals gesehen haben, besteht kein Grund, die besonders symmetrisch-kunstvolle Form als sekundär anzusehen; denn prophetische Improvisation und rhythmisch-kunstvolle Form bildeten in diesem Enthusiasmus eine untrennbare Einheit!" Reconstructions: **Harnack** 1907, ET 142. **Polag** 1979, 68-69. **Denaux** 1982, 322, 327.
Matt = Q: (τί στενὴ ἡ πύλη καὶ τεθλιμμένη ἡ ὁδὸς ἡ ἀπάγουσα εἰς τὴν ζωὴν)[13]
Pro: **Schmid** 1930, 243-44: "Dass Mt 7 13f die ursprüngliche Fassung des ersten Spruches bewahrt haben dürfte, die Lk verkürzt hat, wird vor allem durch den streng durchgeführten Parallelismus nahegelegt." **Marshall** 1978, 563: "No certain answer to the problem of priority can be given, and the possibility of separate developments in the tradition is perhaps most likely"; 565: "It seems highly improbable that if Luke had known of the metaphor of 'the way' in Mt. he would have omitted it; on the other hand, there is nothing to suggest Matthaean formulation of the metaphor in Mt. The same basic thought of the narrow entrance has been developed in two different ways, probably in Christian catechetical usage." Reconstructions: **Harnack** 1907, ET 142 (inserts ὅτι [א N 700 1010] for τί). **Polag** 1979, 68-69. **Schenk** 1981, 102. **Steinhauser** 1981, 152.
Con: **Loisy** 1907, 635: "Matthieu aurait combiné l'image de la porte étroite avec celle des deux chemins, familière a l'ancienne tradition chrétienne, mais qui paraît venir de la tradition juive." **Haupt** 1913, 82: "Q^3 [the final form of Q] hat ζωή nicht aber im Sondergut des Mt steht es noch 25,46." **Streeter** 1924, 283-84: "But the words ἡ πύλη ("*is* the gate") are omitted in Matthew on their second (א Old Lat.) and third (544 Old Lat.) occurrence. If this reading is original, Q had the Lucan saying about "the narrow *gate*," M had one quite different – the antithesis between the "broad and the narrow *ways*." (The contrast of the Two Ways occurs in the Didache and

elsewhere.) Matthew has conflated Q and M." **Dupont** 1958, 99: "On peut se demander si le texte de Matthieu ne résulte pas de la combinaison du thème habituel des deux voies avec la sentence sur la porte étroite." 993: ". . . ainsi **Soiron**, *Logia*, pp. 33s; **Klostermann**, *Mat.*, 68) . . ." **Marguerat** 1981, 175: ". . . la version mt est probablement le fruit d'une jonction secondaire du motif de la porte étroite avec le thème des deux chemins au sein de QMt; une tell combinaison est attestée dans le bas-judaïsme (4 Esd 7,6-8)." **Denaux** 1982, 318: "Mt hat das Q-Logion mit dem Bild von den zwei Wegen bereichert; er ist wahrscheinlich auch verantwortlich für die straffe Symmetrie des Logions." **Lambrecht** 1985, 196: "Matthew has expanded Q a great deal and constructed two long antithetical-symmetrical sentences after 'Enter by the narrow gate.'" **Luz** 1985, 396: "Der semitisierende Parallelismus membrorum ist ein mt Stilelement. Vom 'Finden' des Lebens (allerdings: ψυχή!) spricht Mt red. in 10,39; 16,25"; 396[9]: "Die von der Metaphorik her unsachgemässe Reihenfolge Tor-Weg (vgl. u.S. 397 und Anm. 15-17) wird am besten verständlich, wenn das Motiv des Wegs sekundär zum Motiv des Tors hinzugekommen ist."

Evaluation:

CJ 18 ii 88: {B}, ( )[13]

The rationale for this decision is based upon the choice against the presence of the path to destruction in the original Q text (see the discussion of variant [8] above).

APPENDIX B: TABLE OF SOURCES FOR THE DIDACHE

No.	*Saying*	*Probable Source(s)*	*NT Parallel(s)*
1	1.1 Two Ways	Deut 30:15 Two Ways source (for position)	Matt 7:13b, 14a
2	1.2 Love of God	Deut 6:5 Two Ways source (for position)	Matt 22:37; Mark 2:30; Luke 10:27a
3	1.2b Love of Neighbor	Lev 19:18	Matt 19:19; 22:39; Mark 12:31; Luke 10:27b; Rom 13:9; Gal 5:14; Jas 2:8
4	1.2c Golden Rule	Independent sayings tradition	Matt 7:12; Luke 6:31
5	1.3b Love of Enemies	Sayings Gospel Q	Matt 5:43-48; Luke 6:27-28, 32-36
		Tob 12.8	Matt 6:2-6, 16-18
6	1.4b-5a Retaliation	Sayings Gospel Q	Matt 5:38-42; Luke 6:29-30
7	1.5b Blessed to Give	Independent sayings tradition	(Acts 20:35)
8	1.5c The Last Penny	Sayings Gospel Q	Matt 5:26; Luke 12:59
9	1.6 Sweat and Alms	Sir 12.1	
(10)	2.2-3 Decalogue	Exod 20:13-16 [A]	Matt 19:18; Mark 10:19; Luke 18:20; Matt 5:21-32
11	2.7 Do not Hate	Lev 19:17-18	Matt 18:15-17
(12)	3.2-6 Decalogue	Independent tradition	Matt 19:18; Mark 10:19;
		Exod 20:13-16 [A]	Luke 18:20f; Matt 5:21-32
13	3.7 The Meek	Ps 37:11a	Matt 5:3, 5; (Luke 6:20b)
14	5.1 Way of Death	Exod 20:13-16	Matt 15:19; Mark 7:21-22
15	6.1a Do Not Err	Independent sayings tradition	Matt 24:4; Mark 13:5b; Luke 21:8
16	7.1c Father/Son/Spirit	Matthean tradition	Matt 28:19
17	7.3c Father/Son/Spirit	Matthean tradition	Matt 28:19
18	8.1a Correct Fasting	Matthean tradition	Matt 6:16-18
19	8.2 Lord's Prayer	Matthean tradition	Matt 6:9-13; Luke 11:2-4
20	9.5b Holy to the Dogs	Matthean tradition	Matt 7:6
21	11.7 Unforgivable Sin (not discussed)	Synoptic tradition	Matt 12:31; Mark 3:28-30; Luke 12:10
22	12.1 Name of the Lord (not discussed)	Matthean tradition Ps 118:26	Matt 21:9; Matt 23:39

23	13.1 Worthy of Food (not discussed)	Sayings Gospel Q	Matt 10:10; Luke 10:7
24	16.1a Watch out	Synoptic tradition (?)	Matt 24:42; Mark 13:35
25	16.1b Loins/Lamps	Lucan tradition	Luke 12:35
26	16.1c Be Ready	Synoptic tradition (?)	Matt. 24:44; Luke 12:40
27	16.1d The Hour	Synoptic tradition (?)	Matt 24:42b; 24:44b; 25:13b; Mark13:33b; 13:35b; Luke 12:40b
28	16.2 Gather Together	Independent sayings tradition Two Ways source (?)	
29	16.3-5 Last Days	Synoptic tradition (?)	Matt 24:10b-13; Mark 13:13
30	16.6 The Signs	Synoptic tradition (?)	Matt 24:30-31
31	16.7 The Holy Ones	Zech 14:5	Matt 25:31
32	16.8 The Coming	Synoptic tradition (?)	Matt 24:30b; Mark 13:26; Luke 21:27

SELECTED BIBLIOGRAPHY

ARTICLES IN JOURNALS AND COLLECTED ESSAYS, UNPUBLISHED PAPERS

Allegro, J. M. "A Newly Discovered Fragment of a Commentary on Psalm XXXVII from Qumran." *PEQ* 86 (May-October 1954): 69-75.

Audet, Jean-Paul. "Affinités littéraires et doctrinales du 'Manuel de Discipline.'" *RB* 59 (1952): 219-38.

Bammel, E. "Schema und Vorlage von *Didache* 16." In *StPatr*, no. 4/2 (= TU, no. 79), pp. 253-62. Edited by F. L. Cross. Berlin: Akademie-Verlag, 1961.

Benigne, H. "Didachê Coptica." *Bess* 3 (Novembre-Decembre 1898): 311-29.

Best, Ernest. "I Peter and the Gospel Tradition." *NTS* 16 (January 1970): 95-113.

Betz, Hans Dieter. "Eine Episode im Jüngsten Gericht (Mt 7,21-23)." *ZTK* 78 (1981): 1-30.

Bornkamm, Günther. "πρέσβυς, κ.τ.λ." *TDNT* 6 (1968): 651-83.

Burkitt, F. "Barnabas and the Didache." *JTS* 33 (1932): 25-27.

Butler, B. "The Literary Relations of the Didache, Ch. XVI." *JTS* 11 (October 1986): 265-83.

Chadwick, Henry. "The Rise of the Christian Bishop in Ancient Society." *CHS* 35 (1980): 1-14.

Connolly, R. H. "The 'Didache' in Relation to the Epistle of Barnabas." *JTS* 33 (1932): 237-53.

——. "New Fragments of the *Didache*." *JTS* 25 (1924): 151-53.

——. "The Use of the *Didache* in the *Didascalia*." *JTS* 24 (1923): 147-57.

Cothenet, E. "Les prophètes chrétiens dans l'Evangile selon saint Matthieu." In *L'Evangile selon Matthieu: Rédaction et théologie*, pp. 281-308. Edited by M. Didier. BETL, no. 29. Gembloux: J. Duculot, 1972.

Creed, J. M. "The Didache." *JTS* 39 (1938): 370-87.

Denaux, Adelbert. "Der Spruch von den zwei Wegen im Rahmen des Epilogs der Bergpredigt (Mt 7,13-14 par. Lk 13,23-24). Tradition und Redaktion." In *Logia: The Sayings of Jesus*, pp. 305-35. BETL, no. 49. Edited by Joël Delobel. Leuven: Uitgeverij Peeters, 1982; Leuven: University Press, 1982.

Dibelius, Martin. "Die Mahl-Gebete der Didache." *ZNW* 37 (1938): 32-41.

Dietzfelbinger, Christian. "Die Frömmigkeitsregeln von Mt 6 1-18 als Zeugnisse frühchristlicher Geschichte." *ZNW* 76 (1984): 184-201.

Di Lella, A. "Qumrân and the Geniza Fragments of Sirach." *CBQ* 24 (April 1962): 245-67.

Dix, Gregory. "The Ministry in the Early Church." In *The Apostolic Ministry*, pp. 183-303. Edited by Kenneth E. Kirk. London: Hodder & Stoughton, 1962.

Draper, Jonathan. "The Jesus Tradition in the Didache." In *Gospel Perspectives*. Vol. 5: *The Jesus Tradition Outside the Gospels*, pp. 269-87. Edited by David Wenham. Sheffield, England: JSOT, 1985.

Drews, Paul. "Einleitung." In *Neutestamentliche Apocryphen*. Vol. 1: *Kirchenordnungen*. Edited by Edgar Hennecke. Tübingen and Leipzig: J.C..B. Mohr (Paul Siebeck), 1904.

——. "Untersuchungen zur Didache." *ZNW* 5 (1904): 53-79.

Farrar, F. W. "The Bearing of the 'Teaching' on the Canon." *Exp* 8 (1884): 81-91.

Finkel, Asher. "The Prayer of Jesus in Matthew." In *Standing Before God: Studies on Prayer in Scriptures and in Tradition with Essays*, pp. 131-70. Edited by Asher Finkel and Lawrence Frizzell. New York: KTAV Publishing House, 1981.

Fuller, Reginald H. "The Double Commandment of Love: A Test Case for the Criteria of Authenticity." In *Essays on the Love Commandment*, pp. 41-56. Translated by Reginald H. Fuller and Ilse Fuller. Philadelphia: Fortress, 1978.

Funk, F. X. "Die Doctrina Apostolorum." *TQ* 3 (1884): 381-401.

Gerhardsson, Birger. "Geistiger Opferdienst nach Matth 6,1-6.16-21." In *Neues Testament und Geschichte: Historisches Geschehen und Deutung im Neuen Testament*, pp. 69-77. Edited by Heinrich Baltensweiler and Bo Reicke. Zürich: Theologischer Verlag, 1972; Tübingen: J. C. B. Mohr (Paul Siebeck), 1972.

Gibbins, H. J. "The Problem of the Liturgical Sections of the Didache." *JTS* 36 (1935): 373-86.

Giet, Stanislas. "L'énigme de la Didachè." In *StPatr*, no. 10/1 (= TU, no. 107), pp. 84-94. Edited by F. L. Cross. Berlin: Akademie-Verlag, 1970.

Glover, Richard. "The 'Didache's' Quotations and the Synoptic Gospels." *NTS* 5 (October 1958): 12-29.

——. "Patristic Quotations and Gospel Sources." *NTS* 31 (April 1985): 234-51.

Goodspeed, Edgar J. "The Didache, Barnabas and the Doctrina." *ATR* 27 (1945): 228-47.

Hagner, Donald A. "The Sayings of Jesus in the Apostolic Fathers and Justin Martyr." In *Gospel Perspectives*. Vol. 5: *The Jesus Tradition Outside the Gospels*, pp. 233-68. Edited by David Wenham. Sheffield, England: JSOT, 1985.

Harnack, Adolf. "Analecten" to *Die Gesellschaftsverfassung der christlichen Kirchen im Altertum*, by Edwin Hatch. Giessen: J. Ricker, 1883.

——. "Apostellehre." *In Realencyklopädie für protestantische Theologie und Kirche*. Vol. 1, pp. 711-30. 3rd ed. Leipzig: J. C. Hinrichs'sche Buchhandlung, 1896.

Hoffmann, Paul. "Πάντες ἐργάται ἀδικίας: Redaktion und Tradition in Lc 13 22-30." *ZNW* 58 (1967): 188-214.

Horner, G. "A New Fragment of the *Didaché* in Coptic." *JTS* 25 (April 1924): 225-31.

Hultgren, Arland J. "The Double Commandment of Love in Mt 22:34-40: Its Sources and Compositions." *CBQ* 36 (July 1974): 373-78.

Jefford, Clayton N. "Presbyters in the Community of the *Didache*." In *StPatr*, no. 21, pp. 122-28. Edited by Elizabeth A. Livingstone. Leuven: Peeters Press, 1989.

Johnson, S. E. "A Subsidiary Motive for the Writing of the Didache." In *Munera Studiosa*, pp. 107-22. Edited by Masey Hamilton Shepherd, Jr. and Sherman Elbridge Johnson. Cambridge, Mass.: Episcopal Theological School Press, 1946.

Kloppenborg, John S. "Didache 16 6-8 and Special Matthean Tradition." *ZNW* 70 (1979): 54-67.

Koch, Klaus. "Gibt es ein Vergeltungsdogma im Alten Testament?" *ZNK* 52 (1955): 1-42.

Krawutzcky, Adam. "Ueber die sog. Zwölfapostellehre, ihre hauptsächlichsten Quellen und ihre erste Ausnahme." *TQ* 4 (1884): 547-606.

Kretschmar, Georg. "Ein Beitrag zur Frage nach dem Ursprung frühchristlicher Askese." *ZTK* 61 (April 1964): 27-67.

Layton, Bentley. "The Sources, Date and Transmission of *Didache* 1.3b-2.1." *HTR* 61 (July 1968): 343-83.

L'Eplattenier, C. "Présentation de la Didachè." *FV* 21 (Octobre 1982): 48-54.

Lightfoot, J. B. "Results of Recent Historical and Topographical Research upon the Old and New Testament Scriptures." *Exp* 9 (1885): 1-11.

Lührmann, Dieter. "Liebet euer Feinde (Lk 6,27-36/Mt 5,38-48)." *ZTK* 69 (1972): 412-38.

Malina, Bruce J. "Jewish Christianity or Christian Judaism: Toward a Hypothetical Definition." *JSJ* 7 (July 1976): 46-57.

McGiffert, Arthur C. "The 'Didache' Viewed in its Relations to Other Writings." *AndRev* 5 (April 1886): 430-44.

Mees, M. "Di Bedeutung der Sentenzen und ihrer *auxesis* für den Formung der Jesusworte nach Didache 1,3b-2,1." *VetChr* 8 (1971) 55-76.

Middleton, R. D. "The Eucharistic Prayers of the Didache." *JTS* 36 (1935): 259-67.

Neusner, Jacob. "Max Weber Revisited: Religions and Society in Ancient Judaism with Special Reference to the Late First and Second Centuries." *SecCent* 1 (Summer 1981): 61-84.

Noakes, K. W. "From New Testament Times until St. Cyprian." In *The Study of Liturgy*, pp. 80-94. Edited by Cheslyn Jones, Geoffrey Wainwright and Edward Yarnold, SJ. New York: Oxford University Press, 1978.

Peradse, Gregor. "Die 'Lehre der zwölf Apostel' in der georgischen Überlieferung." *ZNW* 31 (1932): 111-16.

Pickett, Nancy D. "Apocalyptic Eschatology in the Genre 'Church Order': Didache 16." Paper presented at the annual meeting of the Society of Biblical Literature, Atlanta, GA., 22-25 November 1986.

Potwin, Thomas Stoughton. "The Last Chapter of 'The Teaching of the Twelve Apostles,' Illustrated from Passages in the Early Christian Fathers." *AndRev* 5 (April 1886): 445-46.

Rife, J. Merle. "Matthew's Beatitudes and the Septuagint." In *Studies in the History and Text of the New Testament in Honor of Kenneth Willis Clark Ph.D.*, pp. 107-12. Edited by Boyd L. Daniels and M. Jack Suggs. SD, no. 29. Salt Lake City: University of Utah Press, 1967.

Riggs, John W. "From Gracious Table to Sacramental Elements: The Tradition-History of Didache 9 and 10." *SecCent* 4 (Summer 1984): 83-102.

Robinson, James M. "World in Modern Theology and in New Testament Theology." In *Soli Dei Gloria: New Testament Studies in Honor of William Childs Robinson*, pp. 88-110. Edited by J. McDowell Richards. Richmond, VA: John Knox, 1968.

Robinson, J. Armitage. "The Christian Ministry in the Apostolic and sub-Apostolic Periods." In *Essays on the Early History of the Church and the Ministry*, pp. 57-92. Edited by H. B. Swete. London: Macmillan and Co., 1918.

——. "The Epistle of Barnabas and the Didache." *JTS* 35 (April 1934): 113-46.

——. "The Didache." *JTS* 35 (July 1934): 225-49.

Rordorf, Willy. "Une nouvelle édition (Problèmes exégetiques, historiques et théologiques)." In *StPatr*, no. 15/1 (=TU, no. 128), pp. 26-30. Edited by Elizabeth A. Livingstone. Berlin: Akademie-Verlag, 1984.

Sand, Alexander. "Propheten, Weise, und Schriftkundige in der Gemeinde des Matthäusevangeliums." In *Kirche im Werden: Studien zum Thema Amt und Gemeinde im Neuen Testament*, pp. 167-85. Edited by Josef Hainz. Munich: Ferdinand Schöningh, 1976.

Schmidt, Carl. "Das koptische Didache-Fragment des British Museum." *ZNW* 24 (1925): 81-99.

Schmidt, Josef. "Matthäus und Lukas: Eine Untersuchung des Verhältnisses ihrer Evangelien." *BibS(F)* 23 (1930): 183-364.

Schoedel, William R. "Jewish Wisdom and the Formation of the Christian Ascetic." In *Aspects of Wisdom in Judaism and Early Christianity*, pp. 169-99. Edited by Robert L. Wilken. CSJCA, no. 1. Notre Dame and London: University of Notre Dame Press, 1970.

Schöllgen, Georg. "Monepiskopat und monarchischer Episkopat: Eine Bemerkung zur Terminologie." *ZNW* 77 (1986): 146-51.

Schweizer, Eduard. "Observance of the Law and Charismatic Activity in Matthew." *NTS* 16 (April 1970): 213-30.

Seguy, J. "From Revolution to Monastic and Sectarian Conversion: Intimations on Everyday Life and History." In *Religion, Values, and Daily Life*, pp. 97-116. ICSR, no. 16. Paris: Centre National de la Recherche Scientifique de France, 1981.

Skehan, Patrick Wm. "*Didache* 1,6 and Sirach 12,1." *Bib* 44 (1963): 533-36.

Smith, Jonathan Z. "The Social Description of Early Christianity." *RelSRev* 1 (September 1975): 17-25.

Smith, M. A. "Did Justin Know the Didache?" In *StPatr*, no. 7/1 (= TU, no. 92), pp. 287-90. Edited by F. L. Cross. Berlin: Akademie-Verlag, 1966.

Spicq, C. "Benignité, mansuétude, douceur, clémence." *RB* 54 (1947): 321-39.

Stanton, Graham N. "The Gospel of Matthew and Judaism." *BJRL* 66 (Spring 1984): 264-84.

Stern, M. "The Jewish Diaspora." In *The Jewish People in the First Century: Historical Geography, Political History, Social, Cultural and Religious Life and Institutions*. Vol. 1, pp. 117-83. Edited by S. Safrai and M. Stern. Philadelphia: Fortress, 1974; Assen, Netherlands: Van Gorcum, 1974.

Strecker, Georg. "Die Antithesen der Bergpredigt (Mt 5 21-48 par)." *ZNW* 69 (1978): 36-72.

Streeter, B. H. "The Much-Belaboured Didache." *JTS* 37 (1936): 369-74.

Suggs, M. Jack. "The Christian Two Ways Tradition: Its Antiquity, Form, and Function." In *Studies in New Testament and Early Christian Literature: Essays in Honor of Allen P. Wikgren*, pp. 60-74. Edited by David Edward Aune. NovTSup, no. 33. Leiden: E. J. Brill, 1972.

Taylor, Charles. "Traces of a Saying of the Didache." *JTS* 8 (1907): 115-17.

Telfer, W. "The *Didache* and the Apostolic Synod of Antioch." *JTS* 40 (1939): 133-46.

Theissen, Gerd. "Wanderradikalismus. Literatursoziologische Aspekte der Überlieferung von Worten Jesu im Urchristentum." *ZTK* 70 (1973): 245-71.

Troeltsch, Ernst. "The Relationship of Religion to the World." In *Readings on the Sociology of Religion*, pp. 124-28. Edited by Thomas F. O'Dea and Janet K. O'Dea. Englewood Cliffs, NJ: Prentice-Hall, 1973.

Tuilier, André. "Une nouvelle édition (Problèmes de méthode et de critique textuelle)." In *StPatr*, no. 15/1 (= TU, no. 128), pp. 31-36. Edited by Elizabeth A. Livingstone. Berlin: Akademie-Verlag, 1984.

Vassiliadis, P. "The Nature and Extent of the Q Document." *NovT* 20 (1978): 49-73.

Vokes, F. E. "The Didache – Still Debated." *CQ* 3 (1970): 57-62.

Walker, Joan Hazelden. "An Argument from the Chinese for the Antiochene Origen of the *Didache*." In *StPatr*, no. 8/2 (= TU, no. 93), pp. 44-50. Edited by F. L. Cross. Berlin: Akademie-Verlag, 1966.

Warfield, Benjamin B. "Book Reviews and Notices." *AndRev* 4 (December 1985): 593-99.

——. "Text, Sources, and Contents of 'The Two Ways' or First Section of the Didache." *BSac* 43 (1886): 100-61.

BOOKS, MONOGRAPHS AND THESES

Andresen, Carl. *Die Kirchen der alten Christenheit.* RM, no. 29/1,2. Stuttgart: Kohlhammer, 1971.

Audet, Jean-Paul. *La Didachè: Instructions des apôtres.* Ebib. Paris: J. Gabalda & Cie., 1958.

Aune, David E. *Prophecy in Early Christianity and the Ancient Mediterranean World.* Grand Rapids: William B. Eerdmans, 1983.

Baltzer, Klaus. *The Covenant Formulary: In Old Testament, Jewish, and Early Christian Writings.* Translated by David E. Green. Philadelphia: Fortress, 1971.

Beare, F. W. *The Earliest Records of Jesus.* New York and Nashville: Abingdon, 1962; Oxford: Basil Blackwell, 1962.

——. *The Gospel according to Matthew.* San Francisco: Harper & Row, 1981.

Berger, Klaus. *Die Gesetzesauslegung Jesu.* WMANT, no. 40. Neukirchen-Vluyn: Neukirchener Verlag, 1972.

Betz, Hans Dieter. *Essays on the Sermon on the Mount.* Philadelphia: Fortress, 1985.

Bigg, Charles. *The Doctrine of the Twelve Apostles.* Introduced and revised by Arthur John MacLean. London: J.P.C.K., 1922.

Bonnard, Pierre. *L'évangile selon Saint Matthieu.* CNT, no. 1. Neuchatel: Delachaux & Niestlé, 1963.

Bornkamm, Günther, Barth, Gerhard, and Held, Heinz Joachim. *Tradition and Interpretation in Matthew.* Philadelphia: Westminster, 1976.

Boring, M. Eugene. *Sayings of the Risen Jesus: Christian Prophecy in the Synoptic Tradition.* SNTSMS, no. 46. Cambridge: Cambridge University Press, 1982.

Brooks, Stephenson H. "The History of the Matthean Community as Reflected in the M Sayings Traditions." Ph.D. dissertation, Columbia University, 1986.

Brown, Raymond E., and Meier, John P. *Antioch and Rome.* New York: Paulist, 1983.

Brueggemann, Walter. *The Land.* Philadelphia: Fortress, 1977.

Bultmann, Rudolf. *The History of the Synoptic Tradition.* Translated by John Marsh. New York: Harper & Row, 1963.

Bussmann, Wilhelm. *Synoptische Studien.* Vol. 2: *Zur Redenquelle.* Halle: Waisenhaus, 1929.

Cadbury, H. J. *The Style and Literary Method of Luke.* Cambridge, MA: Harvard University Press, 1920.

A Committee of the Oxford Society of Historical Theology. *The New Testament in the Apostolic Fathers.* Oxford: Clarendon, 1905.

Conzelmann, Hans. *Acts of the Apostles: A Commentary on the Acts of the Apostles.* Translated by James Limburg, A. Thomas Kraabel and Donald H. Juel. Edited by Eldon Jay Epp with Christopher R. Matthews. Philadelphia: Fortress, 1987.

Craigie, Peter C. *Psalms 1-50.* WBC, no. 19. Waco: Word Books, 1983.

Cross, Frank Moore, Jr. *The Ancient Library of Qumran and Modern Biblical Studies.* Garden City: NY: Doubleday & Co., 1958.

Crossan, John Dominic. *Four Other Gospels: Shadows on the Contours of Canon.* Minneapolis: Winston, 1985.

——. *In Fragments: The Aphorisms of Jesus.* San Francisco: Harper & Row, 1983.

Davies, W. D. *The Gospel and the Land.* Berkeley: University of California Press, 1974.

Dibelius, Martin, and Conzelmann, Hans. *The Pastoral Epistles*. Translated by Philip Buttolph and Adela Yarbro. Edited by Helmut Koester. Philadelphia: Fortress, 1972.
Dihle, Albrecht. *Die Goldene Regel: Eine Einführung in die Geschichte der antiken und frühchristlichen Vulgärethik*. SAW, no. 7. Göttingen: Vandenhoeck & Ruprecht, 1962.
Downey, Glanville, *A History of Antioch in Syria from Seleucus to the Arab Conquest*. Princeton, NJ: Princeton University Press, 1961.
Dupont, Jacques. *Les béatitudes*. Ebib. 3 vols. Paris: Gabalda, 1969-73.
——. *Etudes sur les évangiles synoptiques*. BETL, no. 70/1-2. Leuven: Uitgeverij Peeters, 1985; Leuven: University Press, 1985.
Durkheim, Emile. *The Elementary Forms of the Religious Life*. London: Allen & Unwin, 1915.
Easton, Burton Scott. *The Gospel According to St. Luke: A Critical and Exegetical Commentary*. New York: Charles Scribner's Sons, 1926.
Edwards, R. A. *A Concordance to Q*. Missoula: Scholars Press, 1975.
——. *A Theology of Q: Eschatology, Prophecy and Wisdom*. Philadelphia: Fortress, 1976.
Eichholz, Georg. *Auslegung der Bergpredigt*. BibS(N), no. 46. Neukirchen-Vluyn: Neukirchener Verlag, 1965.
Festugière, A.-J. *La révélation d'Hermès Trismegiste*. EBib. 3 vols. Paris: J. Gabalda & Cie., 1950.
Fitzmyer, Joseph A. *The Gospel According to Luke*. AB, no. 28. Garden City, NY: Doubleday & Co., 1981-85.
Frend, W. H. C. *The Rise of Christianity*. Philadelphia: Fortress, 1984.
Friedlander, Gerald. *The Jewish Sources of the Sermon on the Mount*. New York: KTAV, 1969.
Funk, Francis Xavier. *Doctrina duodecim apostolorum*. Tübingen: Libraria Henrici Laupp, 1887.
——. *Patres Apostolici*. 2 vols. Tübingen: Libraria Henrici Laupp, 1901.
Gaechter, Paul. *Das Matthäus Evangelium*. Innsbruck: Tyrolia-Verlag, 1962.
Gager, John G. *Kingdom and Community: The Social World of Early Christianity*. Edited by John P. Reeder, Jr. and John F. Wilson. Englewood, NJ: Prentice-Hall, 1975.
Giet, Stanislaus. *L'énigme de la Didachè*. PFLUS, no. 149. Paris: Editions Ophrys, 1970.
Goppelt, Leonard. *Apostolic and Post-Apostolic Times*. Translated by Robert A. Guelich. Grand Rapids: Baker Book House, 1970.
——. *Christentum und Judentum in ersten und zweiten Jahrhundert*. BFCT, no. 55. 2nd ser. Gütersloh: C. Bertelsmann, 1954.
Grant, Robert M. *The Apostolic Fathers*. AF, no. 1. New York: Thomas Nelson & Sons, 1964.
——. *Early Christianity and Society: Seven Studies*. New York: Harper & Row, 1977.
Greyvenstein, Jan Hendrik Jacobus. "The Original 'Teaching of the Twelve Apostles.'" Ph.D. dissertation, University of Chicago, 1919.
Grundmann, Walter. *Das Evangelium nach Matthäus*. THKNT, no. 1. Berlin: Evangelische Verlagsanstalt, 1968.
Guelich, Robert A. *The Sermon on the Mount*. Waco: Word Books, 1982.
Gundry, Robert H. *Matthew: A Commentary on His Literary and Theological Art*. Grand Rapids: William B. Eerdmans Publishing Company, 1982.
——. *The Use of the Old Testament in St. Matthew's Gospel*. NovTSup, no. 18. Leiden: E. J. Brill, 1967.
Haenchen, Ernst. *The Acts of the Apostles: A Commentary*. Oxford: Basil Blackwell, 1971.
Harnack, Adolf. *Die Apostellehre und die jüdischen Beiden Wege*. Leipzig: J. C. Heinrichs'sche Buchhandlung, 1886.
——. *Geschichte der altchristlichen Literatur bis Eusebius*. Part 1: *Die Überlieferung und der Bestand*. 2nd ed. Leipzig: J. C. Hinrichs, 1958.
——. *Lehre der zwölf Apostel nebst Untersuchungen zur ältesten Geschichte der Kirchenverfassung und des Kirchenrechts*. TU, no. 2/1-2. Leipzig: J. C. Hinrichs'sche Buchhandlung, 1884; rep. ed., Leipzig: J. C. Hinrichs'sche Buchhandlung, 1893.
——. *The Sayings of Jesus: The Second Source of St. Matthew and St. Luke*. NTS, no. 2. Translated by J. R. Wilkinson. New York: Putnam, 1908; London: Williams & Norgate, 1908.

Harris, J. Rendel. *The Teaching of the Twelve Apostles*. London: C. J. Clay & Sons, 1887; Baltimore: Johns Hopkins University Press, 1887.

Hatch, Edwin. *The Organization of the Early Christian Churches*. London: Longmans and Green, 1895.

Haupt, Walther. *Worte Jesu und Gemeindeüberlieferung: Eine Untersuchung zur Quellengeschichte der Synopse*. UNT, no. 3. Leipzig: J. C. Hinrichs'sche Buchhandlung, 1913.

Hendrickx, Herman. *The Sermon on the Mount*. London: Geoffrey Chapman, 1979.

Herrmann, Elisabeth. *Ecclesia in Re Publica: Die Entwicklung der Kirche von pseudostaatlicher zu staatlich inkorporierter Existenz*. EF, no. 2. Frankfurt am Main: Peter D. Lang, 1980.

Hilgenfeld, Adolf. *Novum Testamentum extra canonem receptum*. Vol. 4/2: *Evangeliorum*. Leipzig: T. O. Weigel, 1884.

Hitchcock, Roswell D., and Brown, Francis. *The Teaching of the Twelve Apostles*. London: John C. Nimmo, 1885.

Hummel, R. *Auseinandersetzung zwischen Kirche und Judentum im Matthäusevangelium*. München: Kaiser, 1963.

Hyman, Aaron. *Torah Hakethubah Vehamessurah*. 2nd ed. Edited and revised by Arthur B. Hyman. 3 vols. Tel-Aviv: Dvir, 1979.

Iselin, L. E. *Eine bisher unbekannte Version des ersten Teiles der "Apostellehre"*. TU, no. 13/1b. Leipzig: A. Heusler, 1895.

Jeremias, Johannes. *Das Evangelium nach Matthaeus*. Leipzig: Dörffling & Franke, 1932.

Kamlah, E. *Die Form der katalogischen Paränese im Neuen Testament*. WUNT, no. 7. Tübingen: J. C. B. Mohr (Paul Siebeck), 1964.

Kelber, Werner H. *The Oral and Written Gospel: The Hermeneutics of Speaking and Writing in the Synoptic Tradition, Mark, Paul, and Q*. Philadelphia: Fortress, 1983.

Kilpatrick, G. D. *The Origins of the Gospel According to St. Matthew*. Oxford: Clarendon, 1946.

Klevinghaus, Johannes. *Die theologische Stellung der Apostolischen Väter zur alttestamentlichen Offenbarung*. BFCT, no. 44/1. Gütersloh: C. Bertelsmann, 1948.

Kline, Leslie Lee. *The Sayings of Jesus in the Pseudo-Clementine Homilies*. SBLDS, no. 14. Missoula, MT: Scholars Press, 1975.

Kloppenborg, John S. *The Formation of Q: Trajectories in Ancient Wisdom Collections*. Philadelphia: Fortress, 1987.

——. *Q Parallels: Synopsis, Critical Notes, and Concordance*. Sonoma, CA: Polebridge, 1988.

——. "The Sayings of Jesus in the Didache." M.A. thesis, University of St. Michael's College, 1976.

Knopf, Rudolf. *Die Lehre der zwölf Apostel. Die zwei Clemensbriefe*. Tübingen: J. C. B. Mohr (Paul Siebeck), 1920.

Köhler, Wolf-Dietrich. *Die Rezeption des Matthäusevangeliums in der Zeit vor Irenäus*. WUNT, no. 2/24. Tübingen: J. C. B. Mohr (Paul Siebeck), 1987.

Köster, Helmut. *Synoptische Überlieferung bei den Apostolischen Vätern*. TU, no. 65. Berlin: Akademie-Verlag, 1957.

Kohler, Kaufmann. *The Origins of the Synagogue and the Church*. Edited by H. G. Enelow. New York: Arno, 1973.

Kraft, Robert A. *Barnabas and the Didache*. AF, no. 3. New York: Thomas Nelson & Sons, 1965.

Kraus, Hans-Joachim. *Psalmen*. BKAT, no. 15-16. 2 vols. 5th ed. Neukirchen-Vluyn: Neukirchener Verlag, 1978.

Ladd, George Eldon. "The Eschatology of the Didache." Ph.D. dissertation, Harvard University, 1949.

Lake, Kirsopp. *The Apostolic Fathers*. LCL, no. 24-25. Cambridge: Harvard University Press, 1977; London: William Heinemann, 1977.

Lefort, L.-Th. *Les Pères Apostoliques en copte*. CSCO.C, no. 135/17. Louvain: L. Durbecq, 1952.

Leipoldt, J. *Geschichte des neutestamentliche Kanons*. Leipzig: J. C. Hinrichs'sche Buchhandlung, 1907.

Lietzmann, Hans. *Die Didache*. KlT, no. 6. 2nd ed. Berlin: Walter de Gruyter & Co., 1962.

——. *Mass and Lord's Supper: A Study in the History of the Liturgy*. Translated by Dorothea H. G. Reeve. Introduction by Robert Douglas Richardson. Leiden: E. J. Brill, 1979.

Lightfoot, J. B. *The Apostolic Fathers*. London: Macmillan & Co., 1912.

——. *Saint Paul's Epistle to the Philippians*. London: Macmillan & Co., 1900; New York: Macmillan, 1900.

Lilje, Hans. *Die Lehre der zwölf Apostel: Eine Kirchenordnung des ersten christlichen Jahrhunderts*. Hamburg: Furche-Verlag, 1956.

Linton, Olof. *Das Problem der Urkirche in der neueren Forschung*. Uppsala: Almqvist & Wiksells, 1932.

Lohmeyer, Ernst, and Schmauch, Werner. *Das Evangelium des Matthäus*. 3rd ed. Göttingen: Vandenhoeck & Ruprecht, 1962.

Luz, Ulrich. *Das Evangelium nach Matthäus*. EKKNT, no. 1/1. Zürich: Benziger Verlag, 1985; Neukirchen-Vluyn: Neukirchener Verlag, 1985.

McDonald, James I. H. *Kerygma and Didache: The Articulation and Structure of the Earliest Christian Message*. SNTSMS, no. 37. Cambridge: Cambridge University Press, 1980.

Malherbe, Abraham J. *Social Aspects of Early Christianity*. 2nd ed. Philadelphia: Fortress, 1983.

Manson, T. W. *The Sayings of Jesus*. London: SCM, 1949.

Marguerat, Daniel. *Le jugement dans l'Evangile de Matthieu*. Genève: Labor et Fides, 1981.

Marshall, I. Howard. *The Gospel of Luke: A Commentary on the Greek Text*. Exeter: Paternoster, 1978.

Massaux, Edouard. *Influence de l'évangile de saint Matthieu sur la littérature chrétienne avant saint Irénée*. Louvain: Universitaires de Louvain, 1950; Gembloux: J. Duculot, 1950.

Meeks, Wayne A. *The First Urban Christians: The Social World of the Apostle Paul*. New Haven and London: Yale University Press, 1983.

——. *The Moral World of the First Christians*. LEC, no. 6. Philadelphia: Westminster, 1986.

——, and Wilken, Robert L. *Jews and Christians in Antioch*. Missoula, MT: Scholars Press, 1978.

Meier, John P. *Law and History in Matthew's Gospel*. AnBib, no. 71. Rome: Biblical Institute, 1976.

Meyer, P. D. "The Community of Q." Ph.D. dissertation, University of Iowa, 1967.

Morgenthaler, Robert. *Statistische Synopse*. Zürich and Stuttgart: Gotthelf-Verlag, 1971.

Mowinckel, Sigmund. *The Psalms in Israel's Worship*. Translated by D. R. Ap-Thomas. 2 vols. Oxford: Basil Blackwell, 1962.

Müller, G. H. *Zur Synopse: Untersuchung über die Arbeitsweise de Lukas und Matthäus und ihre Quellen namentlich die Spruchquelle im Anschluss an eine Synopse Mk-Lk-Mt*. FRLANT, no. 11. Göttingen: Vandenhoeck & Ruprecht, 1908.

Muilenburg, James. *The Literary Relations of the Epistle of Barnabas and the Teaching of the Twelve Apostles*. Marburg: 1929.

Neirynck, Frans and Segbroeck, Frans Van. *New Testament Vocabulary: A Companion Volume to the Concordance*. BETL, no. 65. Leuven: Leuven University Press, 1984; Leuven: Peeters, 1984.

O'Dea, Thomas F. *Sociology and the Study of Religion: Theory, Research, Interpretation*. New York and London: Basic Books, 1970.

Oesterley, W. O. E. *The Jewish Background of the Christian Liturgy*. Oxford: Clarendon, 1925.

Otto, Rudolf. *The Idea of the Holy*. 2nd ed. London and New York: Oxford University, 1943.

Parsons, Talcott. *Essays in Sociological Theory*. Rev. ed. New York: Free, 1954; London: Collier-Macmillan, 1954.

Perrin, Norman. *The Kingdom of God in the Teaching of Jesus*. Philadelphia: Westminster, 1963.

Peters, Francis E. *The Harvest of Hellenism: A History of the Near East from Alexander the Great to the Triumph of Christianity*. New York: Simon & Schuster, 1970.

Polag, Athanasius. *Fragmenta Q*. 2nd ed. Neukirchen-Vluyn: Neukirchener Verlag, 1982.

Poschmann, Bernhard. *Paenitentia secunda: Die kirchliche Buße im ältesten Christentum bis Cyprian und Origenes*. Theoph., no. 1. Bonn: Peter Hanstein, 1940.

Roberts, Colin H. *Manuscript, Society and Belief in Early Christian Egypt: The Schweich Lectures of the British Academy 1977*. London: Oxford University Press, 1979.

Robinson, J. *Armitage. Barnabas, Hermas, and the Didache*. London: S.P.C.K., 1920; New York: MacMillan, 1920.

Rordorf, Willy, and Tuilier, André. *La doctrine des douze apôtres (Didachè)*. SC, no. 248. Paris: Les éditions du cerf, 1978.

Sabatier, Paul. *ΔΙΔΑΧΗ ΤΩΝ ΙΒ' ΑΠΟΣΤΟΛΩΝ: La Didachè ou l'enseignement des douze apôtres*. Paris: Charles Noblet, 1885.

Sand, Alexander. *Das Gesetz und die Propheten: Untersuchungen zur Theologie des Evangeliums nach Matthäus*. BU. Regensburg: Friedrich Pustet, 1974.

Schaff, Philip. *The Oldest Church Manual Called the Teaching of the Twelve Apostles*. Edinburg: T. & T. Clark, 1885.

Schenk, W. *Synopse zur Redenquelle der Evangelisten: Q-Synopse und Rekonstruktion in deutscher Übersetzung mit kürzen Erläuterungen*. Düsseldorf: Patmos, 1981.

Schlecht, Joseph. *Doctrina XII apostolorum: Die Apostellehre in der Liturgie der katholischen Kirche*. Freiburg im Breisgau: Herder, 1901.

Schmid, Joseph. *Das Evangelium nach Matthäus*. RNT, no. 1. 5th ed. Regensburg: Friedrich Pustet, 1965.

Schmithals, W. *Das Evangelium nach Lukas*. ZBNT, no. 3/1. Zürich: Theologischer Verlag, 1980.

Schniewind, Julius. *Das Evangelium nach Matthäus*. NTD, no. 2. 4th ed. Göttingen: Vandenhoeck & Ruprecht, 1950.

Schönle, Volker. *Johannes, Jesus und die Juden: Die theologische Position des Matthäus und des Verfassers der Redenquelle in Lichte von Mt. 11*. BBET, no. 17. Frankfurt am Main: Peter Lang, 1982.

Schürmann, Heinz. *Das Lukasevangelium*. HTKNT, no. 3/1. Frieburg im Breisgau: Herder & Co., 1969.

——. *Traditionsgeschichtliche Untersuchungen zu den synoptischen Evangelien*. Düsseldorf: Patmos, 1968.

Schultz, Siegfried. *Q: Die Spruchquelle der Evangelisten*. Zürich: Theologisher Verlag, 1972.

Schweizer, Eduard. *Church Order in the New Testament*. SBT, no. 32. Translated by Frank Clarke. Naperville, IL: Alec R. Allenson, 1961.

——. *Matthäus und seine Gemeinde*. SBS. Stuttgart: KBW, 1974.

Seeberg, D. Alfred. *Die beiden Wege und das Aposteldecret*. Leipzig: A. Deichert (Georg Böhme), 1906.

——. *Der Katchismus der Urchristenheit*. Leipzig: A. Deichert (Georg Böhme), 1903.

Soiron, Thaddäus. *Die Bergpredigt Jesu*. Freiburg im Breisgau: Herder & Co., 1941.

Spence, Canon. *The Teaching of the Twelve Apostles*. London: James Nisbet & Co., 1885.

Steinhauser, Michael G. *Doppelbildworte in den synoptischen Evangelien: Eine form- und traditions-linguistic Studie*. FvB, no. 44. Würzburg: Echter, 1981.

Strack, Hermann L., and Billerbeck, Paul. *Das Evangelium nach Matthäus erläuteret aus Talmud und Midrash*. 6 vols. 5th ed. München: C. H. Beck, 1926.

Strecker, Georg. *Die Bergpredigt: Ein exegetischer Kommentar*. Göttingen: Vandenhoeck & Ruprecht, 1984.

——. *Der Weg der Gerechtigkeit*. 3rd ed. Göttingen: Vandenhoeck & Ruprecht, 1971.

Streeter, B. H. *The Four Gospels: A Study of Origins*. London: Macmillan & Co., 1936.

——. *The Primitive Church*. New York: Macmillan & Co., 1929.

Suggs, M. Jack. *Wisdom, Christology, and Law in Matthew's Gospel*. Cambridge, MA: Harvard University Press, 1970.

Syreeni, Kari. *The Making of the Sermon on the Mount: A Procedural Analysis of Matthew's Redactoral Activity*. Part 1: *Methodology & Compositional Analysis*. AASF, no. 44. Helsinki: Suomalainen Tiedeakatemia, 1987.

Taylor, C. *An Essay on the Theology of the Didache*. Cambridge: Deighton Bell & Co., 1889; London: George Bell & Sons, 1889.

——. *The Teaching of the Twelve Apostles*. Cambridge: Deighton Bell & Co., 1886; London: George Bell & Sons, 1886.

Tcherikover, Victor. *Hellenistic Civilization and the Jews*. Translated by S. Applebaum. Philadelphia and Jerusalem: Jewish Publication Society of America, 1959.

Theissen, Gerd. *The Social Setting of Pauline Christianity*. Translated by John H. Schütz. Philadelphia: Fortress, 1982.

——. *Sociology of Early Palestinian Christianity*. Translated by John Bowden. Philadelphia: Fortress, 1978.

Turner, E. G. *Greek Papyri: An Introduction*. Oxford: Clarendon, 1968.

Van Tilborg, Sjef. *The Jewish Leaders in Matthew*. Leiden: E. J. Brill, 1972.

Vögtle, Anton. *Das Evangelium und die Evangelien. Beiträge zur evangelischen Forschung*. Düsseldorf: Patmos, 1971.

——. *Die Tugend- und Lasterkataloge im Neuen Testament*. NTAbh, no. 16/4-5. Münster: Aschendorffschen Verlagsbuchhandlung, 1936.

Vööbus, Arthur. *Liturgical Traditions in the Didache*. PETSE, no. 16. Stockholm: ETSE, 1968.

Vokes, F. E. *The Riddle of the Didache: Fact or Fiction, Heresy or Catholicism?*. London: S.P.C.K., 1938; New York: Macmillan, 1938.

Von Campenhausen, Hans. *Ecclesiastical Authority and Spiritual Power in the Church of the First Three Centuries*. Stanford: Stanford University Press, 1969.

——. *The Formation of the Christian Bible*. Translated by J. A. Baker. Philadelphia: Fortress, 1972.

Wallace-Hadrill, D. S. *Christian Antioch: A Study of Early Christian Thought in the East*. Cambridge: Cambridge University Press, 1982.

Weber, Max. *Max Weber: The Theory of Social and Economic Organization*. Translated by A. M. Henderson and Talcott Parsons. Edited by Talcott Parsons. New York: Free, 1947; London: Collier-Macmillan, 1947.

Wegner, Uwe. *Der Hauptmann von Kafarnam*. Tübingen: J. C. B. Mohr (Paul Siebeck), 1985.

Weiss, Bernhard. *Das Matthäusevangelium und seine Lukasparallelen*. Halle: Waisenhaus, 1876.

——. *Die Quellen des Lukasevangeliums*. Stuttgart and Berlin: J. G. Cotta'sche Buchhundlung, 1907.

Weiss, Johannes. *Die Schriften des Neuen Testaments*. Vol 1: *Die drei ältern Evangelien. Die Apostelgeschichte*. Göttingen: Vandenhoeck & Ruprecht, 1907.

Wellhausen, Julius. *Das Evangelium Matthaei*. 2nd ed. Berlin: Georg Reimer, 1914.

Wengst, Klaus. *Schriften des Urchristentums: Didache (Apostellehre), Barnabasbrief, Zweiter Klemensbrief, Schrift an Diognet*. München: Kösel-Verlag, 1984.

Wernle, Paul. *Die synoptische Frage*. Freiburg: J. C. B. Mohr (Paul Siebeck), 1899.

White, John L. *Light from Ancient Letters*. Philadelphia: Fortress, 1986.

Wilson, Bryan R. *Magic and the Millennium. A Sociological Study of Religious Movements of Protest among Tribal and Third-world Peoples*. New York: Harper & Row, 1973.

Wohleb, Leo. *Die lateinische bersetzung der Didache*. SGKA, no. 7/1. Paderborn: Ferdinand Schöningh, 1913.

Wohlenberg, G. *Die Lehre der zwölf Apostel in ihre Verhältnis zum neutestamentlichen Schrifttum*. Erlangen: Andreas Deichert, 1888.

Wolf, Eric. *Ordnung der Kirche: Lehr- und Handbuch des Kirchenrechts auf ökumenischer Basis*. Frankfurt am Main: Vittorio Klostermann, 1961.

Wrege, Hans-Theo. *Die Überlieferungsgeschichte der Bergpredigt*. WUNT, no. 9. Tübingen: J. C. B. Mohr (Paul Siebeck), 1968.

Zahn, Theodor. *Das Evangelium des Matthäus*. KNT, no. 1. 3rd ed. Leipzig: A. Deichert, 1910.

——. *Forschungen zur Geschichte des neutestamentlichen Kanons und der altkirchlichen Literatur*. Vol. 3: *Supplementum Clementinum*. Erlangen: Andreas Deichert, 1884.

Zeller, Dieter. *Kommentar zur Logienquelle*. SKK.NT, no. 21. Stuttgart: Katholisches Bibelwerk, 1984.

Ziegler, Joseph, ed. *Isaias*. SVTG, no. 14. Göttingen: Vanderhoeck & Ruprecht, 1939.

Zumstein, Jean. *La condition du croyant dans l'évangile selon Matthieu*. OBO, no. 16. Göttingen: Vandenhoeck & Ruprecht, 1977.

INDEX OF TEXTS

OLD TESTAMENT

APOCRYPHA AND PSEUDEPIGRAPHA

NEW TESTAMENT

PATRISTIC LITERATURE

MISCELLANEOUS TEXTS

INDEX OF AUTHORS

GENERAL INDEX